MEAN BABY

Mean Baby

A MEMOIR
OF GROWING UP

Selma Blair

ALFRED A. KNOPF

NEW YORK 2022

THIS IS A BORZOI BOOK
PUBLISHED BY ALFRED A. KNOPF

www.aaknopf.com

Knopf, Borzoi Books, and the colophon are registered
trademarks of Penguin Random House LLC.

Library of Congress Control Number: 2021950379
ISBN: 978-0-525-65949-5 (hardcover)
ISBN: 978-0-525-65950-1 (ebook)

Front-of-jacket photograph by Peggy Sirota
Jacket design by Janet Hansen

Manufactured in the United States of America

First Edition

To my dearest Mommy
while we were apart

And to my greatest love,
Arthur Saint Bleick

And did you get what
you wanted from this life, even so?

—RAYMOND CARVER,
"LATE FRAGMENT," *A NEW PATH
TO THE WATERFALL*

I don't hate hardly ever, and when I love,
I love for miles and miles. A love so big it
should either be outlawed or it should
have a capital and its own currency.

—CARRIE FISHER, *SHOCKAHOLIC*

Let me begin again.

—OCEAN VUONG,
ON EARTH WE'RE BRIEFLY GORGEOUS

MEAN BABY

Prologue

In the fall of 2002, I saw a tarot reader in Los Angeles. I had just been cast in a movie that was about to film in Prague for six months. I was thirty years old, anxious and searching. My mind was a void, and I wanted someone to fill it. I wanted to hear the story of who I would become, what signs I should seek along the way. I wanted an outline, if not an epiphany. After all, that's why we open our checkbooks to fortune-tellers. Tell us a tale. Make it wild. Make it entertaining. But make it our own.

The reader was named T—, and she looked a bit like a Berkeley professor, very thin, very intellectual. Large eyes framed by black bangs falling straight across her forehead. She kept a hankie tucked in one palm. Her breath smelled of Altoids. A skinny black cat curled up at her feet. As we spoke, I learned that T— used to be a lawyer, a profession she left to fully utilize her gifts. In all ways, she seemed like a good captain to have on this metaphysical journey, the right person to relay the drama of my life.

T— was not my first intuitive. For much of my life, I'd sought out such stories from mystics and chakra healers, mediums and numerologists, past-life therapists and astrologers. My fascination goes way back to when I was a child growing up in Southfield, Michigan. At a birthday party in second grade, my friend Melissa Stern's glamorous mother dressed up as a fortune-teller, a sparkling vision in a headscarf and layers of necklaces and bracelets. Melissa's mom was beautiful and lived in a giant house, which felt like evidence enough that she could see into the future, or at the very least that her words must have some merit. When it was my turn, she stared into a crystal ball, traced the lines on both my palms, closed her eyes, held my little hands, and told me that when I grew up, I was going to be a beautiful actress.

"There will be so many boys throughout your life that there will be a line," Mrs. Stern said as she swept the air with her finger to indicate a long queue of men waiting to swoop me off my feet. Seven-year-old me couldn't imagine why on earth she thought this. I had heavy eyebrows and stringy hair and did not believe myself to be an especially attractive child. And though I was prone to dramatic outbursts, the idea of performing in front of an audience terrified me. But I wanted so desperately to believe it. So convinced was I by Mrs. Stern's future-predicting abilities that I internalized every word. I couldn't wait to tell my mother, who would delight in the news.

As soon as my mom drove up in her navy blue 1979 Corvette, the *Evita* soundtrack blaring, I climbed into the back. Our cute neighbor Todd, a little older than I was, settled into the white leather bucket seat that was tinged yellow from cigarette smoke. I wanted them both to know what was predicted for me, so I spilled it all. "Mrs. Stern read my fortune and she said I'm going to be a beautiful actress," I bragged. I wanted my mother to be impressed. I wanted Todd to notice me. Even at age seven I knew beauty was a rare prize.

"Yeah, right," Todd scoffed.

"That's ridiculous," my mother said as she pulled out of the Sterns' long driveway. Once we were safely out of view, she took a drag off her Vantage cigarette. She exhaled against the dashboard, filling the car with curls of smoke. "Why would she tell you that? Besides. If you do grow up to be beautiful"—emphasis on the "if"—"and tall"—emphasis on the "and"—"you'll be a model. Or you'll marry an oilman and spend your days on his yacht." That settled it. My mother's word was gospel. End of discussion. I looked out the window.

As it happened, Mrs. Stern's prediction for me came true, at least in part: I was an actress. And by this point, I'd gone through my fair share of men. Even an oilman, whom I eventually found lacking. But I was still searching, still unsatisfied, still restless and stuck, still desperate to please, still prone to periods of over-whelming despair. Still binge drinking when I couldn't make sense of what to do next or needed to escape my body. I wanted clues, signs, good fortune. I wanted someone to tell me how the story unfolded. I wanted someone to spell out what came next.

Now, many years and many seers later, here I was again. T— studied the cards for a long time and then stacked them up in a neat deck. She tented her fingers, her unpolished nails touching, and said with the kind of conviction that one expects from a tarot reader: "Your life is going to change in Prague." The cat at her feet looked up at me as if in agreement.

I smiled. There it was: my life was going to change in Prague. She went on to say that I would meet a little man who would become important to me and that the true meaning of my life would be revealed. This, too, sounded fine. In fact, this whole visit was turning out to be much better than the last psychic I'd seen, who informed me that in my past life I'd been held captive by my own father and locked in a cement tomb in the woods, where I was burned alive, unknown by anyone.

I was going to Prague to shoot the movie *Hellboy*, in which I'd been cast as Liz Sherman, a pyro-telekinetic who, in a rage, accidentally burned her family to death and now must learn to control her powers. The director, Guillermo del Toro, had seen me in an indie film called *Storytelling* and thought my face held great loss. Loss was at the pit of Liz, he said. She couldn't touch anyone. Any feeling made her burn. It was a fitting role for me because, for years of my life beginning in my twenties, I often had the sensation that my arms were on fire. The feeling would come and go inexplicably: a tingle all the way down to my fingertips like tiny electric shocks, then a burning so intense I felt I might combust, then gone. Though it nagged at me, I never said anything about this to anyone, not even my mother. It was just one more mystery about my body that I didn't understand.

So, I went to Prague, where I waited for the magical life-changing moment T— predicted. A short man—T— was right about that bit—sought me out, a refugee from the former Yugoslavia, and we spent every night together, drinking slivovitz and champagne in bars. We fought, made up, made out, got drunk, fought, made up, made out, drank more. I felt as if I were living inside a Bukowski novel. In the morning, I woke up wondering who this tiny, tattooed, hot-tempered, blue-eyed man next to me was. Only to realize he was now mine. This wasn't the change I wanted.

When the film wrapped, I returned to L.A., once again flailing. My life hadn't transformed in Prague, except that I got even better, and also worse, at drinking, a skill at which I already excelled. In retrospect, I see now that I did learn some things. How to play the part of a woman who was trying to gain control over her own disobedient body. How to distract myself from the pain in my arms when I felt them begin to flare. How to spend long, lonely nights in bars and somehow get through the next day.

But at the time, I felt hopeless.

What I didn't know then, but what I'm starting to learn now, is that I don't need a fortune-teller to tell me a story about who I am or where I'm going. I don't need a psychic to make connections between my past and my present. I know how the story unfolds. I've seen how the pieces fit together. And I want to be the one to tell it.

PART I

SIGNS

7DM   1962

SINAI HOSPITAL
DETROIT, MICHIGAN

Name_ Beitner

Date of birth_ 6 - 23 - 72

Sex_ Girl

Room no._

Mean Baby

I'M NOT SURE how to harness my meandering thoughts into words and sentences that make sense. So I'll start with what I know.

We are all in search of a story that explains who we are.

As Joan Didion wrote, "We tell ourselves stories in order to live." We are made not only by the stories we tell ourselves but by the tales of others—the stories they tell us, and the stories they tell about us.

The first story I was told about myself—other than the one about how my mother watched as the doctor pulled me out from her insides—is that I was a mean, mean baby.

I came into this world with my mouth pulled into a perpetual snarl. I was born with a glower, my face defined by a heavy brow that adults coveted. But on a child—an infant, no less—my face looked judgmental, scrutinizing. No one knew quite what to make of it.

When I arrived home from the hospital, only one of my three sisters, Katie, who was five, was waiting in our driveway. Mimi, aged twelve, and Lizzie, almost two, were elsewhere. Katie rushed out to meet me, my mother holding me on her lap. Katie asked if I was a baby doll for her. No, I wasn't, my expression said. A few days later, some of the neighborhood kids came over to meet the new

Beitner child. Within minutes, they left screaming, warning any-one who would listen, "Do *not* go over there. The Beitners have a mean baby." Can you imagine! Have you ever heard an infant described in this way? What could I have done? I was just days old! An infant with a snarl. I only wanted someone to pick me up, I think. Or put me down! But instead they all went and gossiped. From the very beginning, I was misunderstood.

Nevertheless, the label stuck, as labels are wont to do. What people call you does matter. The words we use hold weight. We say this sometimes, as lip service, but it's true. It's like having a sticker affixed to your back that the rest of the world can read but you can't. Before I could even speak, I was told who and what I was. I was mean.

In my defense, I did not have a proper name for the first few years of my life. My birth certificate reads, simply, "Baby Girl Beit-ner." In babyhood, I was given the nickname Baby Bear. My mom said they called me Bear because I had such a furry head that they would have to rub it to make way for my forehead. (I used to feel bad about this bit of my history, until I read that Rene Russo was born with the same affliction.)

Eventually, my family started calling me Blair—after Blair Moody, my mother told me. A U.S. senator and circuit court judge from Michigan whom she admired. This was funny, because I was so moody. (To this I say: Be careful what you name your kid!) I remember being a Blair, because they would all spell it out when-ever they talked about me, as though I wouldn't piece it together. "B-L-A-I-R was mean," or "B-L-A-I-R wants to come."

This continued until I was three, when I went to preschool and needed a legal name. My mother decided to name me Selma, after her much-adored friend who died around the time I was born. In the Jewish tradition, babies are never named after a living person, and this seemed like a fitting tribute. The other names in contention were Ethel, Gretel—which I would have liked—Marta, Martha, and Gwyneth. (Gwyneth! To think, I could have been one, too!) There came a point where I loudly proclaimed, "When am I going to get one of those names?" referring to my sisters' nicknames of Ducky, Precious, and Princess. I wanted a pretty name. But it was not to be. From this point forward, I was Selma Blaire Bear Beitner, though my mother eventually removed the *e* from "Blaire," because she said it was "too pretentious." And there you have it.

For my entire life, I have been both. Selma and Blair. My two names would come to define me, as much as the stories around them.

As a child, I never took to the name Selma. It seemed to me an old lady's name, not a name befitting a little girl. When given a choice, I always asked to be called Blair, but I got a real boatload of "Selma" in elementary school. Whenever the teacher did roll call, I was too shy to ask, "Can you call me Blair?" So all day long I was Selma, or Bat Sheva, the Hebrew name used by the teachers at my Jewish day school, and at home I was Blair. Mom was always sorry I didn't like Selma. A feminine of Saint Anselm, the Benedictine monk. Or a reference to Selma, Alabama. It was a good name, she often reminded me.

When I was five years old, Mom, Dad, and I went on a weekend trip where I struck up a friendship with a family with a baby. As we lounged poolside, the mother asked my name, and I casually replied that it was Lisa—a nice, normal name. As Lisa, I played with that baby for three hours, helping her navigate the hotel pool in her floaties. When the afternoon sun sank low in the sky, the woman approached my mother and told her that her daughter Lisa had been so helpful.

"Lisa!" My mother let out a wail. "Her name's not Lisa! What a crock! What a liar!"

The woman looked at me as though she were seeing me for the first time. My lovely afternoon had been erased. I was no longer Lisa, and now I was a liar as well.

⁕

My mother nicknamed me Saintly, but it was tongue in cheek. I was no saint. I could sometimes be saintly to my mother, but to everyone else I was a mean baby.

Growing up, I shared a bedroom with my sister Lizzie, since we were closest in age. Our parents let us choose the wallpaper, and since Lizzie didn't care, I picked a pattern with little pink and blue flowers floating against white. I chose it because it looked similar to what Jessica Lange describes as her childhood wallpaper in the movie *Tootsie*. Movies, even then, were what gave me ideas and hope.

Our room had two twin beds and those vinyl shades you needed to tug in order to pull them up or down. Every morning, I got out of bed very, very quickly. I had never been one to linger. (Can you believe it?) I rushed to pull the shade down, so it would snap to attention and rip-roll up loudly, sending the diffused morning sun straight into Lizzie's eyes.

"*Yehi or!*" I'd yell at the top of my lungs, quoting from the first lines of Genesis, the Hebrew words for "Let there be light!"

"Blair!" she would croak, rubbing her eyes. "Why do you do this?"

Next I made my way around the room, throwing open the door, turning on the television atop Mom's childhood maple dresser, her mother's before her, and flicking on the lights. I needed life, immediately. I needed every bit of everything, every bit of help, anything I could reach in order to cheerlead myself into embracing my day. Even then, I did this.

This was how our days began. I made Lizzie crazy. But she put up with me. Every night, we said good night back and forth until one of us fell asleep. She was always there with me.

I was three years old and jumping on the bed with Lizzie when I sank my teeth into her back for no good reason I can recall and took out a chunk of flesh, leaving a bluish-reddish dent in her skin. She forgave me for this, too.

When my father's father, Abraham, died, I stood next to my dad as he accepted condolences at the funeral and punched every man who came near us in the nuts. I was at groin level, and somehow I thought it made sense. (After that I was banned from family functions and made to stay home with our nanny.)

Then there was the time our next-door neighbor Mr. Glen was adjusting his sprinkler with this long metal rod, the water-valve key, and with the fervor of a dog chasing an intruder, I ran over to his yard, grabbed the poker out of his hand, swung it, and hit him squarely in the balls. Bridge instantly burned. He told my parents to "keep that mongrel out of my yard."

For a moment when I was six, I had a babysitter who was the daughter of a family friend. She had an amputation at the knuckle of her ring finger, chopped off by a paper cutter, she told me after I asked. I would study it as she read *Lassie* to me, imagining what it must be like to be her.

One afternoon, while we were playing checkers, I decided to make her feel better. I tucked my own ring finger under itself, pretending that part of it was gone. In my misguided way, I was attempting to make a connection. I thought she would believe me and think, "We're the same!" and that it would bond us. Instead, she reported to my mother that I was making fun of her.

She never came back.

Sometimes, I hung out by myself at the park behind our house after school, practicing my gymnastics. One of my specialties was the cherry drop, in which you hook your knees over a metal bar and swing and swing, then flip yourself over and land on your feet. "That's impressive," another kid's mom would say, to which I'd reply, "Yes, I'm training for the Olympics." Then I would strike the pose, arms outstretched and aloft, fingers splayed, as if I'd just finished my winning floor routine. As if that weren't enough, I continued spinning the tale, telling her how my trainer was arriving in a bit.

When I was two or three, on a vacation in Puerto Rico, I found myself separated from my parents in a busy plaza. An older woman found me wandering alone; she approached me and asked, "Are you lost, little girl?" I stared her down with my mean baby face, and when she didn't go away, I shouted, "Shut up!" When she asked again if I needed help, I screamed, "Get out of here!" Shaken, the kind woman waited until I was reunited with my family, at which point she reported to my mother what a horrid child I was and promptly fled the scene. "Shut up! Get out of here!" became an oft-repeated line in our household for years to come.

In fourth grade, I dared Ilyssa Wolin to swallow a row of staples so I could have her jeans when she died. I vaguely recall her folding the pointy ends inward with her purple-polished nails and swallowing. Even though I wanted those jeans, I must have been relieved when the day continued without her sudden death.

One of my worst recurring mean baby tricks was to pretend I'd lost my earring. As a child, I was always losing earrings while trying on turtlenecks and pulling them off. Somewhere I had learned that this was a consistent way to get the attention I craved. In kindergarten, I'd cry, "Oh my gosh! Oh no! I lost my earring! It just fell out of my ear on the ground!" Like clockwork, everyone stopped whatever they were doing and crawled around searching for my "missing" jewelry, which was never going to be found because it was safely in my pocket.

Once I successfully performed this trick enough times for a familiar audience, I decided to take it on the road. A boy from my old day-care center was having a birthday party, and I was invited. Once again, I told everyone in attendance that I lost my earring. "My mother will kill me if I don't find it!" I lamented, sending the boy's poor mother scrambling to locate it. She got down on her hands and knees, scouring the ground for my missing stud, patting under party shoes and brushing aside bits of bubble gum, when she should have been enjoying her son's party. Everyone spent most of their time searching.

When my mother came to pick me up, the boy's mom approached her, calmly promising that they would try to find the earring.

"Selma, what on earth!" my mom cried.

"I'm so sorry, Molly," the woman said to my mother in a hushed tone. "Selma said you have a temper—"

"She didn't lose her earring! She's a liar!"

The jig was up.

The boy's mother had been nothing but kind to me until this point, but in that instant everything shifted. The goody bags were all lined up on a table. I was reaching out for mine, and she looked me in the eye and said, "I don't think so." That was a good mom.

Looking back, I think I was jealous of how much that mom loved her son. She put so much effort into throwing her beautiful boy a suitably beautiful party, and I wanted the warm glow of that kind of attention to be lavished on me. I longed to understand how that felt. I thought there needed to be an emergency to get attention, and in the absence of a real emergency I manufactured one.

I didn't realize that I was wrecking someone else's party, or that I was taking away from this boy, until it was over. That was just one of my mean baby–isms, a penchant for ruining everyone's time. I bedeviled people, as my mother said, but I was misunderstood. All I wanted was to be that boy's friend, and instead I destroyed my chances. I still wonder if anyone knows I'm the same Blair who made everyone search for her earring.

To add insult to injury, I also told all the kids at the birthday party that the hot dogs—tiny party franks—resembled my dad's wiener. My mom turned to me in the parking lot as soon as we were out of earshot.

"Selma, when did you ever see your dad's penis?" she asked.

"I didn't," I told her. In fact, I had never seen it. It just seemed like something to say. Something funny.

My mother burst out laughing, so tickled was she that all the kids now thought my dad was equipped with a pig in a blanket. When we arrived home, she made me recount the story so my father would know how I'd slandered him. I don't think he particularly cared, though I'm sure he wouldn't have chosen that narrative.

Over and over, my impulses only cemented me as an evil, awful, but cute and determined bad seed. It felt . . . not so great. And I felt guilty and ashamed about all of it, horrible even, once I realized what I had done. But with no real plan to change who I was. What my label said. Mean baby. I didn't know how to make it better. I didn't understand how to be empathic. Or patient. The truth is, I wasn't wicked; I was merely a child who didn't plan her actions well. But it was no matter. I lived up to my name.

I was a mean baby. As if I'd ever had a choice.

Birth Stories

My three sisters and I were all born at 8:45 on a Friday morning, purposefully scheduled so my mother would have the weekend to recover, as she tells it, and get back to work on Monday. My mom packed a punch with this story, whether or not it was accurate. My sister Katie says this story is a myth, that my mother stayed home for a standard maternity leave of about six weeks. But I like my mom's version better, because it seems like a more accurate reflection of her. The version of herself that she wanted to show off. Strong, resolute, remarkable, formidable—which was certainly the impression she wanted among her colleagues. (And I think, by the time I arrived, she was such a pro that she might have in fact returned to work in three days.)

I came into this world on June 23, 1972, at Sinai Hospital in Detroit. The doctor who delivered me was named Dr. Liptschitz, a fact I've always found very amusing (so does my son). As with much of my folklore, I discovered this tidbit from reading about it later, in a baby book I found in the basement. With its pink quilted taffeta cover that was water-stained from one of the basement floods, it looked old, even when I first stumbled across it as a child, the pages molded out and watermarked, the ink already turning colors. There's a picture of me as a newborn, and underneath it my mother had written, "Her eyes are so blue, and everybody says she looks just like mommy!"

These words thrilled me then and still do now. I wished to be like my mother since the second I was born.

The truly amazing thing about my birth was that my mother, who had never watched one of her C-sections before, told the nurses, "This is my last chance. I want to watch." So, she sat, propped up on her elbows, and observed as they cut into her belly. She loved to tell me this story, usually after dinner, once she'd had a couple glasses of wine. I was proud of my birth story. Proud that my mother was a witness and chose to be.

"Selma, it was wild! They actually took my intestines out," she told me, "and put them on the table!"

"Did it hurt?" I asked.

"No, no real pain," she said. "It just felt like people poking around. I was so thrilled I was going to see my baby!"

She reminded me that the nurses all cried—I loved this part, too—because they had never seen a mother so engaged with the experience of seeing herself be cut open and watching them lift out the fully cooked baby.

"Then they pulled you out, and I said, 'Oh, she's beautiful!'"

Family

SOME PEOPLE LOOK to their family to discover the origin of physical traits. What have they inherited from the past? Do they have their aunt Jean's nose? Their uncle Fred's eyes?

I look to my family for signs of illness, for evidence of sadness. I look to my history to trace where my maladies come from and whether they can be conquered. I also look to them for signs of resilience, for evidence of strength.

To understand the course of any cycle, we must trace it back to the beginning. Before me, there was my mother, Molly. And before her, there was her father, James Cooke, the man I knew as PopPop. When I open the door to the past to try to understand who I am, my maternal grandfather is the first one I see. I am my mother's daughter, fashioned in her image, and she was her father's, fashioned in his. As soon as I close my mind's eye, there he is, neatly pressed and fresh in his bow tie, with that same sideways smile I inherited.

PopPop was born Jewish in Kiev, where his father owned a successful tailoring business, known for his exquisite eye for dressmaking. When the pogroms began in the early twentieth century, his father brought the family to America. PopPop was only two years old. The family was always careful to say that they traveled in second class to Ellis Island. No steerage for them! Appearances mattered to my relatives, even when they were escaping persecution.

The family settled in Philadelphia and drifted away from Judaism in order to assimilate—to become American—though I recently learned that PopPop spoke fluent Yiddish. He was, in fact, a member of the Kohanim, descendants of the biblical Aaron who are conferred special privileges in synagogue. They are chosen beyond chosen. Still, he thought of himself as an ethnic Jew, not a religious one. And an American first and foremost.

My grandfather was one of eleven siblings, and as a child he worked with his older brother Sam, selling peas on Dock Street in Philadelphia. I learned about the pea selling only recently, from my cousin Joanna. "Wait, PopPop had a *vegetable* cart?" My elegant, worldly PopPop. I couldn't believe it. "It's like *My Fair Lady,* in Yiddish!" I was charmed by this detail.

When PopPop was a teenager, his brother Paul was out walking with their father and didn't see the trolley car barreling toward them. Their father looked up just in time to shove Paul out of the trolley's path before he was struck and killed instantly. I'm told my great-grandmother screamed and wailed as her husband's casket was lowered into the ground. She was alone, in a foreign country, with eleven children to feed. The grief was written on her face for the rest of her life. Paul and some of the younger children were sent to live in an orphanage, while PopPop was deemed old enough to live on his own.

PopPop and his brother Sam went on to become successful owners of a national chain of supermarkets called Penn Fruit. As a wealthy man, PopPop reinvented himself. He moved near the posh Main Line of Philadelphia and adopted the WASP uniform of tweed and seersucker.

I knew PopPop only as an unusually urbane and sophisticated American man, a lover of Shakespeare and Saul Bellow, well-heeled and dapperly dressed, with bow ties to match his adorable bowlegs. He was a doting grandfather who signed his letters to me "Oceans of Love, PopPop." For me, those words held all possibilities. An ocean of love. These words are the opposite of feeling unwanted. The promise of something exotic and grand. It's such a beautiful phrase. I still use it sparingly, for the best people.

June 23, 1987

Oceans of love to my dearly beloved Blair on your birthday and many happy returns! Pop Pop

Growing up, my beautiful mother, Molly, was definitely a daddy's girl. She was PopPop's pride and joy, but like so many relationships it was complicated. He had a lock on her insecurities and could be critical. When I was ten or eleven, they had a terrible fight, after which their relationship was never the same. It started when he commented that her face was damp with sweat, an insult that deeply offended my mother, who took meticulous care in her appearance. "Lock him up!" my mother cried. I heard her on the phone, griping about this "dig" to a friend. "I never, ever sweat," she said. "My father of all people should know this." This was true, so far as I could tell. My mother's face was always matte, her skin perfectly powdered. No evidence of perspiration, ever, just as there were no signs of weakness.

PopPop died a few years later, when I was in ninth grade. We made the drive from Michigan to Pennsylvania to bury him; my sister Lizzie stuck a candy cane up my nose, and the blood came down bright and rich where it cut. My mother looked in the backseat to see what had happened. I was careful not to complain. Her father was dead. I knew how much she loved him, in spite of it all.

When we put the dirt on his coffin, my mother cried, wailed into the bleak winter day. "Daddy. My daddy."

There is always one person who gets under our skin, who knows our weak spots and neuroses and can't help but go in for the kill. They are the people who wound us the most, because we care so much about what they think.

For my mother, that person was PopPop.

For me, that person is my mother.

Was my mother a daddy's girl because her mother didn't like her? Or did her mother dislike her because of her devotion to Pop-Pop? I was always told that my grandmother Goggy was sadistic toward my mother, but the details remain unclear. I'll never know if there was one event or just a long series of slights and insults that accumulated over time. No one in my family seems to remember exactly what happened, only that Lillian always favored my aunt Sally, and PopPop favored my mother.

According to Cooke family lore, the first thing PopPop noticed about Lillian Minor were her legs. "Who is the lady with the gorgeous gams?" he inquired about the pretty new gal working as a cashier in the grocery store that he managed. He was sixteen; she was fifteen. They married soon after and had two daughters.

My mother was named after an aunt of Lillian's who died of complications from an abortion—a tragic story that was not sugarcoated and had the intended consequence of making me terrified of having sex and getting pregnant.

Like PopPop, Lillian was the child of first-generation immigrants, and her brother James died of rheumatic fever at thirteen. When the embalmer came to prepare the body for burial, she watched as her brother's blood was drained into a bucket. She developed a lifelong fear of blood, which she passed on to my mother. (Now my son has this aversion, too. A stubbed toe or scraped knee is enough to make him lose his breath.)

Over the years, Lillian grew heavy and unhappy; I'm not sure which came first. Eventually PopPop, who judged women harshly for their weight, lost interest in her. Their marriage floundered, and they became estranged and then divorced.

⁓

When I was little, Lillian lived alone in a luxurious apartment building not far from our house in Southfield, Michigan, and she would invite her granddaughters—Katie, Lizzie, and me—to stay overnight. (Mimi was both too loyal to PopPop and too old for sleepovers by then.) But the three of us loved it. She doted on us in a way our mother did not. She let us have candy, she took us to see *The Wiz,* we played Parcheesi. I quite liked her. Still, I always steeled myself for the day when she would embarrass me or hurt me, because my mother said that was what Goggy did.

I waited. It never came to pass.

I loved my mother and I loved my grandmother. I wanted to

understand what had happened between them, in part because I didn't want the same thing to happen between my mother and me. So, one Saturday night in bed with Goggy, I asked her, "Do you think you were a good mother?"

She paused, considering it, then said, "Yes. I tried to be. Why?"

I admitted, "My mother said you weren't."

She didn't say anything, and we went to sleep.

On the way home the next day, my sister Lizzie reported what I'd said back to my mother. We were never allowed to visit Goggy's apartment again. We hardly ever saw Goggy after that, except at extended family gatherings at aunt Sally's house with uncle Jim and the cousins. Our allegiance was with our mother.

When Lillian was in her final years in a nursing home, she and my mother did reconcile. Enough. My mother was a moderate drinker by then, and for Christmas she would drop off cases of alcohol for Goggy—enough for a sizable wedding. "There, that should last Goggy for a year," she'd say. She literally drove her own mother to drink. But my mother might have meant it as a sign of love. Alcohol was the greatest salve she knew.

࿇

When my mother was a teenager, she became ill with a life-threatening viral infection, and Lillian sent her away to an institution to convalesce. My mother became so sick that her family was told to prepare for her death. She recovered, but it caused her to lose all her hair. One night she'd gone to bed with a full head of dark hair, and when she woke up, every strand was on her pillow. Her hair grew back, damaged and thin. It, and my mother, were never quite the same.

This was a period in her life that she seldom talked about. She even gave herself a different name during that time: Roseanne. She wanted to pretend the entire episode had happened to someone else.

I only learned about this when I found a drawing nestled among her keepsakes. The signature read, "Roseanne."

"This is really good, Mom. Who made this?" I asked.

And she said, "Oh, I did, after high school."

"But the name says 'Roseanne.'" I tilted my head. "Who is Roseanne?"

My mother explained it as if it were a perfectly normal thing to do. She was attempting to create a separate self, almost like a character she had performed in a play. That was all she said. Away into her drawer it went, never to be opened again.

Keeping up appearances mattered so much to PopPop, and my mother followed his lead. She was always impeccably dressed: regal in an Ungaro suit and Charles Jourdan four-inch heels, never without a full face of beauty. Only once did I see her wear sneakers—a pair of chic Keds in a style her idol Jackie O might have worn—paired with her signature red lip.

She was truly stunning; she resembled a young Anne Bancroft. She had good height and a nice figure, and she was thin. The rest, she understood, could be made glamorous. She wanted to make an impact.

My sisters and I were not allowed in our parents' bedroom until our mother was "complete," meaning fully dressed and made up. She wouldn't so much as open the bedroom door unless she had styled hair, red lips, a face contoured by Pattie Boyd's makeup maps, and pink blush. She kept the house lights dim to hide signs of her aging, even removing some of the bulbs. "I look best in low lighting," she would say. A friend of Mimi's once said my mom looked crazy because she wore too much blush, and it made me so angry I never spoke to that friend again.

That my mother had lost the thickness of her hair to the virus remained the biggest secret. She always wore a well-done hairpiece mixed in with her own hair, something I found out only accidentally. One day, I was hiding in her bed, under a blanket, when I saw her emerge from the dressing room. At first, I didn't recognize her; it took me several moments to understand. I was so shocked I couldn't move. Until that moment, I had no idea that her hair was a wig. I'm not sure if she knew I was there, if she knew I knew her secret. We never discussed it.

Roseanne was bald. Molly was not. Now I'd like to think that wouldn't have been such a big deal. But she was from a different generation, and a family that equated illness with weakness, and weakness was to risk becoming a victim, and she guarded her facade of strength above all else.

Once, I saw her lying in her bed asleep without her hair and makeup. I was shocked to see her that way, in a cotton nightgown and a terry cloth turban, pale, sans mascara or lipstick. She looked like a pharaoh. She was quite beautiful this way, actually. But it was also frightening, because this wasn't the mother I knew. How shocking to discover that underneath it all, she just looked like a lovely young woman.

❧

My mother had the ability to stop people in their tracks. Much like PopPop, she possessed a star quality, an inherent spotlight that followed her wherever she went. She was a sphinx; people thought there was a deep mystery about her because her eyes held fun and sadness. And she was well dressed. My mother understood that presentation is everything. PopPop had his bespoke suits. My mother was always elegantly attired. Unsurprisingly, I too love couture.

If ever we passed a child who was dolled up by their mother, my own mother would take note and say, "That child is loved." It was my mother's greatest disappointment whenever I wasn't turned out well. "Selma, please make yourself beautiful," she would say. "It means so much." Once I was capable, I really did try. And I curried favor with her, because nothing was more important than showing off her children. She loved us. And she loved us more when we looked good.

We had very few things, but they were beautiful things. My mom bought me my first Burberry coat when I was twelve. (I remember how the saleswoman's eyes popped out of her young head at the thousand-dollar price tag when she rang up our purchase at the register. "What a lucky girl you are!" she exclaimed.) My mother even had my name embroidered on the inside, just as she did with her minks and sables and snow foxes. (It was the seventies.)

For my mother, fashion was more than just a wardrobe. It was a character. It was from her that I learned that the right clothes could protect you against a world that wants to tear you down, that people will treat you with more respect when you look cared for. Every day she got dressed to play a role. She was, in many ways, the first great stage actress I saw up close.

As soon as my mother left for work at 5:00 a.m. for the two-hour drive to the capital of Lansing, I'd head right for her immaculate closet. I'd try on her makeup at her vanity sink, examine her silk YSL shirts and Givenchy dresses, slip on her Maud Frizon heels. Everything she owned was quality. She always warned us against trends, telling us only to buy what would still be classic in ten years. She understood the power of a uniform, another lesson she passed down to me. People would ask her, "Why do you stay so skinny?" and she would say, "I can fit more in my closet this way!" A joke I never got until much later in life. But I also came to understand it was part of her frugality. If you're going to buy expensive clothes, you want to keep them for life. Her philosophy was spend as much as you can afford; then do whatever you must to continue to fit into it. She was very practical in that way.

At the same time, she cautioned against becoming too stuck in one's ways. If we were out somewhere and she caught sight of someone with a dated look—if our server at the steak house was an old-time broad, with dyed-black hair and cat eyeliner—she made an example out of them. "Careful, girls," she'd say. "You get your look, but you need to adjust it in time."

My mother saved her money. When she spent, she did so carefully. She was offended if ever I bought something cheap and trendy. "Why can't you just spend a little more and make yourself look important, Selma?"

Once when I was in high school, my mom took me to the Chanel counter to buy me a lipstick. I don't look right with lipstick and I never have. My face doesn't tolerate it; I look severe, not soft. But my mother always loved a lip on me, and I wanted to make her happy. When the person at the makeup counter said it was twenty dollars, I remember how she carried on. "Twenty dollars?! I like nice things, but twenty dollars!" She bought it anyway. It was hot pink. After all that fuss, it was so perfume-y and tasted so strongly like Chanel lipstick that I never wore it. I wore it just once, on Mackinac Island, with a green suede vest and my hair bleached blond and parted on the side, just the way she liked it.

My mother had rules. I followed each one to the letter.

"Don't wear anything you wouldn't still wear in ten years."
"Classic is best."
"Go high drama, make it worth it."
"A miss is as good as a mile."
"Never chew gum in public."
"People who say 'classy' have no class."
"Never drink and drive."
"People who walk with a lit cigarette have very bad
    taste . . . It stinks."
"When you get to the door to leave, take one thing off."

But the one that I thought of all the time: "A good girl parts her hair on the side." If ever I parted my hair in the middle, she would say I resembled a renegade from an insane asylum. "Selma. Bad girls part their hair in the middle. Good girls part their hair on the side."

Looking back, I see that my mother was so much like her father. She could be simultaneously affectionate and hurtful; like Pop-Pop, she knew how to wound those she loved with her barbs. Her four daughters were frequent targets.

She made fun of me for my lazy eye, my hideous flanks of cheeks, and what she called my "jolie laide" quality. "How can you be so beautiful from one angle and so ugly full face?" My mother said I looked like Lauren Bacall, but only with my head turned three-quarters—never head-on. "Don't look at people head-on, Selma, or they'll know you're a frying pan." Always, always three-quarters. That became my mirror face and, eventually, how I would learn to pose.

Unlike other mothers, who told their children they were beautiful without a stitch of makeup on, she just wanted me to look good.

"Put on some makeup, Selma, your eyes look like piss holes in the snow!"

"Selma! You've got hair above your lip. But it's chic. Very European."

"Oh, Selma, fix your hair. It looks like a plate of worms."

"Selma, get on the stick. Make yourself presentable, please."

If someone said I was beautiful, my mother would squint, as if seeing me for the first time. "You really think so? Her lip sticks out kinda far." But when I fixed myself up, the accolades were so gratifying. The compliments were very few; she doled them out very carefully. I lived for her approval.

She called my feet bear paws, because, though they are flat, I have fallen arches. "Oh, Selma! Walk on your toes!" she called, whenever I got out of a pool. "You're leaving bear prints! It's embarrassing!" It was framed as a joke, but I understood that she meant it. I was never easily embarrassed by my mother. Even when she criticized me, in public or in private, I never minded. Still, it all gets in your head. I'm at a point in my life now when I can no longer walk on my toes, and this devastates me.

My mother always carried herself with the air of an aristocrat or stage actress, even though she wasn't. But she was educated, poised, and worldly.

"To know the rules is to break the rules," she'd say. I always found that fascinating. She was a judge; she *was* the rules.

I loved her, and I feared her, in equal measure. Looking back, I can see she designed it that way.

"You're a witch like me, Selma," my mother once said. She wasn't a witch, at least not in practice. She certainly never put a potion together. But she did give me a certain power, by saying that we were alike.

⌒⁀

When it came to storytellers, my mother was the most gifted one of all. She painted the world with self-fulfilling prophecies. Starting when I was around five or six, whenever we had guests over, my mother lined the four of us up, like the von Trapp children, and introduced us.

"Here is Marie, the student," she said of Mimi.

"Katherine, the overachiever." This drove Katie wild, and still does. "I can't believe Mom would call me that!" she'd lament. "It's really fucking awful. It means you're not capable, but that you've still done shit. Everyone wants to be an underachiever, which is a good, talented person who just hasn't tapped into it yet." (Katie, may the record state: you are not an overachiever.)

"This is Lizzie, the popular athlete," which she sometimes alternated with "Lizzie, the tomboy."

"And last but not least, Selma, the manic-depressive."

I always found this funny because there was nothing manic about me. I have only ever been a depressive. But I didn't dare protest. I considered it my fortune to play the part assigned to me. "Oh, it's true!" my mom would say, in case anyone harbored any doubt.

Just like that, she cemented us with our own identities.

Sometimes, she said cruel things, too. Once, about happy-go-lucky Lizzie, she said, "You could cover her soul with a dime." It wasn't true, of course, but Lizzie internalized it. How could she not?

Because my mother introduced me to her friends as a manic-depressive, she not only convinced herself it was who I was; she convinced me. The part was written for me; she wanted me to play it well, and I wanted to make her proud. Can we ever escape the labels our families bestow upon us?

For my sixth birthday, she brought me to Goldfingers, the very chic boutique jewelry store in Applegate Square, a great eighties shopping center, and picked out a gift—a gold necklace that I still wear. One side featured a girl with a bowl cut and smiley face, the other side, the same girl with a frown.

Does the face inform the personality, or was it the other way around? It's a chicken-and-egg thing, I think. However it happened, I grew into my fate.

"There, Selma! Now we don't have to guess," she said. "You wear the happy side when you're happy and the frown when you frown." It became my signature piece, and everyone knew to look for it. Now they could simply scan my necklace, and if they saw a smile, they knew it was safe to approach me.

Years after I received this gift, my sister Katie wrote a poem about the necklace for a college writing class, which I kept in my journal:

Dangling

You twirl one-handed cartwheels
Each limb moves the air flying
You soar beyond others, hopes and dreams
The smiling pendant dangles at your neck
I see you writing at your desk
Your hair just

Past the childish stringy stage
Hides your eyes as you scribble
I think what you write will be worthwhile
Your happiness sudden then subtle
Is a pink pastel mark
Your soiled fingertips move the colors on the page
These few motions make art
The smile fades
A halfhearted leap flips the pendant
Blair where has it all gone?
A stream of dazzlement has dried
A frown now dangles at your heart.

⸺

My mother admired Waspy women well turned out, so I did, too. She especially adored Grace Kelly. In my mind, I built the impression that they were friends, and that vague story led me to admire all things flaxen-haired and athletic, especially if it came along with big white teeth and some generational wealth. That was the thing back then, and it always came with that rarefied air of belonging—something I never felt. I loved thinking my mom was so important that she had a direct line to the world of celebrities. I believed that everyone she knew was really important, though in reality they were nothing more than acquaintances whom she sometimes mentioned.

When Grace Kelly died, my mother was so sad, quite possibly the saddest I'd ever seen her. No one was more revered than Grace, although Natalie Wood was a close second. When Natalie died, I came home and told the horrible joke I'd heard on the bus to school. "What kind of wood doesn't float?" That was so typical of the 1980s, to tell those types of insensitive jokes without any awareness of how inappropriate they were. Needless to say, it didn't go over well. My mother was sickened and furious when I repeated what I heard.

Elizabeth Taylor did not garner the same esteem, at least not in my mother's eyes. She said she once saw her in a mall and was not impressed. "She looked like the cleaning lady!" I think she never forgave her for what she did to Debbie Reynolds, another of my mom's favorites. (I found this especially fascinating in light of the fact that the two women eventually mended their friendship. Elizabeth and Debbie might have been able to forgive, but my mother was not.) My mom also placed such a premium on skinniness and height, and Elizabeth was not known for either, especially in her later years.

I didn't have many connections to the outer world, our social circle was small, so these tokens from my family came to mean so much. An anecdote meant someone was my mother's best friend, and a gift or a photo meant we were connected. I had a yellow T-shirt with a photo of Elvis ironed on it, a gift from my aunt Anna when I was five. My sisters all got one, too, so I wore that same shirt, in all the different sizes, throughout my life. I always believed Elvis might secretly be my father, because we looked alike. I told other kids that he might be a close family friend! I sometimes claimed Muhammad Ali was my cousin. I was a total liar for much of my life, but it's only because I liked a good story. I didn't mean to lie; I just didn't do a lot of fact-checking.

Even though we could claim no connection to her, my mother and I both loved Brooke Shields. We had a Scavullo coffee-table book, and I looked at it every day. There was a photo of Brooke without a top on, with that long hair and those eyes. I would gaze at it and think, *I wish, I wish, I wish.* I knew I could never measure

up, but it was no matter. These figures loomed larger than life. To this day, I still can't get them out of my mind.

❧

My mother's love of Waspy women went all the way back to her childhood. She grew up in an enclave with the kinds of blue-blooded women that Grace Kelly or Katharine Hepburn might play in a movie. After her illness, she attended Vassar, but she bristled at authority, so she dropped out after one semester. She married at age twenty, to an aspiring doctor, and was pregnant right away. Her parents put her new husband through medical school, which he thanked them for by abandoning his wife and infant daughter. Soon after the baby, my sister Mimi, was born, when she and Mom were attending Sally's wedding to Uncle Jimmy, Mom's husband skipped town for California and never returned. He started a new life with a new family, without ever acknowledging he'd had a family before. By telegram he told her: "Don't bother coming back for your things. I shipped them to Detroit." Then he charged her for shipping.

After her first husband left, my mother moved in with her parents, who by then had relocated to Michigan in order to expand PopPop's grocery store chain into the Midwest. She spent one whole week playing double solitaire, crying, smoking cigarettes, and watching her baby daughter, Mimi, play on the carpet. Then she dried her eyes and decided to up and go to law school. That would be the thing. She would not be vulnerable again.

Even though she didn't have a college degree, she managed to get herself into the University of Detroit Law School. The day she graduated, her mother, Goggy, gave her a pair of emerald earrings, which are now among my most treasured possessions, and she began her career as an attorney. She was a single working mother, beholden to no one. Powerful, brilliant, fully independent. A few years later, she agreed to marry the first—and, my mother claims, the only—man who would have her, a Jewish lawyer named Elliot Isser Beitner. "What else was I going to do? Who else would have me? I was damaged goods," she said. Looking back, their relationship was imbalanced from the start: Elliot worshipped his dazzling, ambitious wife, and she merely tolerated him.

Elliot's nonreligious, Eastern European–born parents, Esther and Abraham, didn't approve of my mother right away—she was, after all, a "shiksa." An East Coast gentile divorcée with a toddler—but Molly and Esther eventually warmed up to each other well enough. Esther's first and only question about Molly was, "But can she drive?" and she was thrilled when the answer was yes. Elliot and Molly married under a chuppah.

What my mother wanted—more than a husband—was a successful career and financial autonomy. She also wanted to stay stylish and beautiful till the end. I used to study her high school yearbook photo for hours, looking for clues about who she was before she became my mother. The picture showed her looking impossibly elegant (to me), her dark, sharp eyes alert and determined. Underneath her photo, it read, "Molly Ann Cooke is a sophisticated gal with a flair for dressing attractively." I longed for those same words to be written about me.

Elliot adopted Mimi, who was so grateful to have a father figure in her life that it seems she developed a bit of a crush on him at first. One day while sitting poolside together on vacation, she took his hand, squinted, and said, "'Haps we kill Mommy?" Elliot found this hilarious and reported the quip back to my mother, who was amused. But Mimi and Dad didn't become close.

My mother went on to have three more daughters. The four brown-haired Beitner girls. We would've given Louisa May Alcott a run for her money.

Molly was not particularly maternal. Usually, when I'd ask what we were having for dinner, she'd say "poison" without skipping a beat. I thought it funny. Poison was the easiest conversation ender. She had a full day of work as a judge and then came home to make dinner. She was a mother at a time when work-life balance wasn't a goal that women thought about or talked about or strove to achieve. Most of the women in our comfortable Michigan suburb stayed home and raised their children. She could not have known that it was possible to both have a powerful career and be an engaged mother. Life didn't cater to children and mothers so much then. It was a different generation. She chose her work because she didn't have a choice. To do both would have been impossible.

As much as I missed her because she worked long hours, I was impressed with her. It was my mother whom I revered and emulated more than anyone. I was mesmerized by her—her smile, her makeup, her clothes, the small grape-sized birthmark on her right calf, her throaty laugh. The way she smoked, sometimes blowing out plumes through her nostrils when Lizzie yelled, "Dragon!" The way she sat behind the wheel of her car, leather-gloved hands turning up the heat in winter. The way she held her martini glass, with her painted red nails, during our parents' nightly cocktail hour. I was riveted by her. She was my first great love. I wanted every cell of her body to repopulate itself into mine. I wanted to become her. This feeling never faltered. Decades later, when she was suffering from neurological distress, my mother was the person whose approval meant the most to me. Even when she had no idea I was there.

⁓

I did not share all of these feelings with her. She was not gooey. Like PopPop, my mom was a woman who believed in decorum, that there was a real dignity in keeping quiet, in being stoic and private about one's personal affairs. "Never talk about religion or politics," she reminded us. Part of this was informed by the 1950s world in which she was an adolescent. Most of it was innate to her.

Growing up, I knew better than to complain about the sparks in my arms and hands that came and went, the repeating nightmares and dark thoughts that I recorded in my diary, the moments of existential anguish I felt even as a little girl. Nor did I disclose my deep desire to feel needed by her. Held by her. Because I was born terrified. I needed to keep very still so she wouldn't see the fear. And disapprove.

Still, my mother and I related through sadness in a way I think the other kids didn't. We didn't acknowledge it; it was more of an intuitive bond. I think she understood this about me, that she recognized my natural tendency toward despair because she was similarly afflicted. We were linked in this way.

Once, when I was in middle school, she told me that if things ever got really bad, we could always go into the garage together. We could turn on the Corvette, seal the doors, and breathe until we didn't. "We'd be together," she said. "So, you tell me." I thought she was trying to be kind; it was her wildly inappropriate way of recognizing my pain, even if it's horrifying to contemplate that a mother would suggest this to her daughter. My sisters were shocked! I see it now. She knew I was depressive, but if I told her—Yes, let's do it—she could stop me.

My mother never wore her heart on her sleeve, save for some periodic displays of anger or jest. She rarely shared anything personal, except occasionally when she was well into her cups. For as much as I watched her, for as much as I studied and revered her, sometimes I think I still don't know anything about her. All I know is that we both saw the world with a critical eye. "Realists!" she'd declare about us. I also inherited her deep appreciation for a body of water, a drink and a cigarette, and a great suit.

Sustenance

EVERY EVENING at 7:00 p.m., our family sat down to dinner. My mother worked a full day, drove the two hours home, and had a full dinner—steak or chicken with greens and potatoes, spaghetti with salad—on the table. "Girls! Dinner!" she called, right on time. We each reported to our places in the kitchen, at the Saarinen tulip table. And then we ate.

Dinner on Coventry Woods Lane was almost formal, my mother still in her pencil skirt and heels, red lipstick staining the rim of the martini glass that was forever sweating at her side, my father in a cashmere sweater and tweed jacket, eyeglasses his constant prop. It was also very civilized. My mother was a Republican and Elliot was a Democrat. This was a time when people could sit at the same table and talk respectfully about the issues of the day and their day, so they did.

Our meals were rather simple: steak, salad, spaghetti. But on the rare occasions when we had luxury, we were always aware of it, though in her fashion my mother was very fatalistic about it. "Girls, these scallops are very special," she would say. "The estuaries are going away. By the time you're grown up, there won't even be scallops left!"

We ate off the blue-and-white china. Before I was able to cut my own food, my mother, who sat to my left in the master chair with the molded arms, cut my steak into bite-sized pieces, thin and pink, blood pooling around the chunk. "Now make a clock," my mother would direct, before going back to her meal, the martini glass having been replaced with a long-stemmed goblet more than half full of red wine.

When we were all young, my parents shared a single bottle of wine with our meal. By the time I was ten or so, the bottle became a Rossi jug, and the glass would be refilled until she and my father were done. After dinner, as I cleared the plates and the crumpled, stained paper napkins, she stayed at the table, smoking a cigarette in the dim kitchen light.

When I was about five, with a lopsided bowl cut and a hard, round tummy, my favorite meal was spaghetti. I liked the al dente pasta with the jarred pasta sauce and especially the grated parmesan cheese from the green Kraft canister.

One night, when my mother called us in for dinner, I was hungrier than usual. It was summer and Lizzie and I had played outside all day. Sweaty, salty, ravenous girls. We took our places at the table, as always, with Katie to my right, my mother on my left.

My mom served me first, a plate of spaghetti with sauce and cheese. As I tried to wait for the rest of the family to be served, Lizzie's eyes were on me as I took a big bite from my plate. She announced this loudly to my mother. "Blair didn't mix her cheese in and she ate it!" She said it in such an alarming way, as if I'd committed a mortal sin. I felt terror, endangered.

I was mortified. I was a sensitive soul (despite biting my sister's back), and my favorite Lizzie, my twin, my everything, had just looked at me with such disdain and told the wrong I'd done. Her tone turned my body cold. My mother, plating our spaghetti, didn't say anything, which meant she must agree. I didn't wait for the ax to fall. To me, this was my army, and they had turned.

I didn't know how to translate shame, which in that moment felt as big as death. In my mind, I surmised I'd poisoned myself. If I didn't know I was not allowed to put unmixed Kraft in my mouth, then nothing was safe. I pushed back my chair and ran to the other end of the house. When I reached our room, I slid myself under my bed, into my own little bomb shelter. I would now die under this bed, with the stained carpeting, evening already settling in. I had no compass. I didn't know! "I am sorry," I whispered inside this space. For me, for my life, for unmixed plates of spaghetti. *I am sorry I am bad. I am sorry I am bad.* I'd later learn that old pets often go under the bed to die.

After a minute, Lizzie came in. She coaxed me out. My mother called us back to the table. Unsure, I sat down and watched my sisters eat. They were careful to mix the parmesan cheese into their sauce before they ate it.

As I gaze through the lens at a life's worth of moments, a plate of Barilla spaghetti and a reprimand from my beloved sister are seemingly unimportant, but it filled in my heart from such a young age. This was one of my first introductions to shame. The same shame would keep coming as years went on. There was a whole system, I saw, that wasn't about being good or even just being. It was about authority, with rules we are not born knowing. If this was how the world worked, I was in for a rough ride.

We don't know what stains a pure heart. We may not remember all those times, when we follow the wrong woman in the grocery store and reach for her hand and feel the red-hot shame for this understandable error. By the time we reach adulthood, we are so accustomed to being here that we forget how big everything used to be. The trespasses that to us seem light once felt like life and death.

If someone had held me and said, "Oh, honey, you're just a child, it will be okay," it might have felt okay. But I kept my secret. I became very anxious when eating in front of people. I tried to avoid meals with friends or boys. I would not eat spaghetti again until long after high school and the shame had faded into the black of the hallway inside me. Flat under the bed of my mind. Even then, the shame spilled out from under the dusty ruffles. Shame upon shame. For years to come, I would believe I should not eat what was put before me.

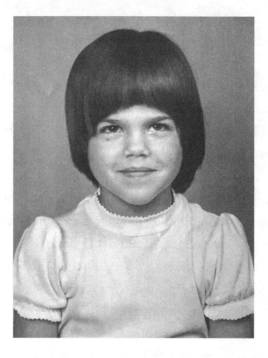

The first time I remember feeling self-conscious about my body was on picture day at Stevenson Elementary. I was in kindergarten, dressed in a royal blue pantsuit with a white cotton top. When I was brought in to have my portrait taken, the photographer looked at me and said, "What a bluebird!" He meant it affection-ately, a term of endearment. I still have the picture from that day, and I can now say I am objectively adorable. But at the time what I heard was: Bluebirds are fat. Bluebirds have fat chests and round bellies. I didn't want to look like a bluebird. I would not be fat.

In due course I grew out of being a bluebird and was, in fact, skinny. My mother would always exclaim how skinny and bony I was. I could tell by her voice that she didn't mind it. But she asked the doctor what she could do so I wouldn't look so fragile.

"Beer!" he said. "Put beer in her cereal. Beer is fattening!"

So, my mother advised beer in my cereal. It tasted awful. I like cereal and I grew to like beer, but not together. The prescription didn't take, in any event. I didn't gain a pound.

In fourth grade, a teacher told me I was very thin and that it looked nice. I pointed to another girl, Miri Bernard, and said, "Look at her, though. She's skinnier than I am." And the teacher said, "No, she's *small*. You're *thin*. Enjoy it."

⁓

My mother valued thinness, so I wanted to be thin. Like PopPop, she prized beauty above all. I had a lazy eye as a girl, which made me feel invisible, but she still believed I was the one daughter of hers who might be pretty enough to model, a profession she seemed to think my only prospect of employment. (I always found this curious coming from a judge who also claimed to value education above all else.) She warned me that once I got my period, I would stop growing, so she said I should try to postpone menstruation for as long as possible, as if it were a biological process I could control. "You need to be at least five feet eight to be a model," she'd say.

When I saw the first drops of brown blood at the age of eleven, I hid the evidence from my mother. I prayed I'd continue to grow taller, longer, leaner. I did not.

When I was in seventh grade, I told my mother I had started my period. I acted surprised, as if it had only just begun. She asked how much I weighed. "Ninety pounds," I said. She told me not to get a pound heavier. Not a single pound. "This is your weight," she said. "This is your size." I have been wary of weight gain ever since.

My mother was dictatorial about weight, perhaps because she had watched her own mother grow heavy when Molly was young. She saw weight gain as a lack of control, a sign of weakness (another bias handed down from PopPop), and as usually unflattering in clothing. My mother kept a diary of her weight and went through phases when she weighed herself obsessively. A few years ago, my sister and I found a detailed chart in one of her notebooks. It looked like an EKG printout. We had no idea what it was until we looked more carefully at the graph paper and realized that it was a record of her weight at every hour of the day for several years.

After she retired, she'd hole up at home alone, smoking and drinking with various suitors. I'd call her to see if she'd like company. "I can come out for a visit," I said. "Oh, don't come visit me, I'm too fat," she'd say. I knew better than to argue.

Sometimes, on weekends when I was little, my mother would invite me to take a nap with her, a special treat. She didn't like to be touched, so any chance to be close to her, my body aligned with hers, was sacred.

I remember one time in particular, when I was eight years old. The sky was a blank wash of gray, the few trees on the property were naked. I knew I was too old to nap, but I wanted to be near her, to smell her Fracas perfume and to be near the idea of her. She beckoned me beside her, and of course I accepted. I would do anything she wanted, anything at all.

I climbed into her giant bed, resting my head on her shoulder as we lay side by side.

She told me a story. I listened quietly. We were on a dogsled. "Look up at the stars, Blair!" she said. "It's snowing. We're on a sled, wrapped in fur rugs, and it's *so cold*!" I giggled, wanting her to go on. She did. "But we are safe on the sled; the dogs are running through the night. There are so many stars, like sparklers held high up in the night sky. It is so beautiful and exciting!"

I wanted to believe her tale. I could see it then. It was a magic carpet ride, an insulation from ordinary life. I longed to turn to her and whisper, "Mother, I am scared of everything but this moment, right now." But I didn't say a thing, because I didn't want her to stop. I scooted my butt closer to her. "Be still," she said. "Stop moving so much." I obeyed. She went on a bit longer, describing the sliver of moon, the frozen wind. And then she drifted off to sleep.

My mother's stories were my sustenance. I repeated this one over and over in my head, feeling the furs and the stars and the snow, the rushing and whistling wind, the dogs leaping. I wondered how they knew where to go. I fell asleep. Afraid as always, but safe in our sleep.

But those were not the only stories she told.

Sometimes she'd call me in for a nap, and I could tell by the look on her face that she was in no mood to tell me a whimsical tale. No dogsleds, no stars, no fur blanket. Instead, she'd tell me the story of how she didn't know if she wanted me, when I ask if she loved me from the start. "I already had three daughters," she said. She was older. She had a career. She didn't want to have another child.

Elliot didn't want this baby, either. Elliot pressured her to go to New York, she said, where abortion was legal.

Oh! When she got to this part, I felt so worried for her, my mom. I was only seven or eight, but I had heard the nightmare stories. I knew the woman she was named after had died from complications of an abortion. "Oh, Mommy," I'd say. "That sounds so scary."

Then she told me how she couldn't go through with it, didn't go through with it. And then I'd let out a breath.

I was always too scared to breathe during these stories. I knew I must stay still, silent. Any interruption was an attack, and she would retreat. When she was done, I always asked questions. But she said nothing more and eventually we fell asleep. Molly and the girl she chose to keep.

Later, when she was awake, I asked, "If I was never born, who would be Blair?" And she roared with laughter. I let out a small giggle. I had pleased her with my wit. She laughed so hard, clearly and deeply. I burrowed underneath the blanket next to her, close, breathing her in.

"Who would be Blair?" my mom says, when I visit her for the last time.

❧

I've been told that story all my life, in many ways been defined by it.

Unwanted.

I wonder if I absorbed my mother's ambivalence about having me even in utero. I wonder if it's embedded deep within me, a part of my DNA.

❧

Perhaps feeling guilty that she often told me how she hadn't wanted me, my mother took pains to show me I had earned the right to be here, that I was special to her.

Dear Mom, Don't show Lizzie,
I want to spend a day alone with you. you Said today was the day, but you are spending more Time with Lizzie, Do you love her better? Its awful staying here while you are having fun with Lizzie.
I wanted to make ~~what~~ whatever Bronia is making but Katie told me that she was. Katie is a Brat, she didn't even use the tape recorder once. I rike to hear tapes all the time but I Cant because you like to hear you're Books ontape and you told me to give it to Katie, you don't care when I'm hurt.
P.S. I'm crying I wish you'd send Katie away from me unloved

(margin notes: you HATE ME SHOW LOVE PLEASE / I never DI If It you don't T / tear drops)

When I was five, my mother entrusted to me her beloved doll named Skinny, a childhood relic she had swiped from a store. Skinny was well worn and well loved, her face covered in filmy, gossamer fabric, small stitches for two blue eyes and a red mouth. I found the doll in Katie's closet one Sunday in October and begged her to let me keep her. My mother told me to be careful, because Skinny was her prized possession. Along with her other doll Checkers who was too fragile to touch.

When she left for work the next day, I missed her as always, but now I had Skinny, a part of Mom, my prize. Our nanny, Mrs. Ross, asked me what that filthy doll was. It wasn't filthy, I said. It was old. I told her it had been my mother's. She yanked it out of my hands and threw it in the garbage.

When Mrs. Ross returned her attention to the small black-and-white portable television set that she watched during the day at our kitchen table, I took Skinny out of the trash. I carried Skinny around all week and showed her my world, carefully avoiding Mrs. Ross. Until she opened the door to my bedroom and found me cradling the little rag doll. In two giant steps, she strode across the room, pulled Skinny from my hands. Mrs. Ross's own soft skin pulled apart Skinny's blue-cloth flesh and ripped her limb from limb. I watched, stricken. When she was done, she tossed the pieces in the garbage. "I told you not to play with that doll," she said. And then she left the room.

After dinner that night, I showed my mother the tragedy that had befallen Skinny under my care. I felt horrible, guilty, and unworthy. Most of all, I felt so sad for my mother. She picked the limbs out of the garbage one by one and examined them. She took Skinny's parts back to her room and sewed her up with pink thread as I watched silently from the doorway. Then she hid Skinny from me.

She never said a word about it to Mrs. Ross.

Another morning, when I was in kindergarten, I was down in the basement when I heard a shriek.

"Get out of my house!"

It was my mother's voice, directed at Mrs. Ross.

I raced up the stairs to see what was going on.

When I reached the top, I cracked open the dark wooden door

to the kitchen just as a coffee cup flew through the air. A skid followed by a smash. The mug landed on the tulip table, scarring its polished white top, before falling to the floor. Fragments of blue-and-white china scattered like confetti. Brown coffee dripped from the wallpaper. Mrs. Ross looked stunned.

"You. Are. Crazy," she said.

I retreated down the steps, back to the safety of the basement.

I didn't know what to do. I pulled out one of the mildewed books from the shelf, *A Very Young Dancer* by Jill Krementz. It was my favorite. In a series of black-and-white photographs, a girl demonstrated each ballet position: first, second, third, fourth, fifth. I took solace in the photos of the girl, who looked so sure and unblemished. I felt a solidarity with her; she was forever trapped in the book, just as I felt trapped in this home, in my family's basement. Unsure of what was unfolding above me, I made myself get lost in the pages. There she was, preparing to be Clara in *The Nutcracker*. There she was, eating dinner with her family. There she was, riding a sled through the snow with her handsome prince.

I looked up and saw Mrs. Ross standing before me, in this downstairs realm adults so rarely entered. She stood over me, wringing her fat hands. "Your mother no longer wants me to work for her. I won't be coming here again." She paused. "I hope you'll be okay."

I didn't say anything to her, the only other constant in my life. A long moment passed. Finally, I looked back at my book. I heard Mrs. Ross gather her things and leave through the back door. I didn't even say goodbye. I stared at the wooden veneer walls, the plastic tea set on the shelf. I wondered who would take me to school.

A few minutes later, my mother came down the steps. Now this was a first! My mother in my territory! I was mildly excited and nervous. She looked around, as if seeing it all for the first time. Then she looked back at me.

"Mrs. Ross is gone for good," she said, conclusively. "I guess you will have to go to day care in the morning, because I will be at work." And that was all.

My mother disappeared up the stairs and out of my view, back into the kitchen. I heard footsteps, the sound of sweeping. A chair scraping the floor. Footsteps retreating back into my mother's bedroom. Double doors shut.

Upstairs, I pieced some things together. When I tiptoed past my mother's room later, and the door was ajar again, I could see piles of folded laundry on the bed. And then I knew: Mrs. Ross had entered my mother's room, which was forbidden. Perhaps she thought my mother had already left for work. The underwear and socks were the witnesses of her transgression.

In the kitchen, the coffee-stained wallpaper stayed that way for the remainder of my childhood. I never knew if nobody cared enough to wipe it clean, or if my mother wanted a visual reminder of what happened when her privacy was violated. The white table, with its small brown gash, like the end of a scream, was never replaced.

After Mrs. Ross was fired, my mother found me the least terrible of the day-care centers in our area. I hated it, but I loved the journey to get there. My mother drove me herself in her new silver Monte Carlo with red velour interior, a red exterior pinstripe. The car had a sunroof and an eight-track player. I would spend two hours at the dismal day-care center, and then I'd shuttle over to Stevenson Elementary.

I hated day care, mostly because one of my classmates swiped the treat out of my lunch every day. With Mrs. Ross gone, I could tell a real confidante that someone was stealing the best part of my day. My mother knew exactly what to do: she started stapling the bag shut. "There. Now the thief will have to find someone else to prey on." And that was the end of that.

From the time we were very little, Lizzie and I wanted to ride horses. Anytime I'd see a field—which typically meant the big stretches of grass off the road on our two-mile walk to the mall—I could picture galloping over the land on a horse. I'd tell Lizzie, and she agreed. Oh, we'd declare, "If only we could cross this country on horseback!"

One evening, after we'd begged my mom for years, she came home from work and said, "Guess what! You girls are getting riding lessons." And I thought, "My life is going to change."

This was a big deal. Because my mom worked, and because Hillel, my parochial day school, didn't do sports, I never played anything until high school. Though I was athletic when it came to solo pursuits like gymnastics or figure skating, I was not an athlete. Even in the best of times, I couldn't run a mile, because I could never catch my breath.

That weekend, my mother took Lizzie and me to Haverhill Farms, a riding school and the only place near us where you could get lessons without having your own horse. Lizzie, wearing a plaid shirt, got right on her horse and trotted off, her head going up and down, a dust cloud billowing behind her. I got a horse named Humphrey whose only interest was eating grass. I couldn't get him to do anything; I had no idea how to make a horse go. I spent the entire lesson sitting on top of a grazing horse, pulling on reins with too much slack.

Piling into the Corvette afterward, my mother said, impressed,

"Oh, Lizzie, you really went!" I knew how I did. I didn't need to ask.

When we got home, I asked if I could take lessons still. My mom turned to me and said, "You're not ready." And that was that. My mother believed in spending money on people who were ready; otherwise it was a waste. It was a real heartbreak.

A year later, she let me try again a few times. It was winter, and a half-dozen students were in the indoor barn. They put me on a white horse named Cloud. We were trotting in a circle when I started sliding sideways toward the inside of the ring. The saddle slipped down, and so I fell. I was given a leg up again, but I was shaken. "Well, that was that again, Selma." I never pushed my mom to let me keep riding. I knew that I wasn't good enough. So Lizzie got to put on the velvet hat and learn to ride, to live my dream. Every week when Lizzie was at her lesson, my mother and I would go to the bakery to pick up a nice challah, to have ready when she got home.

Sometimes I would hold Lizzie's helmet and wish it were mine. In our room she would saddle up with our towels and let me ride her, instead. I'd climb onto her back, watching my posture in the mirror, her hands on the bed. Lizzie, as a horse, taught me everything she learned at her lessons, which was useful, actually, when I finally learned to ride in young adulthood. She was (and still is) the best big sister.

❧

But my mom was still my favorite person, and it made me sad to miss her when she was away at work all day. But as we grew, weekends became reserved for me and Lizzie. Every Saturday, we crammed into my mom's navy blue Stingray, with the white leather bucket seats. The car had a tape deck, which was a new thing then. If Katie was with us, she sat in the front seat, Lizzie and I in the back. My mom smoked Vantage cigarette after Vantage cigarette, and as she would say, we tooled around all day.

We mostly accompanied her on shopping trips, admiring as she tried on clothes at the nicest boutiques we had—beautiful shops with sofas and mirrors and candy in pretty dishes. My mother loved to be treated well, and I loved to watch her be treated well. She wrote a check for whatever she bought, lighting a cigarette as she filled it out. Every time, she would say, "It calms me, thank you." Most of those pieces remained part of her wardrobe until the day she died.

On all our shopping trips, I never drank water; because those Saturdays were so special, I wouldn't do anything to derail them. I learned early that with three girls, if we needed a bathroom and couldn't find one, my mother would throw up her hands and say, "Forget it! We're all going home!" So I went without water, and if I did need the restroom, I learned not to say anything about it, whimpering to Lizzie, who begged me to stay quiet.

I had constant bladder infections, but I didn't often report about those either, because it would irritate my mother. If I had to go pee in a cup, it would mean she needed to take the day off work to bring me to the doctor. Then she would get more irritated if I got a stage-fright bladder, and say, "We're going to be stuck in rush hour!" I tried to keep my ailments to myself.

In addition to bladder problems, I often had a fever. "FUO," they called it, fever of unknown origin. For years, I kept a graph of my temperature, per the doctor's instructions. I had a fever almost every single day in fourth, fifth, and sixth grades.

Often, my body felt out of control, as if the connection between my brain and my limbs had been severed. One morning when I was in kindergarten, I discovered a pain in my left leg. "My leg hurts," I said as my mother was racing off to work. She didn't pay it much mind. "It really, really hurts." I dragged my leg across her bedroom to demonstrate the pain and how it gave out. Perhaps this was unnecessary, but it felt, to me, as if I should be dragging it. My mother just laughed. She kept on laughing as she told the story for years. "What a drama queen! What an actress! Dragging that leg across the floor!"

I learned that I couldn't show pain, and I certainly couldn't talk about it. To do so would only provoke laughter.

Now, as an adult, I happen to experience pain in the same leg. A drop foot. Looking back, it's hard to know what was real and what was drama. As a kid, you have new pains, but you don't have a vocabulary for them. Maybe it was a sign. Or maybe it was nothing at all.

꩜

As I grew up, it became apparent that I wasn't just dramatic. I was also unusually coordinated, limber, stretchy. Since early playground years I knew how to use my body in a physical way. I was quick and nimble, and I entertained with my physicality. My mother didn't believe in enrolling us in organized athletics; she was no soccer mom cheering on the sidelines. But certain individual sports came so easily—skiing, diving, ice-skating, tennis— I could become proficient in a matter of days. Without any formal gymnastics training, I could stand and do a backflip. A back handspring punctuated a sentence. I used my body dramatically, to dramatic ends.

Because I was so acrobatic, my mother hired a wonderful girl, Beth Willis, from my sister Katie's class at Kingswood, to come teach Lizzie and me gymnastics. She was a competitive gymnast (the exact thing I pretended to be at the park!), which felt quite official. The curriculum was a very homemade hodgepodge— a teenage girl demonstrating moves in a low-ceilinged suburban basement—but I took it seriously. My mom bought us some mats, and Beth taught us how to do back handsprings. She brought over her old balance beam, and I learned how to do a back walkover on it as my mom had her evening martini admiring my basic talent.

I was adept at doing flips, but I had to keep them low. My aerial cartwheel stayed close to the ground, because if I went any higher, I would hit the ceiling. That's the funny thing about limitations; sometimes they aren't about you at all. The ceiling was always there, and I didn't know any better. So I kept low to the ground, causing my audience to wince, afraid my neck would break.

When I got to college, I went through a period where I tried to be a real gymnast. It blew me away. There was a whole wide world out there. Space! Height! Breathing room! When I did an aerial cartwheel for the first time, I flew. I didn't know, without the limitations of a ceiling, I could do a double.

I still find myself looking for the safety of the ground. I still think small. "Accommodate for the low ceiling." I'm just now learning that the ceiling is imaginary. It's a relief, and also disorienting. Nothing is what I thought.

I felt very connected to that dark, smoky home, because it was my life. It was my mother. It was what I knew in that house. As a kid, I held tight to the belief that I never wanted to leave. "When I grow up," I'd think, "I'll come back and live here." I hadn't realized that in some ways that's exactly what I did. I brought that house, and its limitations, with me everywhere I went.

My son is a natural gymnast, much like me, and as I watched him practicing his flips, I saw he had a tendency to go low. Like his mother before him, he looks for the safety of the ground. "You gotta go up, kid," I told him, pointing to the sky. And he did a clear, high flip. I bought him a trampoline, because I want him to go higher. I pray that he always will.

⌘

There is so much that adults do, unknowingly, to children. To a child's mind (any mind, really), the smallest moments can become the biggest stories, images that change our lives forever.

It was a weeknight, September 1981, and Mom took Lizzie and me in the Corvette to see *An American Werewolf in London*. It was a big deal to be out with our mom, on a school night, after dark. She bought Jujubes and parceled them out, immediately taking out a filling.

I was eight or nine at the time, and I had no business seeing this movie. It's a comedy gore horror, and for all I know, the movie is hilarious; I haven't seen it since. What I do know is that I didn't recognize the comedy at that age. I saw only the terror.

The movie opens on a scene where the young leads, Jack and David, whose dark hair reminded me of mine and Lizzie's, leave this bar in the Yorkshire countryside. They're jubilant and singing, maybe drunk, when they're viciously attacked by a werewolf. Jack is mauled to death; David goes on, seeing his decomposing friend throughout the film.

That moment was the end of my childhood.

I hadn't grasped, until that moment, the reality of what death does. Until then, it had been an afterthought, a vague, distant mystery that happened to people you didn't know. But that night, I understood: Death is real, and it can happen unexpectedly. I would be dead someday. My mother would be dead someday. It took my breath away. I hadn't considered it really since I learned about death at age three.

This is what I carried home, in my mother's navy blue Stingray.

At home, I put my head on the pillow and tried to push out the images of dead bodies. It was too much for me. I felt unsafe everywhere, convinced that Lizzie and I would be ambushed like the men in the movie.

For weeks, I told my friends at school everything I could remember about the story. For nearly two years, I couldn't be alone in a room at night. When the lights went out, the dark pictures haunted me. A charred corpse beckoned from Lizzie's bed. I cowered in the shadows, sobbing softly into my pillow, wishing someone would come in and hold me. No matter how much I cried, my mother wouldn't come; she needed to get up early for work. She did not allow me to sleep in the big bed with her. Whenever I tried, my dad carried me back to my room, where I stayed awake most of the night. It went on this way, every day, for a year and a half. I kept my aunt Anna's fox stole in my arms as a protection.

I was sensitive and deeply affected by things, which I think made my childhood quite different from my sisters'. (I still need to edit what I watch.) My experiences were all or nothing, an exercise in extremes. This was a story I carried throughout my life, and still do, to some degree.

Lizzie is a mom to two children who are everything to her, and we rarely discuss our own childhoods. But the other day I asked her if she remembered the movie, this night that irrevocably terrorized me. A movie she seemed to have been unfazed by.

"That movie really fucked me up, Blair. It changed my life." Gobsmacked! I had no idea she ever felt that way. I can still see her, sitting in that passenger bucket seat, saying how much she liked it. "I remember getting out of Mom's Corvette that night, thinking, 'I don't know how I'm ever going to be okay.'"

It was a revelation to me. Lizzy was the tough one, acting nonchalant about big scary things. My big sister, always so brave. She pretended she enjoyed it. I didn't know the truth.

We play the parts we are given. We become the stories that are told about us. Lizzie was tough, her assigned role. She was the one who carried me on her back, and she wasn't going to let me down. Still, she wasn't able to help me, and my misery saddened her beyond my understanding. When I cried every night and she didn't console me, I never imagined she was silently experiencing her own brand of terror.

Lizzie grew up to embody everything strong and tough. She was stronger than most boys in her class; she ran hurdles and rode on the back of a motorcycle, embraced an athletic lifestyle. She became a cop after college, a hostage negotiator. To discover that deep down she had been just as afraid, but she never said a word. That rocked me almost as much as that scene had so many years before.

"I'm so sorry," she cried into the phone. "Blair, I am so sorry." And I was sorry, too.

As adults, we pull our childhoods with us wherever we go.

Elliot

WHEN I LOOK BACK on the characters of the past, my memories of my father are indistinct. I don't think I ever saw him clearly. I wish I could go back with wiser eyes.

I always liked his name, Elliot. But I never responded to the man with it. From early on, it was apparent that I was proudly my mother's daughter, and she required all my love and devotion. I could tell my mother was impartial toward her husband, with whom she maintained a cordial, if not cold, relationship throughout their marriage, so I didn't try very hard to please him.

It was my mother who commanded my attention. She was the person I wanted to kiss me good night, every night. She had the footsteps I ran out of my room toward. She had tremendous power over me. But some nights, when she was working late, my only option was Elliot. When he came to the bedroom I shared with Lizzie, he would jokingly ask her, "Who is your favorite? Mom or Dad?" And she would answer, "Tasca!" who was the German shepherd down the street. She knew how to handle his questions; she knew how to play him. And he would be amused. He never dared ask me that. He already knew the answer.

༄

While our home life was humble compared with that of my wealthier friends, vacations were utopian. Where our house was marked by grim darkness and a shag pea green family room carpet, for me, vacations meant sunshine and pools, fresh pineapple, platters of breakfast room service, and chance encounters with other

kids. As children, we had such beautiful vacations that it became my life's pleasure to try to re-create them. To this day, a good hotel is still what I think of as the highest luxury.

In the 1970s and 1980s, my family would go on these gambling junkets, Elliot's thing, over Christmas and spring break. We kids would all get one suite, my parents another. There was coconut ice cream and Shasta with more fresh pineapple and a pink umbrella, which we could charge to the room! Most thrilling was the sense of adventure and independence. In my own house, I felt I was waiting for my turn to begin.

In my school day, I never ate the lunches packed for me—

typically salami or peanut butter sandwiches. I had a nervous stomach, Maalox in my backpack. I was embarrassed to eat in front of people. It was too vulnerable. Too sensual. But on vacation, I ate everything. I returned to my normal life feeling sated.

One year, when I was in third grade, we took a trip to Aruba that was comped by the hotel, another junket. I don't know the details beyond that my father hadn't gambled at the prescribed hour, or that he hadn't lost enough. Though they certainly had enough money to cover the rooms, my dad decided to leave in the middle of the night to avoid the unexpected expenditure of the vacation, on principle. I never really understood why my mom went along with this, only that Elliot was quite careful with a dollar, one of a collection of things my mother hated about him.

Early in the morning, under the cover of darkness, we secretly left the hotel without checking out and sped to the airport. Katie was so afraid. She kept saying that we were "like the von Trapp children," fleeing in the night. I somehow wasn't scared, merely inconvenienced, and was fine just as long as I didn't get separated from my mother.

Even at eight years old, I couldn't make sense of why he didn't just settle up. I remember asking, "Is this really worth it?" Sure enough, someone from the hotel met us at the airport, and Elliot was forced to settle his bill. In the end, we weren't criminals; we were just people who ended our vacation early. We still took trips as a family, but that was the last junket we went on.

Hillel

THE ROLE OF JUDAISM in my family was a tricky thing.

My sisters and I were all raised in the Jewish tradition, even though my mother never called herself Jewish. Judaism is matrilineal. Still, I always found it curious, given that her beloved father was Jewish and her mother—for whom she had only disdain—was Scottish and not a Jew, that she chose to identify as Anglican. In her jewelry box, she kept a cross that read, "In case of emergency, contact an Episcopal priest." She never wore it, out of deference to Elliot and our family, but I always knew it was there.

Even though my mother herself didn't identify as Jewish, it was important to her that I did. I was her chosen one. This became my first big role: to perform Jewishness. Over the years, it became a strange interweaving, where she would pit me against myself, telling me that I needed to be Jewish, telling me that I could never truly be.

My mother never socialized with any Jewish people. As a kid, I used to think she believed they were beneath her. As my sister Katie would say, "She would've hidden a Jew, but she doesn't want to be friends with one." But now, in hindsight, I suspect she felt as if she didn't truly belong.

Growing up, we never had a Christmas tree. We celebrated Hanukkah and fasted on Yom Kippur. Even my mother fasted. She was always respectful of our Jewish rituals. Her disdain ran somewhere beneath the surface, never outwardly visible. The Holocaust was at the front of her mind at all times. She referred to it often, citing the atrocity of *Sophie's Choice* and anchoring me firmly in the mindset of "do not forget."

My parents sent their three younger daughters to Hillel Day School, partly out of respect for Elliot, but mostly out of convenience. We could take the bus to Hillel, which meant my mother wouldn't have to drive us to school every morning. (Never mind that the bus ride took an hour and a half, because we were the first to get on.) It was a fully immersive Jewish education—Talmud study, prayer every morning, minyan, a congregation of students engaging in daily Hebrew instruction. I remember feeling grateful to have had this education. Still, my mother made it clear that in her view Hillel was not the be-all and end-all.

Once we were part of the Hillel community, we pretended to be good Jews. We played the part well. We overcompensated. We opposite-of-Anne-Franked. Our family went above and beyond in our Jewish calling. We stopped eating ham at home, in case one of our more observant friends came over and wanted to stay for dinner. My mother kept two sets of dishes, which she liked to brag about. "I keep two sets of dishes!" she would say to shopkeepers, who nodded politely. "One for milk and one for meat." The truth was, we didn't really keep the plates separate, so none of them were kosher. Thank God we never hosted an Orthodox person in our home, so these lies didn't actually harm anyone.

In my journals I wrestled with whether I believed in God. I wanted to believe; I loved the idea of God. "Dear Book," I wrote, ending each searching entry with "The End" in case I died before the next one, then crossing it out every time I sat down to write. At school, the fear of God was put into me, as well as the idea that we the Jews were his chosen people. I knew, given the usual metric of Judaism passing down through the matrilineal line, I wasn't really a Jew. But at school, no one could know this. We needed to keep it a secret.

I officially became a Jew when I was in second grade. My mother asked if I wanted to convert, because Katie had wanted to when she was the same age, and bat mitzvah time was approaching. "Selma, do you want to be Jewish, too?" She sat at the table after a dinner our new housekeeper made, smoking and drinking a glass of wine, dabbing her red lips.

I said that I did.

My conversion took place during the time I wore an eye patch. In first grade at Hillel we were all given an eye test, and mine came back saying I needed glasses. So we went to the eye doctor Leonard Lerner (coincidentally, the father of the kids who screamed about the mean Beitner baby). It was here I discovered I had a severe lazy eye. "We must take care of this right away!" he said. I was told I'd need to wear an eye patch for exactly two years. "We must trick the brain!" he said. A speech I came to imitate. Whenever anyone asked why I wore an eye patch, I would repeat, "We must trick the brain!" Emphasis on "trick."

We bought patches from the drugstore, black fabric with a little point in the center like the dart of a dress. They were a bit Gaultier, like Madonna's cone bra. The patch was sweaty in the summer, with a smell like a wet Band-Aid. It pushed my face down into an even meaner scowl—a mean baby pirate. I knew I wasn't pretty with my eye patch on, but my mother was supportive. She would draw on my patches, to make them cuter. I followed the doctor's words like the gospel. I never removed the eye patch.

The conversion process is immersion in a mikveh, a bath from which you emerge from holy water reborn as a Jew. Mine was lined with salmon-colored tiles, like something you'd find in a hospital bathroom. Before entering the mikveh, you are instructed to remove everything from your person—clothes, earrings, even traces of nail polish. But I refused to take off my eye patch. Dr. Lerner had been clear. I must never, ever remove it.

"You know, you're not really Jewish if you keep that on," said the woman at the synagogue who was presiding over us girls, gesturing to my eye patch. But the rabbi (coincidentally, the senior rabbi at Hillel) let it slide and gave me my conversion papers. For many years afterward, Katie would tease, "You didn't remove the eye patch, so you aren't really a Jew." To which I would say, "Shut up."

The day we removed the patch, my vision was perfect. Twenty-twenty.

"*Yehi or!*" I yelled. Let there be light. Everyone laughed.

Three days later, my vision went back to the way it had been. The brain was not tricked. It will always choose the easiest way, and the easiest way in this case was to turn that eye off. To this day, if I put one hand over my good eye, I cannot see.

I still have a patch. I put it on every once in a while, thinking maybe I'll trick the brain. But the brain and I both know better.

~

The first time I got drunk it was a revelation.

I always liked Passover. Every year, as my family and I celebrated the exodus of the Jews, I actually felt that hope of next year in Jerusalem, as we sang in the Haggadah. I dunked my parsley in the salt water and tasted the pain of our tears. I loaded my matzo with horseradish. And as I took small sips of the small glasses of Manischewitz I was allowed throughout the seder, I felt warm, at one with my ancestors. A light flooded through me, filling me up with the warmth of God. (As a little kid, I *loved* God. Huge fan.)

But the year I was seven, when we basically had Manischewitz on tap and no one at the table was paying attention to my consumption level, I put it together. In that moment in the dining room, with the plagues and the frogs and the hail and the locusts, there came an epiphany. I realized, as I kept refilling my glass, the feeling was not God but fermentation.

That was heartbreaking to me, because it was like finding out Santa Claus wasn't real, if I'd cared about Santa Claus. It was also very convenient that I made this discovery at the table, where there was a glass of wine already in front of me. I thought, "Well, this is a huge disappointment, but since it turns out I can get the warmth of the Lord from a bottle, thank God there's one right here."

Because I wasn't very much of a planner, nor an in-the-moment critical thinker, I got drunk that night. Very drunk. The kind of drunk that would make most people never drink again. I rolled around the living room floor, then clung to my cousin Matt's leg, weeping and begging him not to leave me. I was out of control. Eventually, I was put in Katie's bigger bed with her, where I slept next to her all night long (a clear sign that I was gone if ever there was one). In the morning, I woke up and didn't remember how I'd gotten there.

So, now I knew. The relief I sought could be found in an inexpensive, sticky-sweet bottle—or *any* bottle. It wasn't spiritual; it was scientific. I didn't go back to it right away, but I knew it was there.

A few months later, there was this fly in the house that wouldn't leave me alone. It buzzed around and around the living room before landing on the cream carpet right next to the bookshelf. I squatted near the fly, attempting to swat it, but there was no need. It was already dead. That's when I saw it—an old paperback, wedged between S. E. Hinton's *Outsiders* and Judy Blume's *Forever.* I pulled it out and looked at the cover, intrigued. *Sarah T.: Portrait of a Teen-Age Alcoholic.* The book's pages were well-worn and stained, indicating it must have made the rounds with my sisters.

The book was about a sad misfit girl who turns to alcohol as a coping mechanism. I opened it up and started reading. With that bleak, dead fly as my witness, I read the book from cover to cover. What an adventure! As my eyes scanned the pages, I thought, "This is how I'm going to be okay." I was gloomy and sensitive, haunted by a nagging sense of loss I'd felt since the day I was born. Here was a girl who felt the same loneliness I did and for a few sparkly scenes found her fun in vodka-spiked watermelon. What was I waiting for? The answer to my pain was right here.

Of course, it was intended as a cautionary tale—a chaotic, problematic story, with an awful, tragic ending of a dead horse on a road. But I sidestepped the consequences and saw it as a how-to guide. I held the slim novel in my hands, knowing exactly what came next. As I slid the book back into its place on the shelf, I said,

"I'm gonna do this." I made a promise to myself: I would be the best alcoholic a girl could possibly be.

I stood up and went over to the game cabinet. Behind the green poker chips and the card-shuffling machine my dad would sometimes bring out for Saturday night card games stood the dusty bottles of party drinks. I reached for the tallest. It was a bottle of Amaretto. I screwed off the top and removed the wax paper stopper. In a sense, this was my last warning, but I didn't see it that way. I saw it as hope.

I took a swig. Not great, but not bad. It tasted like almonds, syrupy and sweet. I took a longer pull. "You're safe now, Baby Bear," I whispered aloud.

From that moment forward, Sarah T. became my inspiration, a mentor for how to crawl out of my timid body. Somehow, no one in my family took notice. I drank Beefeater gin. Miller Lite. Any bottle I could find. Just nips at first, then quick and burning sips whenever my anxiety would alight. Sunday mornings, I'd wake up early and take sips from the half-empty cocktails my parents left overnight in the sink. Every once in a while, I stole a bottle of Tanqueray and kept it hidden under my bed. I felt almost proud, as if I were grown up because I was doing this adult thing. I usually didn't get fall-down drunk; I barely even got tipsy. I just let myself have a little check-in, a tiny bit of warmth.

It wasn't until third grade that I got wasted again. My mother wasn't home. That night, after my sisters and I cleared the dishes, I crept back to the refrigerator. The light turned on, illuminating my face along with the jug of Gallo. I took just a little bit, a tiny sip, nothing to be alarmed over. But it kept calling to me. And as it did, I returned to the fridge for another swig, and another.

By the tenth trip, I was falling-down drunk. I staggered across the kitchen floor, past my dad on the couch bathed in the glow

of the nightly news, and finally into the powder room, where my stomach began to lurch. I vomited. (And vomited. And vomited. Sour splashes, evidence of my lack of impulse control.) My dad came in, held my hair away, and rubbed my back. Only then did he realize what had happened.

"Oh my God, Selma, you're drunk," he moaned, genuine concern playing across his face. "You can't drink this stuff; it's not for kids. It will make you really sick." He spoke in a soothing voice as he helped me clean up the sick. "I won't tell your mother about this," he said. I was grateful.

After that, I was on my own. I became an expert alcoholic, adept at hiding my secret from anyone and everyone. I was very careful. And no one was ever the wiser, at least until high school.

Some people say everything happens for a reason. I don't know if that's true, or just a line we repeat, over and over, to justify our bad choices. What I do know is that drinking happened to me. And once it did, it became my safety, a way of softening my jagged edges. As time went on, it happened with more and more frequency. It became the lede of my story. When I drank, I didn't know what drama I would find, but I knew it was drama that I would *feel*. I needed it. I looked forward to it. It was always my way out.

At Hillel, the families were very intact. Traditional. Parents knew what their kids were doing, and the kids seemed to have an instinct about what was healthy and what was not. I, on the other hand, had a different kind of family. Naturally, my parents wanted the best for me, and obviously that didn't include drinking. But there were four of us girls and I was the baby and both of my parents worked, so it was easy for things to go unnoticed. I was neglected, but not on purpose. Everyone did the best they could. No one hovered over me, and I was fast and secretive. I wanted to be older, to fast-forward to adulthood. I wanted to be my mother. So, I tried to follow adult social cues.

My school friends and I were in different places. I was reading *The Bell Jar* and trying to cultivate a profound, William Styron–esque depth. Meanwhile, they only cared about amazing bar and bat mitzvah parties and sweaters from The Limited. I didn't get a kick out of friendship bracelets and kid stuff. I was drawn to extreme situations, but my everyday life was very simple—wake up, take the bus, go to school, come home. I created my own drama.

My very best school friend was Marla. By fourth grade, we were inseparable, completely in love. We made each other barrettes braided with thin strands of ribbons, friendship safety pins with small glass beads, Keds painted with each other's names on the sides down in the basement.

One morning after a sleepover, Marla went home and my friend Ilysa and I walked over to play in the cool new park, past the field beyond my yard. We were the only ones there that morning, so I called my neighbor and kinda boyfriend, Danny, over to join us. I found a few half-empty forty-ounce bottles of Miller beer sitting on the platform that led to the slide. A nice drink before lunch. I wasn't worried about the alcohol, only the germs, but these bottles seemed clean enough. I figured the morning sun would have washed away any herpes germs.

I picked one up. It smelled warm and yeasty. I put the glass bottle to my lips and finished it, then burped so loudly that the two of them had no choice but to loosen up. But my peers were quiet. They took a purse-lipped sip when I handed it to them. We played a bit and the day petered out. I had no idea I'd shown my cards.

And then, in fifth grade, I got drunk in front of Marla. I misjudged. She was at my house on a Saturday night, and I drank a glass of wine after dinner. She didn't want any. Cool, I thought. I didn't think a thing. But that's when she disengaged. Before I knew it, she started siding with Ilysa instead of me. I felt ganged up on, confused as to what I'd done wrong. "Why do you hate me?" I asked her. That was my first fallout (due to alcohol). I felt hurt, rejected. It never occurred to me that she was distancing herself from me because of the drinking.

Her head was in *Ziggy* and *Garfield* posters and spending our allowance on bubble gum and greeting cards at the drugstore, not stealing alcohol and cigarettes. I would want my son to do the same. I wouldn't want my kid to hang out with me, either.

I don't think she ever told her parents.

After I lost Marla, the rest of my Hillel experience was hell. I sobbed every day, begging her to tell me why she turned against me. She never said. (In fact, I never knew until adulthood, when Marla visited L.A. and met up with me at the Chateau Marmont. She ordered a glass of wine as I sipped my coffee, then sober for years. "Was it my drinking?" I asked. "Yes, I think it was," she said. She shifted in her chair, still uncomfortable talking about it. "I also think it had something to do with the way you lived. You freaked me out. I'd never seen someone our age behave that way. And you were sick or lied about being sick. I don't even remember.") I'd lost my only best friend, whom I loved. I went through years of missing her, mourning what I'd lost, all the while being made fun of by her and the other girls. This should have made me reconsider my actions, but it didn't. It only made me keep them to myself.

Mimi and Katie weren't drinkers, but sometimes Lizzie would do it on the weekends, with friends. Once, when I was in fifth grade, we got our friend Emily so drunk that she poured a bottle of ink all over my mom's maple desk, which she'd had since childhood. We ran around, taking our clothes off, drunk and crying. We got away with that almost every weekend, Johnny Depp–ing our way around the basement. But that one weekend, Emily spiraled out of control. Ceiling tiles were popped out. Books were ripped, toys torn apart. My baby book—the only artifact I had that told me who I was—got destroyed. I hadn't anticipated this kind of fallout. When I drank, I never resorted to destruction. But what did we expect? You can't get a ten-year-old drunk and think it will go well. It was all my fault.

One Sunday when she was thirteen or fourteen, Lizzie came home hungover, a notch in her belt. "I was with Mia and Lisa Weinberg," she told me—the cool kids—"and we got *so* drunk, and we went to the movies, and they said, 'Lizzie is glassy-eyed.'" Glassy-eyed! It seemed such an achievement of drama. That became my goal for the weekend. "Show me when I'm glassy-eyed," I said as we sat in the bathroom, drinking old bottles of Aperol and Grand Marnier. I would have a whole lifetime to explore that feeling. But I wanted to pack in as much drunk as I could.

Once Marla left me, I became best friends with Becky, the biggest outcast in our grade (who turned out to be an incredible friend). She was once a thumb-sucker and I had been way out of her league, but now blue-eyed Becky in her cool new Esprit clothes and newly ostracized Selma found each other. She had no judgment about any of the choices I made. I was feared, and alone, with her. That I made it through eight years of Hillel is thanks to three things: Becky, the long gulps of Tanqueray I snuck in most days before school, and Bradley Bluestone.

Bradley Bluestone was the Brad Pitt of Hillel Day School. With goyish and boyish features: blue-green eyes, light brown feathered hair, thick eyebrows, and a button nose. To me, his face was delicate and handsome and perfect. He even had a lazy eye, like me. I wanted him on my arm and was determined to do whatever I could to make it happen. Every morning, when we said the prayer to Abraham, I took breaks to stare dreamily at Bradley.

Once, in sixth grade, Becky and I were talking by the swings at the park behind my house when she asked me, "Do you think you'll love Brad forever?"

"Yeah, I think I will, actually," I replied without hesitation. "Forever. He's the one I love."

"You can't be with him; he's a year older," she protested, as if it were impossible for him to "go" with me. But I wasn't having it.

"No, he's going to be my boyfriend. And I will love him forever."

And he was. By the next year, we were officially "going." From that point forward, I again firmly established myself as the most popular girl in school—besides Lizzie—the only one with a boy-friend who was older.

"You're so beautiful," he told me one summer afternoon, as we were lying in the sunlight, his face over mine as I lay back in the grass. "I can see every pore on your face." Mortified, I shut my eyes so he couldn't see me. He was the first boy to ever look at me up close, I guess. His observation shamed me. Bradley was my first kiss. His mouth tasted of sweet raspberries as we made out in front of my house next to the lilac bushes. It was June 24, the week after school let out. He drove over on his Aero moped—on a real high-way! I was nervous and impressed. In my mind, he was all of it, like Jake in *Sixteen Candles*. His dad was a lawyer turned chiropractor! Doubly useful! He made my knees weak. It was young love, and it stayed for a while.

We'd split up and reconcile, as young love goes. I would call and

break up with him—or worse, have a friend call and break up with him on my behalf—just to try out dramatic adult behaviors I saw on TV. I was dead terrified of people so I pushed and bedeviled. "Stop bedeviling Bradley!" my mother would say.

Even later, as I was ending my time in high school at Cranbrook Kingswood, Brad and I confided in each other. We wrote love letters and talked late into the night, cramming as many song titles as possible into our congenial chats. His parents doted on him, though college had its share of emotional stress. He was still golden. He was still golden for me. BB + BB still made me smile when I opened his letters. Bradley Bluestone + Blair Beitner forever.

And then, on February 7, Becky called me. It was my senior year. I was sitting back in bed, taking my temperature while enjoying a Whitesnake song on MTV, watching the blur of motion and spotlights and Tawny Kitaen on a white piano, not a car, this time.

"Bradley is dead."

What? What?

"He died in his dorm room," Becky told me. "The funeral is tomorrow."

"What? How did he die?" I asked, my eyes filling with tears. "What happened?"

She said Anthony found him. His best friend since Hillel. She never knew what happened.

I couldn't speak. I wanted to drop the phone, to stop the words from coming out, to stop this from happening, from being true. But it had already happened. I held the phone with both hands and wept.

The next day, we went to the Ira Kaufman Chapel, where Bradley was interred.

As we shoveled dirt onto his expensive steel coffin, the shovel broke. There was a gasp. Sobs. His mother and I hugged. My heart broke for his parents. He was the love of their lives.

"To outlive your child is the worst grief," my mother said later that night as I sat on her bed crying.

"I can't stop thinking about him, rotting in the ground, all alone in there. Underneath. Mom!" I sobbed, too consumed with grief to care how I sounded. I tried not to think about the movie with the werewolves. I cried and cried. My mother said, "You will never really get over this." She was right. I never did. No one ever spoke of his cause of death; to this day it's still a mystery to me. It's almost as if his parents couldn't bear to put a label on what had happened to their son. They wanted to remember him as he was, unblemished. To me he will always be this golden boy who floated up to heaven like an angel.

I, Selma

THOUGH IT DIDN'T ALIGN with my mother's original ambitions for me, I found I loved to write. Every summer starting when I was six, the whole family would accompany Katie on her way to Camp Ramah, a Jewish sleepaway camp in Ontario, Canada. On our way, we'd make a pit stop in Toronto, where we stayed at the Four Seasons. One of the things I loved most about the Four Seasons was how the rooms had a pad of yellow paper and a pen next to the bed. I'm not joking when I say that before this I don't think I was exposed to a blank piece of paper of my own not meant for a school pad. A piece of paper where I could write something personal? Frivolous? This was a gift.

And so, I set about to write the story of my life.

> I Selma Breitner
> well There was a man
> but he was the life
> guard and I wish he
> wood marry me.
> I wanted to ask
> him but I dont wan't
> To in Paris him
> and he took me in The
> maze and he had hols in his
> Jim shos

"I, Selma, am six years old, and I'm in love with a lifeguard. He has holes in his tennis shoes, and he took me through the maze. I thought he was sexy."

I shared it with my mother, who was so impressed. Praise did not come easily from her, and yet she loved my writing notes. It took only three sentences to win her over. If my mother approved, then I knew it was a worthy venture.

Back home in the basement, I began writing *I, Selma.* I wrote about how my sister Katie had smooth skin or some such irrelevant and clichéd finding. I wrote that I was scared to grow up, because I didn't know how I would make a living. (Valid.) I also wrote that I was fat. (I was not.)

While some of *I, Selma* was scrawled in childish print, some was done in cursive that was at once very pretty and very upright. (Now it slants every which way, like my mind, but at that time it was clear and straight.) It didn't take me long to see it was not a literary masterpiece, and so I gave up and eventually threw it away, embarrassed by my naivete.

Eight years later, I was in a bookstore with my mother when I noticed Tina Turner's new memoir displayed up front. It was called *I, Tina.*

"That's my title!" I said, pointing at the cover.

My mom laughed. "You gotta get up earlier than Tina Turner!"

PopPop was a deeply literate thinker who also loved to write. He said he always hoped to publish a book one day about the pitfalls of conglomerating in the grocery store business. He even had a title for it: *Requiem.* But he never made much progress with it, as far as I know.

I like to think I inherited this yearning to write from him. From a young age, I privately wanted to be a writer, but I was too scared to say this ambition out loud. It felt at once lofty and also disappointing, since I thought it wasn't what my mother wanted, and my greatest wish was to please her. So instead, I wrote all the time in secret—stories and poems, random thoughts on scraps of paper. I poured my fears into my journals, along with details of every crush and rejection. Pretty heady and boring simultaneously.

When I was twelve, our teacher Ms. Nelson gave us a creative writing assignment in school, and I took the task to heart. Looking back, I wrote something incredibly trite but age appropriate, and I was thrilled when my poem won first place. (At a Hebrew day school not known for its writing, managing to open up in any way was worthy of praise.) I had never won a prize for anything academic since the "Pitzel Family" book I made in elementary school, and I couldn't wait to show it to my mother.

We were in the formal living room, the one lined with all the law books and the fly of yore, and I perched beside her on the cream velvet sofa. I wanted so to please her. To have her smile and say, "Wow. This is wonderful, kiddo." But apparently, her standards were higher than Ms. Nelson's.

"What is this?" She peered at the pages. I already suspected it wasn't her dish of tea—something she corrected me about all the time. ("Selma, it's not a cup of tea, it's a dish of tea." To this day, I still don't know which is right.) Still, this was worse than I'd predicted. When she was finished, she put it down and said, "Ugh, Selma. This is drivel. Sheer drivel. I can't believe they gave you something for *this*?" She thrust it back in my direction. "I don't want to see this shit again."

I looked down at my words. Now I could see there was something off about it. My mother was right. There must have been some mistake. I felt ashamed. I crumpled it up and threw it in the garbage.

I didn't view her as being hard on me; I trusted her word. Instead, I went in the other direction and stopped trusting others whenever they offered me praise. I internalized her words. It was the truth. (Later, when I was in high school, my mother actually told me I should write a book one day. "You write, I edit," she said.)

My older sister Mimi had the most beautiful friend, Gina Ferrari. My favorite. She was an artist, a painter, as well as loyal to my sister, a quality we all appreciated even then. When I was in fourth grade, she set me up at the table at her house with some of her watercolors and an iris in a vase. I painted what I saw. As it turned out, it was pretty damn good. It was chosen—again at Hillel—for another award. The painting was displayed at Sinai Hospital, of all places, and my mother was thrilled. (She loved the painting so much she kept it until the day she died.) If my mother praised something, then I knew it was worth pursuing.

I didn't share my writing again for a long time, but whenever I said something that my mom found to be exceptionally clever or nuanced or funny, she would sit up straighter, point her cigarette at me like Princess Anne, and order, "Put it in the box."

One time, my mother and I were in synagogue, and we were starving. I was in middle school. It was Yom Kippur, the Day of Atonement, and we were fasting, we were famished. Miserable. Bad breath all around. Even the handsome stained-glass wall of our Saarinen-designed Shaarey Zedek temple with its Chagall-esque vignettes of Old Testament scenes couldn't distract us. My attention rested on a woman in front of us, an old, old salon-coiffed lady focused on her prayer book, hunched, her clip-on earrings backward. I whispered to my mother, "Mom, look!" and pointed to the earlobes in front of us.

We were the only ones who could see the glimmer of two ersatz diamonds pointing in our direction, like headlights shining only on us. We found this totally hilarious. The backward clip-ons.

"Put it in the box," my mother whispered, laughing. "Put it in the box."

Then we went around critiquing all the other congregants' bad fashion choices. We were the mean girls of shul.

I was pleased. I didn't need a prize when I had my mother's approval. This became our refrain. Through college, through New York, through California, with every phone call. If I made my mother laugh, she pleaded to me between cackles. "Oh, Selma!" she'd cry, hands clapping. "Put it in the box."

❧

"Selma, you must write a book!" my mother would say.

"I have nothing to write about, Mom."

"Then write a song! Be a songwriter."

"But all the good melodies are taken!" I said.

"Put it in the box!" she roared.

❧

For a long time, I thought this box was purely symbolic, her way of acknowledging a funny story. But then, after years and years and countless demands to "put it in the box," I finally asked her, "What is this box? Is it a real thing?"

She told me PopPop had kept a box in his closet, and whenever he had an idea or a funny story for the book he hoped to write, he jotted it down and put it in his special box. I pictured a wooden bird box where all the winged thoughts were held, fluttering around like hummingbirds, until he was ready to write fully and set them free.

As the eldest, Mimi was the family authority on our grandfather. He named her his *ichiban,* a pet name, meaning "my first," that he borrowed from his travels in Japan. Not long ago, while talking to her about PopPop, I asked if she knew anything about a box where he collected his thoughts and musings.

There are people
who live by words
and those who lie
by silence — both
are shits — equally.

"I'm not even sure if there ever was a box," I said. "It's just, like, a metaphor. Something Mom said."

Mimi gasped and almost screamed into the phone, "No, I have the box! I have it!"

When he died, Mimi was given some of the contents of his apartment, including a box that fit this description. I couldn't believe it. She had the famous box.

Recently, Mimi sent me some of the contents. Much of it is random—newspaper clippings about his business, nonsensical quotes, restaurant receipts with a single indecipherable word scribbled on the back. But there are some jewels, little glimpses into his personality and biases.

A newspaper clipping, at the top of which he scrawled, "When the gov't becomes law-breaker—anarchy."

A handwritten note: "A woman should be charming."

And this: "Children make us young, but how can they keep us young when they make us so old?"

And this: "Requiem: In a family, some members often feel they 'own' you—but at the same time, do not feel the responsibility 'to' you."

Another: "Only a success wipes out the disgrace, etc.—but writing it out helps. Catharsis."

And my personal favorite: "There are people who live by words and there are people who live by silence. Both are shits equally."

Whenever I look at it, I feel a kinship with him, a string connecting us. A mystery closer to solving.

Written in a thick red script: "The value of life depends on dignity not success." I noticed the date. It was the last day before he retired.

❧

My mom didn't have a box, at least not in the literal sense. Instead, she had a cherrywood rolltop desk—separate from her makeup vanity, separate from her work desk—which we were *never* to look into on pain of death. The bottom drawer was very deep; from the outside, it looked like two drawers. Everything she liked of mine went in that bottom drawer. There were no photos of me. She kept all my stories, all my drawings, all my little pieces of paper. "Put it in the box." That is what she saved. I was the only child she did it for.

❧

The most important person I met at Hillel was probably Anne Frank. Her diary was the required reading in Ms. Nelson's fifth-grade class. I felt immediate respect. And kinship. Not since Sarah T. had I found a girl who spoke to me as intimately and urgently as Anne Frank did. For a child fifty years my predecessor, she still seemed alive and modern. I can see her face in black and white on the cover, her sweet, ever-familiar smile. Hair parted on the side. I carried that paperback with me everywhere, to keep her alive. My sister Katie once took my copy and hid it, as payback for when I hid her *Tiger Beat* magazine, and I ran through the house screaming, "Katie has hidden Anne Frank! Give her back! Give her back! Hasn't she been through enough already?"

Anne was my glorified shadow. Trapped. Intelligent. Optimistic. Unlike Anne, though, I did not believe people were mostly good at heart, and I didn't understand how she could maintain such faith in humanity. I couldn't wrap my head around what had befallen her. And yet I related to her as if she were a close classmate— romantic, passionate, and outspoken. She fought with her mother. She questioned her faith. She could be petulant and sullen. She had intense mood swings and periods of internal despair. She yearned for one true confidante to whom she could confess her deepest secrets, and the person she found was Kitty, the imaginary friend to whom she addressed most of her diary entries.

"Dearest Kitty," she wrote. "I am seething with rage, yet I can't show it . . . I'm stuck with the character I was born with, and yet I'm sure I'm not a bad person."

Relatable.

Of course, we are reading a diary of a lamb to the slaughter. What I really couldn't believe was that, as far as I could tell, Anne was going through this period of hiding from imminent death without losing sanity or self. I couldn't even manage a day of Hillel without a few sips of alcohol to calm my system, much less years of hiding in a secret annex, fearful each day would be my last. I compared my little life to hers and felt inner guilt and shame for all I had. For safety.

Anne was a different ideal from others I clung to. I loved her depth and that she was a secular Jew who wrestled with her belief in God, like me. I felt conflicted as to my own identity, so I truly, deeply identified with Anne Frank. It is the Selma and the Blair. Selma identifies as Anne Frank, while Blair is off trying to cultivate a Hitchcock blonde look, at least in photographs. Like the smile and the frown, they are equally a part of me.

Years later, in 2010, I was honored to be asked to read Random House's new audio edition of Anne Frank's diary. As we began in the studio, the script laid out on an easel, I was overcome. The first sentences I uttered were difficult; Anne's revered words, every one of which I'd read so many times, coming out of my mouth suddenly sounded so hollow. But once I gave in to the voice, I felt as though I had crossed over into something real.

When I first encountered Anne as a child, I didn't realize how much I would come to relate to her in truly unexpected ways—the experience of feeling trapped, of wanting to interpret her world and the world beyond but not being allowed to have a voice, of feeling as if you were no longer in control of your own destiny. Of wanting to find a way to cope. For Anne, it was through writing. For me, for a long time, it was through alcohol. It took me a long time to find another way. Unlike Anne, I would have the luxury of years to try to get it right.

Now I can say without hesitation that I am, and always will be, Jewish. In my everyday life, I am very Jew-ish: a secular Jew who is deeply spiritual, with a lot of faith and a big voice when it comes to remembrance. I don't belong to a temple. I still remember Passover, though I don't serve Manischewitz. (No fucking way!)

By the end of eighth grade, I came to resent Hillel. The religious curriculum was fine, but I struggled in math and began to clash with teachers who resisted my desire to change and grow up. I was too dramatic, too rebellious and restless. And Brad had gone on to high school, so I felt there was nothing left for me.

It was around this time that I developed constant throbbing headaches. Pain blossomed. My face ached. To soothe the pain, I began drinking more on weekends and feeling poorly as a result. I had little appetite, eating only breakfast and a small dinner when we all sat down as a family. I had even more trouble eating in front of others. It felt garish. Sexual. Provocative. Private. As winter came, I became thinner, my skin tinged with gray. I went repeatedly to the endodontist, believing the pain I suffered was caused by my teeth, and received several root canals, chasing what I now know was trigeminal neuralgia.

One November weekend, the seventh- and eighth-grade classes went away for a retreat called a Shabbaton, and everyone turned on me. My friends iced me out. I was friendless and depressed. When I came back home, I told my mother what a terrible time I'd had, and she suggested that I dye my hair. "You need a change," she said. "It will cheer you up." She called Cousin Helen, a distant relative just out of beauty school, for help.

It took hours, but I went from dark brunette to champagne blond. I looked like a movie star with a dash of Sylvia Plath. Still melancholy, but on the surface I was quite bright now. My face looked pinker. Sweeter. My eyes, framed by my dark, thick eyebrows, suddenly looked stunning. I was happy with my new hair. A lighter bang did mean a lighter face.

Especially as a bleach blonde, I found things at Hillel devolving. The final nail was hammered when my teacher, upon reading my class journal, kept me after the bell to discuss my work. She pursed her lips, holding her glasses in her wrinkled, thin, but manicured hands. Ms. Itzcovitz was always on top of things. She was sharp. Skeletal. Watching. But this time, she read it all wrong.

"Do you think it is peculiar that you go by two names? Selma and Blair equally? As if you are two people?" she asked.

I did not. But clearly she did.

"And now," she continued, pointing her eyeglasses in the direction of my newly dyed hair, "you have this situation."

I found this deeply ironic, because her own hair was dyed a brassy caramel color. I felt accused. Betrayed.

"I have two names," I patiently explained. "I prefer Blair. Some people prefer to call me Selma." It was simple. Sensible. True.

She nodded her head. As if she knew it all. Then she told me to think about it. Not for a journal prompt, but to *really* think about choosing one name only.

I have thought about it. I thought about my mother and the seldom referenced Roseanne. I thought about the two selves I was accused of having, Selma and Blair. About the smile and the frown. And this is where I've landed: There is no schism. My names are a wardrobe. Whatever I felt like wearing on that particular day. Over the years, I have grown into Selma. As I always knew I would. Or rather, as my mom did.

Ms. Itzcovitz was a fine teacher. But both Selma and Blair can now agree. Making me feel wrong was a rotten thing to do to a child.

Brigadoon

𝓕OR NINTH GRADE, my sisters Lizzie and Katie had gone from Hillel to the prominent prep school Cranbrook Kingswood, and I was finally following their lead. Cranbrook was pure enchantment. Reminiscent of *Dead Poets Society* or the dazzling world of F. Scott Fitzgerald. There were buildings by Frank Lloyd Wright hidden within the Saarinen-designed campus. Everywhere you walked, there was something to appreciate. High ceilings and wood paneling, grand foyers with polished brass, shiny malachite tiles. Wrought-iron windows specially made for the school. Every last detail had been chosen in the best taste and craftsmanship. Everything was exclusive, in a welcoming bent. It even *smelled* good, with fireplaces roaring on cold winter days. It still remains the most glorious set I've ever been on.

Classes were held in rooms that looked more like living rooms. Beautiful open spaces to wander, besting even the lobby of the Chateau Marmont, which has a similar lighting scheme. The environments were specifically designed to facilitate open conversation, stimulating questions, and discussions around big ideas.

As soon as I showed up, I saw there were so many people— a whole world, in fact—outside yeshiva. And they looked and dressed so much better. Coming from such an insular community, I was surprised to meet so many sunny blond athletic types who, despite their lack of being chosen ones, were doing just fine. When I was a student, Cranbrook was a haven of dazzling lacrosse players and VW Cabriolets. The students were, by and large, the products of generational wealth—the descendants of people who had important names. They came from beautiful homes in which they hosted parties like something out of a Jay McInerney novel, where the things that got broken were priceless and irreplaceable. I fell right in step anyhow, cultivating an aesthetic that was both dramatic and classically tailored, inspired in large part by my mom. One day I'd wear a full-on riding habit, the next a motorcycle jacket. I studied *The Official Preppy Handbook,* memorizing every word as if it were gospel. It was funny and kitsch, but really enjoyable. I had a new goal, and it was to master prepdom.

I also found that when it came to academics, I was utterly unprepared. At Hillel, I excelled in English and writing and social studies. But when it came time to keep up in math and science, I was in way over my head. I flat out failed, and my attitude was equally out of step.

It can take hitting a kind of bottom for a lazy person (and I counted myself as such) to find motivation. I found I had failed this gorgeous place, a truth far more disappointing than failing myself. For the first time, I saw that my choices affect my future. The positive side of my negative self is that I don't see what I have until it's gone. And then I do change.

I was expelled from Cranbrook, and I went to public school for a week. It did not go well. I didn't understand the hierarchy; I couldn't keep up in the large classes. I was lost. I was verbally bullied and physically pushed. Luckily, fate had other plans. During that first week as a student at Southfield-Lathrup High School, I

Box 801
Bloomfield Hills
Michigan 48013 USA
313 645-3000

Cranbrook
Educational
Community **CRANBROOK KINGSWOOD**

Cranbrook Schools

September 11, 1987

Mr. and Mrs. Elliot Beitner
22445 Coventry Woods
Southfield, Michigan 48034

Dear Mr. and Mrs. Beitner,

I am very pleased to be able to write this letter to tell you that
Blair has been invited back to Cranbrook Kingswood School.

Blair has persuaded the faculty that she is serious about returning
to school. Her attitude has undergone a dramatic change. She has
shown she can be an outstanding citizen by her achievement this summer
at camp. Her willingness to see a counselor and to work with a tutor
in study skills demonstrates clearly to us all that she is actively
seeking to become a successful and self-confident student.

█████████ made a most wonderful presentation of Blair's petition to
return to school. His faith in Blair was the key element, I believe,
in the success of the petition. For a student to return to school in
this way is an exceptional occurrence. I cannot recall this happening
once during my last ten years as a teacher here. It is manifest to me
that the faculty have thought very carefully about Blair's situation,
believe she can be successful in the school, and will do everything it
can to support her and encourage her.

It was, in the end, Blair's own behavior that has persuaded us to readmit
her. I commend her, and I congratulate you.

Sincerely,

Dr. Jeffrey Welch
Academic Dean

JW:bjl

had an anaphylactic reaction to the long-term Bactrim I was prescribed for bladder infections. It grew so severe so quickly that
I couldn't breathe. My mom picked me up in the middle of the
day—I was never more grateful for an early dismissal—and I was
rushed to the emergency room. After that, I never returned.

By the time I was discharged from the hospital, I managed to
get invited back to Cranbrook. There was a meeting in Dean

Arlyce Seibert's office to discuss my future at the school. I fixed my eyes on Arlyce, on her welcoming posture, her gray blazer, the pale fabric of her pants. She told both my parents I would be readmitted, pending some academic and social conditions. My mom sat closer to me, her Burberry trench unfastened but still hanging on her slender frame. Once Arlyce finished speaking, my mom glared at her.

"You can just change the rules?" she said. "You're going to change the rules . . . for her?"

Despite her profession, my mother had a real distrust of authority, let alone one who altered the rules. (She might have said, "To know the rules is to break the rules," but her expectation was for everyone else to abide by them.) The magistrate in her could not let this positive moment pass without offering her two cents.

Elliot, his own Burberry draped across his lap, whispered, "Molly. Please?" He knew how much this school meant to me, that I couldn't manage without it. The grounds. The teachers. The students. The glimmers of hope. And just like that, I was given another chance.

To feel you have a second chance is one of life's greatest victories. I was grateful, humbled, not to mention relieved as all hell. This time, I promised, I would do better. I would never make the same mistakes again. I would remain present. I would try.

⌀

I felt I would not be long for this world if I remained alone, in the basement, without allies. I needed to get on someone's back, to have them navigate for me. I am a true case of someone who needs someone smarter, someone brighter, someone more together in my inner circle, to learn from. My mom often said about creative people, "He'll either be a great actor, or he'll wind up in jail!" You need the right crowd, she reminded me. To keep you in line.

Thank goodness for Sue. She was the only stranger who walked up to me at orientation day. Thank God she did. There I was, leaning against a wall, waiting in my thrift store clothes, at this very rich school, where no one wore such things. Royal blue Repetto ballet flats paired with black denim jeans and a royal blue letter jacket in the same shade as the shoes. It had "Dan Rose" stitched on the left breast. My hair was still blond with dark roots, grown out from the champagne blond bob that caused such a stir back at Hillel. I stood out, though I didn't intend to. I was nervous and curious. Self-conscious and intimidated. So I tried that mood on. I wore my mean baby face to keep people away till I could get sorted. But that didn't deter Sue.

I called her Suzy Sunshine. She was perpetually upbeat, my polar opposite, the best counterpart. Before Cranbrook, I had lived a small life. My entire existence took place between the orbit of Hillel and my home. Meanwhile, Sue was so blond, so Nordic, so never-met-a-Jewish-person-before. She was the light I gathered to.

From the first moment we met, Sue *saw* me. One of the first people who did. She saw me out of my fear. When she looked at me, she saw past the exterior, intuiting who I was at my core. After Sue came up to me, we never let go.

All I really wanted (other than to be tall and a model) was to be kind. I wanted someone to say, "You know Selma Blair Beitner? She is so sweet." I wanted to shake the ghost of the mean baby once and for all. But that's not what people did say about me. Instead, it was more like "Selma is crazy, you have to love her. Don't you love her?" or "That chick's on drugs," even though I wasn't. People either loved me or were repulsed by me. But they didn't see me.

Not for who I really was. Or wanted to be. I had no outline just for me.

Sue did. She understood that I was a likable, sweet girl who was also eccentric and tough. My mother scared people to earn their respect, and I learned that from her. Where there was fear, there was admiration. Where there was admiration, I could keep a distance.

"I feel so seen" is something people say now, often as a joke, but if you really dig down, it gets to the heart of what people want all their lives. I was surprised someone like Sue wanted to be good friends with me. Because she was so *good*. With a big strong family and healthy boundaries. She went to church and studied hard. She took me into her world, and mine became better under her care. I saw what it was like to be part of a loving family, the kind with spotless carpets and a chirping alarm system. Our home was tidy; we had a housekeeper. But it wasn't clean in that cared-for, shiny way. Whenever Sue would borrow something of mine, she

would say, "This smells like your house! It makes me so happy." Finally, one day I asked her what that meant, and she said, "Cigarette smoke."

Sue was *normal.* She was sunlight. My association with Sue kept me grounded. And in turn, I showed her another side, where things that are dark and broken aren't so scary, really.

Even though I was newly happy in my surroundings, I still suffered from depression and melancholy and mystery pains that settled in and went without warning. But I discovered I wasn't depressed when I was moving. For two weeks in March, I found an escape in Wilderness, a modified Outward Bound program and a Cranbrook rite of passage. We were given the opportunity to travel to the Smoky Mountains of Tennessee, to carry our food and shelter. It was extracurricular and very immersive. The teachers, who observed us all year, knew whom you were friends with and purposefully matched you with students not in your own social group.

I loved it. I did not excel in team sports. Though I was agile, I didn't have the stamina or the training for those kinds of endeavors. But realizing I could walk with a sixty-pound pack the same way the big hockey goalie could? That was something! Wilderness was its own team, in a way, where the point wasn't to score a goal. We slept under a tarp, nestling in to stay warm. Once, when it was 16 degrees, I had to put my frozen foot in Andrew Clausson's groin to warm it up. As the designated foot warmer-upper, he took each person's foot and nestled it in his ball area. I've never spoken to Andrew, I thought, and yet he is letting me warm my frozen feet in his sixteen-year-old crotch. What a mensch!

In nature, my depression melted away. Of course, on that trip, I also couldn't drink, which no doubt played a role. Without my usual escape hatch, I discovered camaraderie. Once I'd felt that love, with basic strangers, the sane part of me knew to seek it out again.

Outward Bound became my healthy distraction. Later in life, when I went through periods of depression, or MS flare-ups that I didn't yet recognize as such, I would sign up for Outward Bound. After a big project wrapped in Hollywood, I would take two weeks in the wilderness to restabilize. (Once I was already established as an actress, I registered as James Blair, hoping for anonymity. Which was short-lived because once we met at the airport before our treks someone would say, "You look like that actress." So it was back to Selma.)

It was just one of the many wonderful things to come from my experience at Cranbrook. It was like stumbling upon Briga-doon. Students were made to create art, to write, to think deeply and critically. What amazed me most of all was that everyone I met seemed to be genuinely interested in who I was and what I thought, even when I didn't feel I had much to share. We were valued. I've never encountered teachers like them again, even in college. It was a far cry from my dark house, where the grown-ups didn't seem to care for anything but work and cocktail hour. Here, we were treated as equals.

⁓

"That's the guy," said my sister Lizzie's friend Anna, turning to the field hockey expanse by Kingswood Lake. It was just before the start of my freshman year, and we were at field hockey conditioning, running drills on a humid summer day. Anna was gorgeous and older and drove a Saab and wore Ombre Rose parfum, and like many girls at Cranbrook she had her hopes pinned on Chip. I looked up and there he was—long, lanky, slightly hunched, in

black sport shorts and a plaid shirt worn open over a T-shirt. Our eyes met. He gave me a shy smile. Fleeting, but genuine. And that was it. A match had been lit.

Even as a high school sophomore, Chip Fuller was a most gorgeous human. The high cheekbones, the straight white teeth. His face was framed by thick eyebrows that were slow to arch, like mine. His young, full veins showed visibly on his arms. He was a flesh-and-blood, real-life movie star boy. By the time we met, he was already well established as *the* guy at school. I didn't crush right off. But I was curious.

Our first kiss took place in my friend Cathy's den, her family's iconic art pieces as our witnesses. (I recall that a Rothko was present just outside.) One of us gurgled, an involuntary throat gurgle, prompting a smile. And then came a kiss. It was my first kiss since Brad, the summer before eighth grade. Chip smelled ever so faintly of salami, reassuring. I relaxed into it. And then I fell in love.

I arrived at high school inexperienced; I had only ever kissed one boy, nothing more. The truth is, I was so terrified of getting pregnant that I never had sex while I was in high school. Blow jobs, however, didn't scare me. If you couldn't get pregnant, it seemed okay. (Someone once wrote on a bathroom wall, "Lizzie and Blair Beitner give good head." I couldn't believe it. A good review!)

Nevertheless, Chip's mother was very worried we would soon have a sex life. One day, while meeting at Embers Deli to discuss their children, my mother put a proverbial bagel in her mouth by telling her it was a physical impossibility. "He's six four and she's five two! It's impossible!" And my mom truly believed it. I did not have sex with the love of my teenage life, and to this day Chip and I still laugh about it. (Although it was, in fact, physically possible. Sorry, Mom.)

Instead, he cheated on me with one of my friends. I went away to camp that summer after ninth grade, and he slept with her. (I honestly can't say I blame him. She was cool and worldly and sexy.) I didn't find out until the following winter, and it broke my heart. I forced him to call her right in front of me, as any young, insecure girl might do, and say, "I don't want to be friends anymore." They are still friends.

Later, that same friend gave me a beautiful book of photos, inscribed with the lyrics "When the mountains crumble to the sea, there will still be you and me," which I found ironic, because that was my song with Chip. But I loved her and kind of forgave her.

It was that time of life when many trespasses are made on our hearts. I forgive it all now. I did a lot of bad things myself—lied, apologized, begged for forgiveness. I once kissed the only boy that Sue liked, right in front of her. We had been drinking a bit. Thankfully, we're still okay. I've come to understand it's all part of the process of learning how to be human. And no repeats, please.

Even before I started at Cranbrook, I was acquainted with the Dean. Everyone at Cranbrook knew him. He had tutored my sister Lizzie in math before she enrolled and offered the same help to me in the summer before school began to catch me up to speed. (Coming from a parochial school, none of us Beitner girls were equipped for the academic rigor of Cranbrook, and we needed the extra preparation.)

The summer before ninth grade, I met with him in his office every afternoon after field hockey practice. It was warm and inviting, with wood paneling and built-in bookshelves. I can still picture the way the sunlight came through the wavy glass panes in his office, bathing the space in August light. If every corner of Cranbrook was like a big-budget set, the Dean's office was no exception. There wasn't a bad angle to be found.

For me, that office was a place of safety and comfort. He helped me understand polynomials and slopes and algebraic equations (barely—I'm still hopeless at math), and he helped me to be patient with my potential. He was kind and comfortable. He was funny. He was also handsome and deeply respected by the community. Everyone adored him. I was lucky to have this man in my corner.

He took me under his wing. He counseled me on everything—friendships, boyfriends, schoolwork. He began to treat me like his family. I thought he was the greatest man I had ever met. So thoughtful and well dressed. Handsome. Tall. So generous. I joked with him and sought him out and reveled in his attention. He was a kind and authoritative guiding force, the father figure I longed for but hadn't found in Elliot. All of my friends melted in the Dean's presence. Sue and I would say how much we hoped we'd find a man just like him when we grew up.

I'm sure you can see where this is all going. The pattern is so familiar, so obvious, it feels inevitable. But at that time, I couldn't have predicted it. I didn't know anything about consent. I trusted authority. I was just a teenager.

A few months into school, the Dean's embraces started to linger. He remarked I was pretty. Maybe inappropriate, but of course he was also married. To a woman I respected and found lovely. In fact, he and his wife once took me and my three best friends, Sue, Kelly, and Frances—we called ourselves the Fab Four—away for the weekend to their beach home in Tawas, Michigan. We all sang "Don't Leave Me This Way" together and threw spaghetti at the walls in the kitchen. I snapped pictures with my drugstore Kodak. I felt cherished by both the Dean and his wife, and I cherished them back, taking walks with them along the autumn paths.

I couldn't overlook how my interactions with him had started to seem romantic. But as best I could, I ignored the signs, as though my denial would somehow prevent them from getting too real. In my mind, we were more like peers. He cared about me and he helped me, and in my young point of view, that made us friends.

The problem was my grades were not up to par. I was failing. I was overwhelmed with math. I started to drink even more. I couldn't keep up with French. The only foreign language I'd learned at Hillel was Hebrew, and now I was far behind my classmates. I was so happy in my social life—I had a great circle of friends, I'd been a Homecoming Princess already as a freshman, I had Chip—but academically, I was lost, and as the weeks ticked on, I grew more and more anxious about my grades. More and more I turned to the Dean for help, and more and more he cast me in a romantic light.

One day right before winter break of my freshman year, December 1986, I was in his office. He locked the door. We exchanged gifts. He asked me what my scent was, an Hermès fragrance I'd borrowed from my mom's friend Jane. I didn't know how to pronounce it at the time, and I told him it was "Hermies." I'm sure it was too adult of a fragrance to enjoy in such a small room, a real Saks Fifth Avenue scent. I felt ashamed.

I was already a little disarmed when he asked me to stand. We embraced. It felt too long and too still and too quiet. I was a child. I wasn't equipped for this. His hand went to the small of my back, tracing the space just above my tailbone. His lips were on my mouth. They were closed, but they were there.

I tried, everything I had, to put my faith in this. Please, I thought. Please don't go under my pants, my dress-code-approved Ralph Lauren khakis into which I'd carefully tucked a plaid shirt. Please. You are a grown-up and I love you; please do not put your hand inside my pants. But he did.

It was gentle. It was subtle. It wasn't far. But I was shaken. I froze. My stomach clenched. In one moment, everything I had worked for seemed in jeopardy. I didn't want to lose all the good I'd created at Cranbrook. But I knew I couldn't stay.

It was a simple thing. He didn't rape me. He didn't threaten me. But he broke me. The Dean was my only touchstone there, and he was no longer my friend. He had put me in a situation from which I could not comfortably extricate myself. I wanted him to be the man I met before I started at Cranbrook. The one who taught me algebra. The man with the handsome jaw and eyes and a wife, with such patience and affection and care, both for this school and for me. Now the same man was making me unsafe. He was throwing me away. He was the Dean and he was respected. He was the politician everyone loved. He knew I was fragile at this school and was trying to regain my footing. Now I would have to play along untruthfully.

Box 801
Bloomfield Hills
Michigan 48013 USA
313 645-3000

Cranbrook
Educational
Community **CRANBROOK KINGSWOOD**

Cranbrook Schools   December 7, 1987

Mr. and Mrs. Elliot Beitner
22445 Coventry Woods
Southfield, Michigan 48034

Dear Mr. and Mrs. Beitner:

   I was extremely pleased with Blair's first quarter
performance. She demonstrated that she was sincere about
wanting to return to Cranbrook Kingswood. I did not doubt
that she would have a good year, but it is now reassuring to
know that is the case.

   Blair is a very positive person in our school. She
cares about her friends and our school. Her participantion
in the sports program also speaks of her willingness to be
part of the school in ways other than pure academics.

   I hope the physical problems Blair has been facing will
soon be resolved.

   Please feel free to get in touch.

                    Sincerely,

                    Dean of Students/Adviser

■:js

I didn't know what to do, so I might have giggled when I ran
out of the room, and promptly passed out in the vestibule right
outside the Dean's office. Chip happened to be coming out from a
class down the hall. He saw me and helped me up.

In the safety of Chip's car, I told him what happened. I wanted
an ally. Chip believed me. He saw the Dean's favoritism and how
it was possible. Chip became a good part of that story. He kept
the peace; he was friendly to this man who was my mentor. But I

knew he was always looking out for me. He didn't do much, but it was enough. He waited for me outside the Dean's door as often as he could after that.

I felt sad. I loved the Dean, but not as a lover. And he had dealt a huge blow. I had no designs on grown men. I needed the Dean for so much more than a sexual awakening. I needed him to help me learn to be in this world. I needed him to help me succeed academically, to thrive. I needed to do better in school so I could stay at Cranbrook. I felt shattered. I didn't understand anything. I was angry.

My grades continued to fall; I lost my way. I fell apart.

It was later that spring that I was told I would not be invited to return to Cranbrook for my sophomore year. I was devastated. It was the Dean who lobbied for me to be readmitted, and he prevailed; it was in part because of him that I was given a second chance. Despite his transgressions, he did fight for me. He was my ally. Except when he wasn't. That's why it hurt to discover the Dean was just a regular man. It was a sad awakening. Adults are just like you, but older.

For the rest of my time at Cranbrook, I did what I could to avoid being alone with the Dean. But in order to stay in my beloved school, I was under a contract to meet with him every day. I was in a bad spot. He kept trying to find me—taking me out of class, seeking me out. He was one of the most important men at the school, and I knew I could not refuse him outright. Sometimes when we were together, he tried to hold my hand or kiss me. Nothing ever happened again, but I still felt it could. I never felt safe. I was the mature one, the one to make sure we were never alone together for any extended period of time. I became cagey, laughing and deflecting and making jokes. Distracting. All the while I would pray, *Please just let me get through this year.* Still, I never told him to stop. Cranbrook had taught me so much, offered me a whole new vocabulary, and yet I didn't know how to say those two simple words. "Please. Stop."

Please. Stop. Are there two more important words in this world?

Please. Stop. Are there two words that are harder to say when you're a woman in a position like this?

Every time, I tried to get out of the room, I tried not to engage. But I never asked him to stop. I didn't want to consider what the consequences might be if I refused him. Saying no to him meant losing Cranbrook. And I didn't want to lose Cranbrook.

One night early in my senior year, my mother and I were lying in her bed. She was reading a Robertson Davies novel. I leaned into her shoulder. Apropos of nothing, she closed her book and said, "I think the Dean is in love with you." She paused. "Is he?"

I was overcome. I took a slow, deep breath, exhaled, and said, "I think he might be. He tried to kiss me."

My mother exhaled and said, "I knew it." She took a deep breath. "You must not tell anybody. He's beloved at that school. And you'll just be a troubled girl. Best to get through and get done." I knew she was right in saying this. I put my head on the pillow. I would evade. I would get out. I had done the right thing in confiding in her, and she would not embarrass me and make me react in any public way. My former ally was now an enemy of my ever-loyal mother.

"I'm sorry," she said, her focus far off.

My mother and I didn't speak of the Dean again. I did as she instructed and stayed quiet. But at the end of my senior year, on the night of my baccalaureate, he came over to speak to me. He congratulated me for winning a writing award and told me he was so proud of me. I was still holding the book I'd received in recognition, a hardcover collection of short stories engraved with the words "To Blair Beitner, the 1990 Strickland Writing Award, in Recognition of Her Passionate Commitment to, Joy in, and Success at Creative Writing." I clutched it over my chest. Armor. Then he turned to my mother and said, "And you must be so proud of Selma, too."

She stared at him but didn't say anything. She didn't even crack a smile. She just looked at him, stone-faced. Then: "I know what you did. Stay away from my daughter." He walked away. I graduated the next day.

⁕

When I was a freshman at Kalamazoo College and felt worlds away from the Dean, a call came in from him out of the blue. I was in my dorm room. I don't remember how the conversation began; I had five roommates crowding near, waiting to go out together. But I do remember him telling me, "I need to apologize for what I did. I am so sorry, Selma."

I breezily said, "It's okay."

I hung up the phone. Then I went in the bathroom and threw up.

Two years later, a girl approached me on campus and asked, "What happened with the Dean? My mother is friends with his wife. She said she's furious with you. You ruined their marriage."

That broke my heart. I'd never have the chance to explain his transgression. There was no winning. I was the mean baby, the girl who had ruined this house. I was surprised that another adult—an adult I loved—thought I was culpable. I was surprised she couldn't see the truth: that the Dean had ruined me.

⌒

I still think about what happened. How handsome the Dean was, in his suede elbow-patched tweed coats over cashmere sweaters. How he was seen as so fair and great. How I chose him as my father figure because he allowed and encouraged me to. I think about how it all seemed on the up-and-up. He didn't rape me. He was too old-school, old guard and careful. What is so horrible to me, what hurt me then and now, what damages and hurts the scores of women who have been in similar situations, was that he extended the invitation to a vulnerable girl. That he dared to test out the waters, knowing full well I believed he was there for me, in my corner, as a trusted champion, friend, and mentor.

It took tremendous strength to see the situation for what it really was. To my fourteen-year-old brain, I was sensitive and lost and I wanted to trust someone. This man represented the sum total of what I thought I wanted someday. I wanted to grow up and find a man who was just like the Dean. To be a wife who was just like his wife. But his predation changed me. It was an insult to everything I learned to believe in.

I learned that this man, so beloved, was not—at least not entirely—who everyone believed him to be. I learned that when it came to marriage, I did not have much to look forward to. I learned that the people in charge do not always have your best interests at heart.

⌒

Remarkably, my dealings with the Dean did not diminish my total awe and love for the rest of my Cranbrook experience. If anything, I built Cranbrook into a transcendent place. It was remarkable, and it was beautiful and otherworldly, but I made it into a full-blown fairy tale, maybe to compensate for how shattered I was by the actions of a grown man. But the institution of Cranbrook still saved me from my basement.

More than anything, Cranbrook is where I was exposed to great works of literature beyond the books I'd discovered on my mother's shelves. I loved books, just as my mother had always loved books, but Cranbrook gave me a vocabulary. Words, I discovered, are the salve for curiosity. Words are the connection linking me to everyone else, to all the people before and since. Words were a discovery, threads of humanity connecting us across time and place. Words were my saving grace.

The surroundings of Cranbrook made every book even more heartbreaking or winsome. The first book I studied in ninth grade was *The Catcher in the Rye,* taught by my young teacher who looked like a Salinger character himself in his L.L.Bean moccasins and wool socks. *The Scarlet Letter. The Odyssey. The Turn of the Screw. Invisible Man* and the works of C. S. Lewis and James Joyce. If my house were to catch fire, the two things I would save are my son and my first edition of *Till We Have Faces,* gifted by a dear friend.

I preferred the tragic tales then. *The Sorrows of Young Werther. The End of the Affair*—oh, that book broke my heart open! *The Wanderer,* by the doomed French novelist Alain-Fournier, in which the main character is ruined by his passion for an unattainable girl found in a fairy-tale estate in the woods. I fancied myself a chain-smoking writer, living in a garret and writing poems like Sylvia Plath and Ted Hughes.

We also read plays and short stories, by Henrik Ibsen and James Joyce. Shakespeare and Homer and Morrison. I learned that Raymond Carver said he didn't write long stories because he didn't have the endurance. Oh! I thought. You can use your laziness to your advantage. You can use your lack of focus and still create something beautiful.

At Hillel, we learned from the Torah. Our main Hebrew text was the Talmud. They were laws, and they were profound, but they weren't personal to me. At Cranbrook, the canon of literature they chose all felt so personal, an intimate conversation between writer and reader. It could be playful, easy, and sometimes confounding. To me, Cranbrook was a secret garden. Meeting so much literature in that setting, where everything felt so timeless, I found the thing that sang to me.

Books would save my life. I saw how they cracked me open in the best way. Pushed tears out or made me laugh with the fart that did fly in *The Canterbury Tales.* I learned how it feels when someone else's thoughts touch a part of you that you haven't felt before. Books are a great emotional lifesaver. A nightlight. A doormat.

Even if you're stuck in a hospital or in line at the DMV, it's all okay if you have a good book with you.

Books also taught me how to notice things, how a moment can be a whole story. I notice everything these days—the dust bunnies swirling into far corners, the long blades of grass living between the cracks in the sidewalk, the way my son flares his nostrils. These things, if you stop and take note, remind you that you're alive, make you feel that you still count. They silence all the worries for a moment.

By the time I was a young adult, I was just starting to arrive at that point where distance made one wiser. I wanted a permanent record. Something to prove I once existed. Something to hold on to. These books moved me; their words so beautiful that they became a part of me. I wanted to stay inside them forever.

But my hero was Joan Didion, whose work I devoured—*Slouching Towards Bethlehem, Play It as It Lays, The White Album.* I related to her aloofness, the refuge she sought in words. I read and reread her, dazzled by her brilliant mind and understated style. Her whole presentation thrilled me. I felt so pleased that, like her, I kept journals all my life. "Keepers of private notebooks are a different breed altogether, lonely and resistant rearrangers of things, anxious malcontents, children afflicted apparently at birth with some presentiment of loss." It was as if she were speaking straight to me.

If Didion was my idol, my English teacher James Toner was my first real-life mentor—the only person I'd ever met who had actually published stories in literary journals. I worshipped him. As a bonus, he didn't want anything from me other than for me to keep reading and writing.

I entered Mr. Toner's class as if I were walking into his church. For the first time, I was allowed to be seen as a person growing into a writer. It was a far cry from Hillel, where the girls were not even encouraged to study in the same way the boys were. Mr. Toner taught me that literature could be a salve. He nurtured my yearning to be a writer.

The very first short story I wrote was for Mr. Toner's class, and my mother served as my editor. "Selma," she said, her red pen slashing, "this is very rococo." But she had an eye for it. Ever the storyteller, she would find a good sentence and then build a simple narrative out of it. Somehow, without really adding a word of her own, she could turn a story into something great.

I am a procrastinator of writing essays. I saw this in school. They were too structured, too focused. You had to map it out, you had to outline, you had to be clear. Whenever I began to write, I thought, "Who the hell knows where it's going?" I wanted to force the words out. But in Mr. Toner's class, I discovered that writing could be so many things. I felt the power in the pages. He helped open up the possibilities. I wanted to be someone. I wanted to create something, too. In my dreams, I wanted James Toner to someday teach my words to other kids who felt shut down and needed a key out. I wanted to be seen. I wanted to run into the hills like white elephants and come out a writer. Instantly.

꩜

We girls knew that my parents didn't have the sort of commitment to each other that would go the distance happily, and so I was not surprised when one day, I came home after visiting an Ohio college with Sue junior year and found my mother alone on the chaise in her sitting room, a cigarette in one hand and a book open on her lap.

"He's gone," she said, without a trace of emotion.

My father had moved out. My mother didn't make a big deal of it, and neither did I. Elliot had left and never lived on Coventry Woods Lane again. He rented apartments and furniture, as if the split were temporary. They finally divorced when I was twenty-three and never spoke to each other again. My relationship with Elliot was never going to build after the day he moved out. I chose a side, and I chose my mother.

❦

My literary ambitions took a major detour my senior year, when my first foray into acting was made. Ironically, the whole thing was James Toner's idea. I was struggling mightily with Shakespeare; I didn't care for verse and didn't find my way into his plays. This was, Toner thought, a deficiency in my education. He recommended I audition for the school play *As You Like It.* Perhaps onstage I would embrace Shakespeare's brilliance as a playwright. My audition went so badly I didn't even get a callback. I was dreadful! The text fell from my hands, I was unable to find my place.

I continued auditioning, at Mr. Toner's urging, and was rejected again. Finally, I tried one last time, for a student-directed production, and was cast as a lead in T. S. Eliot's *Murder in the Cathedral.* The play was not great in our hands: interminable and boring as hell. At intermission, much of the audience fled, including my mother (although she did comment that I looked gorgeous in my stage makeup and that I should keep it on indefinitely).

Looking down from the stage, I intuited we were losing our momentum and resorted to every trick I could think of to keep the fidgety audience engaged. I could have turned the performance into a burlesque show. The show must go on. It didn't matter what show.

By the end, there were only a few listless souls remaining in the auditorium. To my dread, James Toner was one of them. Mortifying! I wanted to melt into the stage. I couldn't believe he'd witnessed such a boring calamity. I felt certain I'd fallen several rungs in his esteem. After we took our bows, I sheepishly made my way over to him. "Blair!" he exclaimed. "You're an actress!" I was quiet. Crushed. I wanted him to see me as a writer. But he was unequivocal. His words played in my head. *You're an actress.* The power of a label yet again. At least I had more options now.

Later that night, I took a walk in the woods. Deep in the trees on Cranbrook's campus, there's a statue of Zeus's head, a kind of mantelpiece in a clearing, and if you stand on the right spot, tears fall from his eyes. I stood there alone, waiting for Zeus's tears. Mr. Toner's words replayed over and over in my mind. I wasn't a writer. I was an actress. I did not yet think that one could be both a writer *and* an actress, or that I had the power to set my own course. Not an overachiever. Or even much of an achiever. But I had been given another prophecy, and it was my destiny to fulfill it.

PART II

QUESTIONS

Kalamazoo

BECAUSE OF MY early academic struggles at Cranbrook, I didn't have a strong enough GPA or SAT score to get into the University of Michigan, where Katie and Mimi had gone, so I won a partial scholarship to study photography at Kalamazoo College, a small liberal arts school a few hours from home. I didn't think any school would ever compare with Cranbrook, so I never gave the lovely, ivy-covered Kalamazoo a chance.

From the day I arrived on campus, I was a recluse. I worked hard enough, spending hours every week in the photography lab or typing poems at my word processor. I didn't try to make friends. My suite mates were a decent group of misfits, but we never grew close. When I wasn't in class, I drank. But so did everyone.

I grew dangerously depressed and despairing. Away from the reign of my mother, so lonely, I felt lost and adrift. Grateful for the wine coolers, beer, and fancy Godiva liqueur I kept in my room.

My English professor Conrad Hilberry, an accomplished writer and a wonderful older man, became an appropriate mentor. He was elegant, with a wide grin and a big laugh and legs that kept crossing and uncrossing. He was also quite thin; if he turned sideways, his glasses appeared thicker than his torso!

His class gathered in an airy room, like my Cranbrook days. We sat around a table and read our work aloud. We talked about

Arthur Ashe, of whom we were all great fans and who was honored with the tennis courts in his name. He introduced me to the works of Charles Simic, Sharon Olds, John Donne, Joan Didion, Truman Capote. He was so pleased whenever the word would sing. When I was a freshman in college, he told me to keep writing. So, I wrote. Only poems, because I was still too unsure to put more words down on paper. Words that made sense anyway. Recently, I came across one.

Martini Olive

You started with the asking that summer.
Honey, will you hand me the lemon rinds?
My little hands willingly felt past
The warm milk and mushy avocados.

Peculiar how you were so happy in the day,
Buying limes, stirrers and olives
Orange pimiento caught inside that firm green flesh.

Strange to think I came out of you
Like the inside of an olive
As soft and as slippery.

But on the front porch,
Watching the mosquitos,
You never mentioned it.
Night would buzz down.
The glasses were still now,
But only that summer.
Later is a different day.

Before bed, your asking brought me running
Sliding on the pickled oak floor.

Summer, and you were afraid of dying in the tub,
Naked—undignified, you called it
And that made me cry.

Somehow, silently, my nose pressed against
Plaster, I waited for you outside our little bathroom
While you undid yourself and soaked.
I listened for the clink of glasses or
The smell of a martini that reminded me of
The geraniums we planted.

I imagined you floating down
Bloating with water like a martini olive
Sponging up the gin.

Conrad Hilberry died in 2017. I miss him. He sent word once in a blue moon and continued to be a supportive presence in my life, until I left for California. He encouraged me to dig deeper. "Let yourself be provoked. Don't be afraid to get agitated," he said. "What if I don't have anything to say?" I would ask him. "Just keep searching," he'd respond. He always urged another story, a closer look. I think he knew how much he meant to me. I hope he did.

❧

When I was a freshman at Kalamazoo, I started dating Jason K., a pretty boy who lived upstairs in the dorms. He was a catch, in that college-boy way, easily cuter than anyone else there. One night, we rode the bus into Kalamazoo for dinner and a movie, and he kissed me. For months I walked the stairwell to his small and cozy room, where I was greeted by the scent of his Calvin Klein Eternity cologne and the glow of the Christmas lights strung above his bed.

We tried, very sweetly, to make ours a love story. But we weren't cut from the same cloth. He didn't really fancy me deeply, a fact that became evident soon enough. He typed up a list of all the things he thought I needed to change about myself. How to Fix Blair.

I took up with another handsome fellow, Todd, a trainer at the barn where I rode for PE credit. We fell in love. One night, he told me he didn't love me anymore and that he wanted to break up. Devastated, I waited for him to fall asleep. Then I went into his closet, sat down on the brown marble shag carpeting, and decided my life was not worth living.

Tucked among his clothing, I took a full bottle of extra-strength Tylenol, which I got down with half a bottle of tequila. Then I closed my eyes and waited. I don't think I wanted to die in that moment. I just didn't want to be in pain anymore. Aka: alive. I believed I was unlovable. I wanted to go to sleep and maybe I could wake up as someone else. Someone right.

As I was about to pass out, I had regret. I woke up Todd and showed him what I had done. He found his mom upstairs and she called poison control. They drove me to the nearest hospital.

In the ER, they gave me a supersized charcoal slushie the consistency of blended Oreo cookies. I couldn't keep it down, retching violently, so the nurses pumped my stomach. The large tube they threaded through my nostrils broke my nose but sucked out most of the offending acetaminophen. I had diarrhea in the bedpan. By morning, I was released.

```
                    BLAIR'S GOALS

    I. Gain five pounds in muscle.
       A. Run
       B. Eat good foods
       C. Stretches and aerobics before bed

    II. Stay at "K" for this year
        A. Don't let Jason make me miss class
        B. Can't get stoned more than once a month
       *C. Learn to use "Mac"
        D. Schedule time wisely
        E. Study for at least three to four hours after dinner
        F. Run tuesday, thursday, and friday 2:30 to 3:30

    III. Learn to be independent
         A. Avoid Tony and express your true feelings to him,
            even if it may hurt him
        *B. Don't push away Jason's friendship
        *C. Don't get into another relationship until counseling
            with Jason
         D. Get out of your mom's backpocket
            1. Call only once a week (unless absolutely
               necessary, then must ask Jason if you can).
            2. Express to your mom, when she upsets you and
               don't take everything so hard
           *3. Think for yourself and about what's good for
               you and don't worry about anyone else

    IV. DON'T BE AN ALCOHOLIC
        A. Blair can only drink three times a week (maximum of
           eight drinks at a time).  You can only drink the
           maximum once a week.
```

I GOT A Sense of Humor

```
    I have read the above arrangement and have agreed to the
    terms of it, and understand certain consequences that may
    entail due to the abuse of this agreement.


                          Signed
                                 Selma Blair Beither
```

I didn't say a word about it to anyone until months later, when I confessed to my father, who forced me to tell my mother before she saw it on the insurance bill. Over the phone, she calmly told me, "You are dead to me. How could you have done that to me?" I held the receiver to my ear and held back fat tears as my suite mates looked over. I thought she understood who I was. I thought she understood everything. So angry was she that we didn't speak much for two years. Todd, however, took me back, and we stayed together until I left for University of Michigan and then New York City.

❧

Aside from Conrad Hilberry, the other bright spot of my time at Kalamazoo was that I finally had the space to pursue my childhood passion for riding horses. They offered riding for a gym credit, and I immediately enrolled. I was pleased to discover that somehow I was okay at it, a pretty enough rider. My body had learned more, I thought, and this time I was ready to ride.

That's how I met Todd. I noticed a trainer who was gorgeous in his riding outfit. He had a natural way with horses, and I wasn't surprised to learn he'd been riding since he could walk. He taught me how to jump. He taught me proper form. We spent frigid days watering horses and dropping hay bales in stables.

For two years, I kept riding and jumping. It was like a time-lapse sequence in a movie, where I worked at it daily, blundered and prevailed, and eventually I progressed into a decent rider. Practically, this meant that if I got on a good horse, I'd win a couple ribbons. If I got on a horse that wasn't so good, I'd fall. I didn't show a tremendous amount of promise, but I was obsessed.

My daydream was to be like Tatum O'Neal in *International Velvet*. I wanted to be a good rider. And like any actress, I also wanted to look the part. The style part I could manage. Ordering a hot dog and Diet Coke at a horse show, I looked like a serious contender. But when it came time to ride, it was anybody's guess. Where other girls would cry when they fell off, I would laugh it off, get back up, and finish the course. Everyone thought I had such a good attitude, but really I was just a mediocre rider who was pleased to get to ride instead of watching my sister.

My mom only opted to view one horse show. She was very disappointed in the dusty ring in Kalamazoo. "Where's my mint julep?" she asked. If my mom had to be somewhere she didn't want to be, there had better be a cocktail; otherwise she wasn't coming back. One and done. I'm sure she had a good book with her to get through.

Where riding brought me joy, it also caused pain. I broke bones, including my lower back. I crushed half my face in a bad fall. After college, when I left Michigan to pursue acting, I put it behind me. I left showing, I left the injuries, I left the dream of opening up a barn with Todd. But I never really left my love of riding. It would be waiting for me to return, someday, when I was ready.

⁓

I once stole a pair of jeans from the college laundry room. I didn't intend to; I was carrying my clothes back to my room when I saw a green pair of jeans crumpled in the pile. I didn't have a pair of green Guess jeans. They definitely weren't mine. But I made no attempt to return them.

Three years later, I rented a bright red summer-term house with a girl named Tammy. I wore those jeans all summer long, and it turned out they had been hers. By that point, I'd forgotten about it. She never said a word to me, but later she told a boyfriend that she knew I stole her jeans. Cringey.

Even though they were not particularly flattering, I remember feeling really solid in those jeans, because they felt like a hand-me-down from someone who wasn't my family. Meanwhile, the whole summer long, she thought she was living with a thief and said nothing to me. I wish she had told me! I would have said, "Oh my God! These are yours? Here, I'll give them back to you right now." And off they would go, returned safe and sound. I would have told her my side of the story and made it right. But she didn't have the same casual outlook on thievery that I had.

I'm still embarrassed about it. There is surely someone out there saying, "Selma Blair? From *Cruel Intentions*? She stole my jeans." I want you to know, Tammy, I've thought about you a lot. I was an ass, but only a one-time thief of jeans. I'm sorry.

Over the years, I've come to find that it means something big to have something of someone else's. Having another person's possessions feels a bit like love. A sharing. Maybe it started when I stole Marla's purple nail polish in fourth grade. Once I'd swiped it, I could never wear it, because then she'd know I had it. I just liked keeping it at home, because it belonged to Marla. A small way of keeping her close. I didn't tell her and felt guilty. I still do. For all the things I did wrong.

Of course, stealing things from people is in fact not an act of love. But I've discovered you can ask them. I stole a shirt from my high school boyfriend, Chip, well into our adult years. I went right into his closet and took it. I told him about it, after the fact. The next day. "It reminded me of you, and I wanted to have it." He was very unfazed by it, in a very cool way, and he said I could keep it. So, I'm still a bit of a thief, I guess. But now, at least, I go about it in a more kosher way. He told me to ask next time. Copy that.

❧

My junior year, I transferred to the University of Michigan. A chance for a fresh college start. Still, I didn't stop drinking. I couldn't. Alcohol was too much a part of me, a part of college life, a necessary emotional sustenance, as essential as air. I became anxious and scared if I didn't have a drink come evening. It was my regulator, a way to quiet myself quickly. I drank some before class. I drank after class. I drank all weekend long. I drank alone in my dorm room. I drank in the darkroom while developing photographs. I never drank water, only alcohol—wine or gin or whiskey or vodka. I fell down, I threw up, I stood up, I went to class.

My drinking grew worse when I befriended the hard-partying sorority girls of Kappa Alpha Theta, who invited me to join them on spring break. The whole group of us drove down to Key West, all the way from Michigan. My dad offered to get me a plane ticket, but I declined. I wanted to have a real college road-trip experience. As a solo drinker, I was curious to know what it felt like to be normal and sociable.

The day after we arrived at our rental, a few of us went deep-sea fishing. It was sunny, humid, and frankly kind of boring. There was a stocked cooler full of beer, and I made quick work of it. I was so bombed catching barracuda on that boat in the hot Florida sun that I began shamelessly flirting with the first mate. By the time we came ashore, I was dead drunk. Our group ended up at a fancy restaurant for dinner, where I retched in the bathroom nonstop. I could barely make it back to the table without vomiting more.

After I'd discharged a day's worth of sun poisoning and beer, I found the boy from the boat at the club. We went back to his little house, where his tiny bedroom smelled like fish, his work clothes piled in a corner. I knew nothing about him other than his first name, Tom. In a blackout, I started to have sex with him. Right away, he said, "We need a condom," and those words brought me back. What the fuck was I doing? "I have to go," I said. "I will call you a cab," he responded courteously.

But I needed air. I fled Tom's apartment and ran into the street, but I had no idea how to get back to our rental. I didn't know where I was. That I was miles away. This was before cell phones. I was alone.

I stumbled down the sidewalk, trying to find my way back to the house, or someone who could take me. The street was pitch black. I sat over by a cropping of trees. That's when two men found me. They held my hands down, kissed me, touched my breasts, laughed with each other. They were very aggressive; they didn't leave bruises, but they hurt me just the same. They flipped me over on my stomach. I don't know if both of them raped me. One of them definitely did. I made myself small and quiet and waited for it to be over.

I lied plenty when I was little, but I am not a liar now. I've never accused anyone of anything false, never spun a tale with details that aren't real. I wish I could say what happened to me that night was an anomaly, an isolated incident. But it wasn't. I didn't think of them as traumas. I have been raped, multiple times, because I was too drunk to say the words "Please. Stop." Only that one time was violent. They were total strangers. It was always awful, and it was always wrong, and I came out of each event quiet and ashamed.

Over the course of my youth, this type of thing happened more than I care to recall or admit. Crawling out of bars, waking up bloated and sick in hotel rooms. Not remembering how I got there. Not understanding what was taking place at the time. It is painful to write these truths even now. Looking back is the way to move forward. To meet it. There are many plot points I don't remember clearly, so many time frames upon frames lost. I numbed my body and left it an empty shell for the taking. I still don't know a lot of the details, and it's safe to say I never want to.

It started the very first time I got drunk at the Passover table and screamed and cried to my cousin Matthew, who was just a kid himself. Even then, when I drank too much, I would look to a male for comfort. In eighth grade, I hung out with a boy from the gas station, drinking and making out in a bathroom stall. As a teenager, I'd drink and wake up with a boy I didn't fancy on top of me. I was taken advantage of so many times. And then grown men—true strangers—overpowering, trespassing. I left my body and other people entered it. The real ways I was assaulted were not, and will never be, okay. Now I see how tragic and embarrassing this is. Reading it over on this one small page, all I can wonder is, how did this happen? How did I let this go on? Where was Blair?

I never said a word to the sorority girls I was with about the rape. That crowd wasn't as messy; I imagined they had better sense to never put themselves in such situations alone. So I didn't tell anyone, ever, until now.

These were the things I drank to forget. I didn't drink for attention; I drank to disappear. To find relief. I drank to numb the pain I was in. The mysterious aches and ever-present pains. And the more I drank, the more I drank out of the need to erase what I had done and who I was when drunk. It was a vicious cycle. But it was no matter. The desire to drink as much as I could, as often as I could, stayed with me and did not let go for more than twenty years.

New York

IN THE SUMMER OF *1993,* I received a postcard in the mail at our home on Coventry Woods Lane. It said I could take summer classes at an acting school in New York City for college credit. My parents agreed to let me go, only because Katie was living in Manhattan and could keep an eye on me.

I lived on Twenty-Ninth and Second, in a grad student dorm that smelled of mildew and Clorox. The whole place was infested with tiny cockroaches. I had never seen a cockroach in person before, until one spun out of the toilet paper roll when I was ripping off a few squares. They hid everywhere—in the walls, under the bed, in the phone books. (I was forever scared to open the Yellow Pages, terrified a little roach might shimmy out and find its way inexplicably straight to my mouth.)

The acting school was through the Column Theater and Studio in Chelsea. All the students were around the same age as me. One pretty redhead named Dierdre had been in a Cherry 7UP commercial years before and I was in full admiration. She was the first person I'd ever known who carried around a water bottle. Odd but also sensible. She was ahead of the curve clearly, as well as the only one who'd signed with a real modeling agency, Wilhelmina. She had big, glossy white teeth and freckles, and was a full head taller than I.

One night after class we all went out drinking, and spied Matt Dillon across the bar. I'd been in love with him ever since he played Dallas in *The Outsiders,* and like my childhood poster come to life, there he was. Brooding, unattainable, absolutely gorgeous. Dierdre kept getting up from our table to walk past him, hoping he'd notice her. She was quite confident! But I knew I should stay put. I didn't stand up until I was ready to leave, and then I shuffled right past him, out of the bar, and back to my roachy apartment. Still, I couldn't sleep. Something about seeing Matt Dillon in person had flipped a switch in me. I had a goal: to be the one at the bar who captured others' attention.

After that summer, I returned to Ann Arbor for my senior year of college, but I was itching to get back to New York. I had to get closer to the energy I'd felt that summer. My aim now was clearer: I wanted to try to make it as an actor.

⁓

One week after graduation, I moved to New York City. My mom helped me pack my Hartmann suitcase, with "Blair" embossed in gold lettering on the side. She snuck in a pink-and-blue cotton quilt, so old and thin it was flat as a penny found pancaked on the tracks. (I have carried that blanket from house to house for more than twenty years.) I passed the long winter nights tucked under that blanket, rereading every story James Toner had assigned me and desperately wanting to be safe and successful and near my mother.

We wrote long letters to each other. She'd write that she missed me so much she'd go into my bedroom and put on my old clothes just to feel close to me. Sometimes we spoke on the black rotary phone, but only occasionally, because I had nothing glorious to report. I only wanted to share achievements that would make her proud. The struggle would not be of interest.

My sister Katie was just starting her career as a book publicist in New York, and we saw each other often, which helped our relationship. She showed me how to use the subway. She lived with a roommate in Murray Hill. For two nights I slept on her couch, but we quickly realized we were not meant to be roommates—ever. The plan was for me to secure my own room at the Parkside Evangeline, a women's residence subsidized by the Salvation Army, situated in the tony neighborhood of Gramercy Park. A prewar building with seventeen floors, the Parkside felt like a college dormitory, with its tiny rooms and simple built-in wooden furniture. My room had a desk with a lamp, a small twin bed, and a shared toilet, which smelled of age and Lysol. It was good. No kitchen, which was fine, since I didn't cook. It wasn't far from the Column, and I drank enough beer to keep my clothing snug.

The larger truth was, I couldn't afford food if I wanted to drink, and I wanted to drink more than I wanted to eat. So, I didn't eat. I was an evening regular at Pete's Tavern, the oldest standing bar in New York, right across from where I lived. Women got free chicken wings during happy hour, so I went there nearly every night for my small supper, where lots of men would buy me drinks. Not knowing what to order, I drank Bushmills, a drink Lizzie ordered. It took me that year to learn that amber alcohol was not for me, causing me to vomit and sway too quickly. I fell off barstools and stumbled back to my room, but the people at Pete's Tavern always took some care of me. I always made it back to my own bed at the all-women's residence. There were a lot of decent bartenders there, and someone usually walked me home.

❧

My first week in the city, I found a palm reader on the street, next to a sign advertising her as both a psychic and a gypsy. She held my hands in hers, carefully studying the lines. I knew that whatever came next was utter BS. But a person holds a little power whenever you ask them to tell you what they see.

She considered my palms. "You will have a horrible disease and you will die a horrible death," she told me, before concluding with "Do not go overseas." Then she told me that if I gave her more money, she could lift the curse and reverse my bad fortune. I didn't go for it, but I told everyone I saw for the next week that I was going to die a horrible death. It wasn't even a good story, but I told it over and over, wearing my curse like a badge of honor.

❧

I gave myself one year to find some traction. At night, in my small wooden bed, I prayed for a miracle. I asked for clarity about what to do with my life. If a job didn't materialize, I'd have to give up, go back to Michigan, and work at Dawn's Donuts, then marry rich. As if, in that fantasy, my mother would be pleased.

In the meantime, I took a job folding T-shirts at the Gap on Seventy-Fifth and Lex. I loved folding clothes on the folding board. I loved the Gap pens we won if we sold the most product that day. I loved the employee discount and the tap of the register keys as I printed out gift certificates and ran exchanges. In a way, working at the Gap was the perfect job for me, a place to channel my deep need for organization. To get there, I rode the subway more than fifty blocks uptown. It was worth it to emerge from underground and find myself on the Upper East Side. That location was regarded as the first class of the Manhattan Gaps, attracting only the finest shoppers. I sold Valentino a stack of white T-shirts, the perfect pocket tee. He couldn't get enough.

Then, after nearly ten months of the struggle, Jana Kogen found me. One night while I workshopped some scenes for this children's agent, a blue-eyed pixie watched me from the velvet row seat where she sat holding her clipboard. She looked amused as I performed a botched monologue from *Top Girls*. I was wearing lingerie and too much lipstick, clutching a cigarette and a highball, and speaking in a wonky southern accent. At least that's what I was going for. The agent said that perhaps my headshot should be updated. And that was all.

(I recently asked her if she remembered the monologue. Her eyes danced. "Terrible," she said with a laugh. "With a horrible southern accent!")

I was pathetic, but promising enough for her to see some potential in me, because she called me the next day at the Parkside. On my pager rather. I rang back. She was energetic and funny and encouraged me to keep going. Get some clothes. A new haircut maybe. She had no idea who I was, but we fell in love with each other. I needed a chance, and Jana is the one who gave it to me. She took me on, and we became a team.

Jana signed me, then sent me out on auditions. I dressed in my wardrobe of pocket tees and shorts from the Gap, purchased with my employee discount. After sixty auditions, I was offered my first movie role, Cousin Linda, in a film called *In & Out*. Three thousand dollars a week for the six-week shoot. I booked it.

It was a golden age for movies. I was on set with Joan Cusack!

Kevin Kline! Tom Selleck! And most exciting of all: Matt Dillon. The very one. The unbelievably model-gorgeous Shalom Harlow also made her debut as Matt Dillon's girlfriend. I remember watching her in the makeup chair, where she magically transformed from a pretty teenage girl with pubescent acne into a Hollywood beauty with clear skin and red lips.

In the end, my scenes were mostly cut, but I didn't care. I'd been "discovered." I had my first role and I was now a hugging acquaintance with Matt Dillon. I was on my way.

A perk of living at the Parkside Evangeline was the free daily breakfast provided in the basement for residents. While I lived there, I became friendly with a woman from Scotland who also lived and worked at the Salvation Army. One morning over breakfast, she told me about a tea leaf and tarot reader she frequented. The woman charged $250 for a reading, which for me at that time was quite the hair ball to swallow. Still, I wasted no time seeking her out.

The reader was an old Turkish woman who looked, dressed, and acted like a vaudeville character of a fortune-teller. Every element of her home and wardrobe was straight out of central casting, right down to the Victorian furniture covered in plastic and the cat perched in the other room. Overall, the apartment was very nice, a spacious walk-up with wood floors and high ceilings.

She read my tea leaves. Gazing into the bottom of her little porcelain cup, she said that I had a boyfriend who recently died and that he was with me. Immediately, I thought of Brad. She said I would be in show business and that I wouldn't do that well, but I would stick with it. She said I would have a little dog that would help me. Then she said that someone with the initials M.W. would be a very important man in my life, that I would come across him later in life, and that he would help save me.

I looked for that M.W. everywhere. I always believed in it. The first job I got was on the series *Matt Waters*—I thought, there's the M.W.! Finally, a prediction that came true. To take it one step further, Matt Waters was played by Montel Williams, another M.W., who became my friend. It didn't dawn on me until recently, but Montel has MS and has been a huge help in my life. I could never have known, when I saw that tea leaf reader, the turns our lives would take. Montel became a hero of mine, and I don't hesitate to say this prophecy was fulfilled.

It was during this time in New York that I got my own place in Murray Hill and took up with a Cranbrook friend's redheaded stepbrother who I knew had a crush on me in high school. He was smart, complicated, and very fashionable. He took me to the Gramercy Tavern, Bice, Mezzaluna. He lavished me with gifts, buying me a new wardrobe at Calvin Klein, shoes at Prada, hats from Dolce & Gabbana. But the clothes did not change my essential character. Once we became a couple, a label he didn't seem to embrace, I drank even more, a cover for my insecurity.

On my twenty-second birthday, after a few too many dramatic arguments and hangovers, I admitted, "I think I need to stop drinking." I arrived at both the conclusion and the confession out of necessity. He rewarded my honesty by leaving the bar with another girl.

I was shook. Devastated. Crushed. In my acute panic, I rushed to self-destruction. I went back to my studio, where he often spent the night. I rummaged through his leather Dopp kit and took all the pills I could find. I didn't actually want to die. I just wanted the pain to end instantly. I wanted comfort and revenge. I hated myself.

I found my favorite Belinda Carlisle album and put on "Mad About You." In a world with Belinda, I didn't want to die. I called his sister and told her what I'd done. She said to call someone I trusted, someone nearby who could help me.

I had no friends in New York at the time, and I wasn't about to tell Katie. So I called a man whose business card I had—a photographer who'd recently taken nude photos of me for a project on alternative beauty. He came over right away, and the plan was to take me to Bellevue Hospital, which was right around the corner.

I was adamant about not using my insurance, because I didn't want my mother to find out and disown me the way she had when I was in college. But my concern was premature. Just as we reached the entrance to Bellevue, I fell and passed out. My face hit the pavement so hard that I broke a bone, the zygomatic arch, just beneath my eye. The photographer picked me up, and instead of taking me into the hospital, he carried me back to my apartment.

I don't remember, in my mental state, exactly what happened next. I don't know what was said, or not said. I don't know what I invited. I don't know what transpired. All I know is that I passed out, and when I opened my eyes, he was having sex with me. I came to just long enough to understand that he was on top of me, with Belinda still playing in the background. And then I passed out again.

The next day, Katie came over. We were supposed to have met earlier that morning for brunch, but I was so far gone I never heard her pounding on the door. She persuaded the super of my building to let her in. When she came inside, she found me sprawled on the floor, mumbling incoherently.

I was not well. After the drinks and the bottles of antidepressants, it was more than I could manage. Katie rushed me to the hospital, where they pumped my stomach again. The doctors told her I'd ingested a lethal amount. But I survived.

There was a lot of damage done. Physical and emotional. The hospital contacted my parents. We all agreed, out of necessity, that I would come back to Michigan and immediately enter an inpatient rehab facility in Pontiac.

Rehab is a tricky thing. It feels a little like going to camp or to boarding school; you're with a bunch of other people who are as messed up as you. This particular treatment center was more of a state lockup. There was no way out. At Fox Center, my roommate was a toothless meth addict from Las Vegas. My closest ally was a man by the name of Bob Evans (no relation to the sausage family), a wheelchair-bound diabetic with blue feet and a winning personality.

While I was in rehab, I fully owned that I was an alcoholic. It was absolutely clear to all of us. With the introduction of AA, I felt hope for the first time in my life. AA was a good tool at the time, though it became more difficult for me to maintain over the years once I became more recognizable, in part because I lost my anonymity. But back then, when I was unknown, the tools of AA forced rigorous honesty. On family visiting night, my mother pulled me into her lap, wailing, and cried, "My baby, my baby," over and over until the nurses told her that she couldn't have me sitting on her lap, because it was inappropriate. But she wouldn't listen. She held me in the way I'd always hoped she would, and we were being separated by the staff. She seemed relieved that I was an alcoholic. "It explains so much, so much," she said. It was a bigger comfort to her than thinking I was only depressed. Alcoholism, she thought, was something that could be fixed.

At Fox Center, we were kept inside, the doors locked. Smoking Newport after Newport in the kitchen lounge, I acclimated to various new prescription drugs, Antabuse and Trexan mostly, ostensibly to curb any wish to drink once I was released. One morning after a dose of Trexan, I felt especially agitated. Rageful, upset, frightened. I was having my first panic attack.

Earlier, my doctor, who was also a friend of my father's, had said I was welcome to read the Merck manual he kept in his office whenever I liked. This was a great comfort to me as a natural researcher and self-diagnostician. I was on my way to read about the side effects of Trexan when I encountered a nurse blocking my path to the doctor's office. Steadying my voice as best I could, I calmly explained to her that I felt out of control—triggered, trapped, distorted. "I've never felt this way before," I told her, adding that it must be because of one of the prescribed drugs in my system. She ignored me then ordered me to class. I repeated my story. I moved closer to the doctor's office door, but she pushed me away. That was it. I lost control. I punched her in the back with all my confusion and anger. She did her best to block my blows until three big security guards rushed over, restrained me, and carried me to a small room where I was given a sedative injection.

The doctors discontinued the Trexan. Poof, I was normal. My rage vanished. What I didn't know at the time was that my father had witnessed this entire episode. He had come to visit me and stood silently in the hallway watching the scene unfold. Later, he would use that episode against me.

❧

While home in Michigan, shortly before my release from rehab, my father checked me out for the day to take me to the eye doctor for a checkup. I'd been having trouble with my vision and was experiencing some unusual pain. I hadn't seen my childhood eye doctor, Leonard Lerner, in several years. But he was the same—thick mustache, kind face framed by round spectacles. I laughed, remembering how sweet he had been when I had to wear the eye patch as a girl. Now I was twenty-two, thin and pale and agitated from weeks of rehab and Antabuse and attempted starts on antidepressants.

In the dark room, staring into my dilated eyes, he asked, "How is your vision? Do you see all right?" I thought for a second before replying. "Um, I think so? Yes, I think so. I don't know."

The doctor looked again, sat back on his little stool, and said, "Well, the interesting thing is you have optical neuritis. An inflammation of the nerves in the eye." He turned on the light and said, "It's usually a symptom of MS. Multiple sclerosis." He looked at me, but I have to say it simply didn't register.

"I think it's all the medication I'm taking," I said. "I don't have MS," I told him.

I was eager to get back to Fox Center and cigarettes, so I imagine we made an appointment to return for a follow-up visit. During that time, the pain subsided or I figured it was my teeth. Or a side effect of the Antabuse, as my copy of the *PDR* informed me. Three weeks later, I was back in Dr. Lerner's chair. He examined both eyes, sat back, and confirmed, "I must have been wrong. The optical neuritis is gone."

On my release from Fox Center, I flew back to New York, newly sober, to pursue my acting career. I booked a real job, a movie with Adrian Grenier called *Arresting Gena,* where I was to play a struggling drug addict. The role was in my wheelhouse, and I was excited for it. Before I told anyone else the news, I called my father. I was proud to report the news after he had kindly covered my Parkside Evangeline bills. We spoke regularly in those days. He had a new girlfriend, a struggling TV anchor who was trying to break into show business, Katie told me. Elliot never mentioned her to me.

That's when the letters started coming. Twenty letters a day arrived via FedEx at the production office of *Arresting Gena,* all of them written by a mysterious sender. They contained bogus information about me and my "violence and addiction." They obliquely referenced my attack on the nurse at Fox Center. The letters mentioned heroin, which I'd never tried, and warned the director to fire me, claiming I was a liability. The return address was always from a place in Chicago called Faces and Places, a fake agency. I was fired before we even started shooting.

The letters continued for a year and a half, during which I was fired from every job I booked. I was quietly hysterical when, finally, I was contacted by a detective who was retained by the talent agency UTA. He said he had been hired to protect Drew Barrymore, the famous and adorable actress to whom I was supposedly writing death threats. After weeks spent trailing me, he realized I wasn't the perpetrator and got in touch to let me know.

He also had information. He said the letters were being mailed from my father's office building in Detroit. He gave me a description of the sender that just happened to match my father's girlfriend at the time, I found out.

The detective, Kevin, told me to lay a trap to find the culprit. I had secured a screen test at Universal for a movie called *Father's Day,* which seemed like as good a time as any to see if my father's girlfriend was the saboteur. At the detective's urging, I told three different stories to three different people: I told my ex-boyfriend that I had a screen test against Alyssa Milano. I told a friend I had a screen test against Alicia Silverstone. I told my father I had a screen test against Drew Barrymore.

Sadly, the name Drew Barrymore became involved in the story

again. The head of casting at Universal received no fewer than fifteen letters saying I was a violent and dangerous person who held a grudge against Drew Barrymore. The casting director showed me and my agent, Jana, the letters. Humiliated, I told my father he was now dead to me. I didn't speak to him for twelve years, and our relationship, already challenging, never fully recovered.

Years later, I begged my agent at UTA to get me an audition with Drew Barrymore for the new *Charlie's Angels*. Nancy Juvonen, Drew's production partner, queried, "Don't you know the history with Selma and Drew?" End of discussion. I was mortified. I had no idea the story had followed me for so long. I opened a bottle of white wine, drank it, and cried. I never tried to audition for Drew again.

When I finally met Drew in person at Tracey Ross, the L.A. clothing store on Sunset popular in the early aughts, much later, I discovered she'd never truly known the whole story, only that it was a father thing, a messed-up situation. I told her I was so, so sorry about the letters she'd received. She hugged me and said, "Don't worry. We all have wild family stuff," and her big embrace smoothed out some of those years-old anxieties. It's still a fright to me. The sabotage. The fear. But I count my lucky stars, the famous star is the dearest Drew. Who seems to have an unending source of compassion.

L.A.

AFTER AT LEAST sixty more auditions in New York, Jana told me it was time for Los Angeles. "You need to go west, young woman." It was pilot season. It was also time for a new era to begin.

I was happy to leave the roaches behind, along with the cold, numbing winters. And so, westward I went.

Jana set me up with two agents, Bonnie Liedtke and fresh-faced Julie Taylor. Perfectly suited, I was happy at the Oakwood corporate housing in Burbank, on Coyote Drive, which was close to the agencies and Warner Bros. I had a Murphy bed that came down from the wall and a cat named I Know, whom I adopted from a shelter back in New York. (The name came out of our first night together, when he cried and cried and I said, "I know, I know. You're hungry. You're sad. I know." It stuck.)

I was immediately taken with Los Angeles. The smell of jasmine at night. The vast highways. The lights. The novelty of eating a bagel while sitting under a palm tree. It was unbelievable to me. A vacation almost.

As part of my fresh start in L.A., I went really blond. Art Luna was *the* guy; he had a chic hair studio in West Hollywood. I saw Sherry, a blonde colorist to the stars. The first time there, Anjelica Huston was getting her hair done beside the wash sink where I sat. The movie *Prizzi's Honor* was a favorite of my mother's and mine, and now here she was, right in front of me. Anjelica complimented my straw wedge shoes. "I had a pair of those back in the day," she told me. Her presence was the perfect balance of commanding and fun. She asked where I got them, and I told her the truth—Steve Madden. The admission hurt. I wished I could say Cacharel, or anything, for that matter. But Steve Madden was within my budget, and Anjelica was kind. "How marvelous," she said, and told me she planned to get a pair of her own.

When it came to my career, Jana was my point person, along with Bonnie and Julie. All three of them were quick-witted and hilarious, pretty and stylish. (Bonnie is still a big deal in the film business; Julie went on to create SoulCycle and sell it.)

The very first job I booked there was a movie with Suzanne Somers and Chad Christ. As soon as I was cast, my brand-new sunny-blond hair was dyed dark brown. Suzanne was the blonde, of course, so I had to go dark. It was darker than I'd ever gone before, and that was how it remained. I already knew Chad from my time in New York, and I found him to be beautiful and cool. And Suzanne! I watched *Three's Company* when I was a kid ad nauseam, and I couldn't believe my great fortune to work with my favorite adult childhood sitcom star. She was glorious. Bubbling with excitement, a grand toothy smile, almost a caricature of herself, that's how strong her real presence is. I liked her immediately.

I remember the imprint of her long, tan toes in her rose-pink suede Bebe wedges. Alan, so in love, was ever by her side. One night, we went to dinner, and I can still picture her long fingers plucking a warm pita slice from the bread basket. "I love this bread," she trilled. "If a place has bad bread, forget it!" I was shocked that the food-combining master ate bread, and I told her so. "I love it. Of course you can. Just with the right things!" she replied.

I continued on audition after audition, learning lines in my green Levi's bought from an ex in New York. There were little sprinkles of fairy dust that kept me going. I got close on so many pilots. But I wasn't pretty enough, I wasn't shiny enough, I wasn't energetic enough. I wasn't "killing" them. I was too tough here.

Unable to afford the Oakwood any longer, I moved out and found a small apartment in a brick apartment building on Gretna Green in Brentwood, around the corner from where Nicole Brown was murdered in her front courtyard. I had a studio over the garage and dumpster. But I was hopeful. I was happy. I liked the warmth, the joggers, finding my way. I knew I was going to need big-time luck. But I also had these three women looking out for me: Jana. Julie. Bonnie. I had an inkling that somehow it would all work out.

My mother casually asked when I was going to come home. "Just come home, Blair. You can work at CVS." She acted as if my interest in acting were very foolish and impractical. She said she didn't understand the appeal at all. If I wasn't a success, why was it worth it? But I wasn't ready to give up and move home, as much as my mother wanted me back in Michigan.

Kevin Williamson wanted me to test for the role of Joey on *Dawson's Creek.* I auditioned and thought that I really nailed the part. I wore a beaded choker, my hair tucked back with a bobby pin, parted on the side. I tested against Katie Holmes. She was so tall, so pretty. She wore headphones and Birkenstocks. She kept to herself. Of course, I didn't get that part, and the rest is history, but I kept getting close.

Alec Baldwin saw a short film I was in at the Hamptons International Film Festival and wrote a little piece about me in a festival paper, calling my performance a display of "flat-out star power like a combination of Marlene Dietrich meets Debra Winger." He said the film "sagged slightly" whenever I was off screen. My mother was over the moon. "Movie stardom in abundance," Alec wrote. (Years later, I saw him in a bar at a restaurant in D.C. and thanked him for his words, which had given me hope. He smiled and said, "You're welcome! Well, I guess you owe your career to me!" I replied, "Don't celebrate quite yet." I haven't seen him since.)

I auditioned for a role in *Amazon High,* to play a cheerleader sent back to Amazonian times to teach women how to tame horses and rule the cannibals. It was a ridiculous premise but I wanted it. I went to the producer's offices at Universal and did the splits, then a cartwheel, then a flip, along with scripted cheers. My body could still do these things easily, without training, I was still a kid really. The next day, I got the part. I spent the next seven weeks in New Zealand for the shoot, most of which found me disoriented and melancholy, with all the time alone in a room while it rained outside during preproduction. I'd been sober since Fox Center, but I went to the land of the long white cloud and became out of sorts and homesick. I walked to the only liquor store I could find and bought the most expensive port I could afford. I gave myself a limit: only one tiny sip a day. I would drink like a normal person, I told myself. But then one night we all went out, and that one night was my undoing; I drank until I blacked out.

When I returned to Los Angeles, I was drinking again. I took on some bit roles here and there, but nothing was real. I was tired. I was always tired. I was in my mid-twenties and figured I would need to start fibbing about my age, telling directors I was eighteen or twenty. I felt ancient. Then I heard about a movie called *Cruel Inventions,* a contemporary riff on the French novel *Dangerous Liaisons* set in private-school New York. I was going to get the part, I decided. And if I didn't, I would consider giving up.

There's no other way to say this: the audition for the upcoming teen drama *Cruel Inventions* (the title was ultimately changed to *Cruel Intentions* in postproduction) was a Big Fucking Deal in Young Hollywood. Everyone was talking about it, buzzing about it, speculating about it. The established young stars Sarah Michelle Gellar and Ryan Phillippe had already been cast as the leads. Ryan's girlfriend, Reese Witherspoon, already a high-profile actress, was pending in the role of the ingenue. He would persuade her to take it.

The casting director, Mary Vernieu, had a small but busy office in Brentwood. I didn't actually yet believe I had any chance of getting the job, so when I went in to see Mary for the part of Cecile Caldwell, I was completely relaxed, not at all invested in the outcome. I had already been crushed losing the Joey Potter role on *Dawson's Creek,* so I chilled out. Like every young person in Hollywood, I wanted the role of Cecile. I had read the script, and while not *The Deer Hunter,* I found the whole thing compelling. At the same time, I felt somewhat drained by the constant rejection, maybe even ready to pack it in. I looked forward to getting back to photography or writing, or even a job in a shop.

When I strolled into the room, nonchalant, my hands in my pockets, the director, Roger Kumble, immediately asked, "So, how old are you?" I was done lying about my age. After fielding this question at so many auditions, I'd had it. I stiffened and spat back brattily, "How old are *you*?" At that, he sat up and listened.

I could see I'd piqued his interest. He was paying attention. I played it up. I told him I'd just gone across the border to Canada with some friends to buy alcohol, hoping he'd buy that I was under twenty-one without my actually lying. And then I did the audition using the same energy he brought out in me. I wasn't angry; I wasn't combative. I think I was just a little fed up that day. After doing seven auditions that week without being noticed, I felt I had nothing to lose. A little mean baby came out of me. But she saved the day, because she made him listen. I suppose Roger realized this was the saving grace for the character of Cecile. She didn't have to be the sad victim. His words: she could work humorously. She could be relentlessly irritating. There's a certain power in annoying the shit out of the people who are scheming to take you down. Clueless confidence saved her from a pathetic existence. In the end, it's often the confident people who are the most successful. And Cecile would be a great success.

A few days later, Roger and I met at a bar to talk about the part and how to get everyone on board. He talked to Ryan; he talked to Sarah. He really went to bat for me. The cast represented young Hollywood. I was so starstruck and happy I could plotz!

I was already acquainted with Sarah Michelle Gellar before we met in person, from a voice-over I'd done on *Scream 2*. Of course, I also knew her from her work. She was the epitome of a young TV star. She had been Kendall on *All My Children*! From day one, she was a friend to me, both in getting the part and in showing me the ropes. In a lot of ways, our real-life relationship mirrored our dynamic in the film, albeit without all the scheming. She is still one of my closest friends in the world. A mighty nurturer and talent is she.

At the table reads, when we first all got together to read the script, I sat next to Reese. She was the most delicate yellow flower. I was completely overwhelmed by the sight. She wore a pale blue cashmere hoodie, Essie Ballet Slippers on her nails, her blond hair thick and straight. She was lovely. It was clear to me she was going to be a superstar. Everything about her was impeccable and still is today: her nails, her cuticles. Her brain! She smelled freshly showered and kept her notebook tidy, her cashmere didn't pill, she never complained. Reese also had the prettiest feet. Even unpedicured, her feet are perfect. My mom loved Reese and her delicate ankles. "You look like you're a different species," she would say. "Don't you feel like a water buffalo when you stand next to her?" I did, actually. I always felt like the awkward outsider around Reese and Ryan. Ryan called her "doll" when we all went out to dinner, like Frank Sinatra and Ava Gardner. Just like Cecile herself, I was the goofy brown mushroom among the Upper East Side elite.

There was only one instance where I felt remotely cool. The cast had moved to New York for the shoot, and one night we all went out to the *Godzilla* premiere. It was a huge movie, and everyone who was anyone at that time was there. Prada lent me a dress, and the entire cast went together. I looked up to Reese and felt as if I couldn't let my guard down. I longed to impress her. At one point, Ryan came up and said, "We want to meet Puff Daddy. Do you know how we can meet him?" I saw an in. "Yes! I know him!" I didn't really, but we shared a manager. In dopey Cecile fashion, confidence in hand with cluelessness, I rushed up to Puff Daddy, Reese and Ryan in step behind me, and embraced him with a gigantic hug. The audacity! I didn't know you don't just walk up to the biggest star of the moment and introduce him to the stars of your own little movie.

The final image of Reese driving off in that 1956 Jaguar roadster while the notes of "Bitter Sweet Symphony" rise along with the camera is still one of the most iconic memories from that film, but I think the kiss between Kathryn and Cecile (me!) is a close second. That kiss! That wet kiss. (I'm reminded of it at almost every meeting with a group of younger people. As in, "Hey! You're that girl who kissed Sarah! Do you remember that?" Now perhaps they think I am so old I wouldn't remember . . .) I wasn't that nervous about kissing Sarah, but I was eager for the scene to be over and done with because we both knew it was going to be somewhat sensational and there was pressure on us to pull it off. We wanted to get it right, certainly.

I remember Sarah's lips were so soft. I wasn't attracted to girls, but I did enjoy the soft, whisker-free lips of SMG on mine. We kissed over and over. During one take, she pulled back and there was this long trail of spit between us. I thought, surely that won't be the one they use. Of course, the spit take won the day. It reminded me of the sexy scene of Marilyn Monroe's spit string in *Niagara*. When my mother saw the film, she was appalled that I was such a graphic, sloppy kisser. ("Honestly, Selma, did you have to use so much tongue? Your tongue, it's massive! Like a creature from *Star Wars* or something! When are you going to come home and get a real job?") Despite her feigned shock, I knew she must be relieved that I at least managed to get one real Hollywood job.

It felt grand. I hoped all movies would be this way, that everything in the world would feel like this. Magazines. Newspapers. My first *Tonight Show* appearance, wearing Dolce & Gabbana. I kept the name plate on my door. It was all easy and fun.

After *Cruel Intentions,* I was offered the role of Vivian Kensington in *Legally Blonde* because Chloë Sevigny, who had just struck big with the movie *Kids,* passed on it. At the time, I was the next logical choice, which made me feel that I was in very good company. I did have to audition for Robert Luketic. A few lines. It didn't seem there was a lot to the role. Fine by me. Reese. Yes, please. In the original script by Karen McCullah, Vivian ended up blond, bubbly, friendly, and best friends with Elle Woods. That part didn't play well, though. Elle was the true and only legal blonde. Vivian was to remain brunette and in the background.

To watch Reese command the room so aptly on *Legally Blonde* was clearly movie star magic. She had just given birth to her beautiful daughter, Ava. She was in excellent shape and worked so hard—always the first one there, always the last one to leave. As ever, she never complained. It made an impression. I learned.

When I was working on the movie, I told Amanda Brown (who wrote the original novel the screenplay was based on) how much I loved *The Wizard of Oz*. So as a gift, she gave me my very own pair of ruby slippers. That was the only time I've ever acted the part of a gleeful child. I jumped up and down, yelling, "I got the slippers! I got the slippers!" although nobody was at my house to witness this exuberant display. They were an exact replica, made especially for me, to my exact foot measurements. They even had the same felt glued to the soles, a sound deadener, which allowed Judy Garland to silently dance on a soundstage. (We use foam these days.) It was such a beautiful, thoughtful, personal gesture—the best gift I had ever received. It seemed to make up for any childhood neglect I ever felt I'd had regarding toys. The shoes live on my mantel, sparkling from the fireplace. More than any role I had, more than any movie, getting those slippers was the most thrilling discovery.

I enjoyed myself on that set; it was the first time I let my guard down in front of other people. Ever the goofy sidekick, I kept the crew and cast entertained while Reese did one great take after another in pink stilettos. One time while I was performing my own shtick outside as some of us stood around the craft services table, I started impersonating a *Billy Elliot* routine and got so amped up that I actually jumped up into the air. I don't know what happened, but my feet went out from under me. I couldn't locate them. Before I could make sense of it, I was parallel to the ground, then landed flat on my face. It was a colossal fall—even a Teamster ran over to make sure I was okay. Now I simply say "Billy Elliot"

to that crowd, and we all start laughing. When entertaining the troops, I go flat out.

❧

The offers came in, some better than others. I was on a roll. I played the titular character in a TV show, Zoe Bean, of *Zoe, Duncan, Jack and Jane.* Zoe was the cute girl next door. It didn't take off. The label I'd been given was too embedded in who I was. I never figured out how to play the sweet, stable, capable, pretty person. I excelled at characters who might be called smug or ridiculous. Eccentric, weird prudes became my bread and butter. I never had an arsenal of gentle, weightless, girl-next-door glances. Always the mean baby, I played the girl who was misunderstood and set apart. Her default expression was a dry stare. A barb, her power. She is all the women in my life—my mother, my sisters—or a ridiculous child woman making her way. Or all these versions combined.

My career was on the rise, but I had a hunch I was not going to be a leading lady. I was a supporting player. That was who I knew how to be. It was also the easier label to give. Stars are few and not like me, I felt. If you take one message away from this book, let it be this: labels are sticky.

Still, I landed the cover of *Seventeen* magazine, a dream get for a young actress in those days. I felt so proud. It was June 1999. I showed up with my freshly cut bangs and was given a chartreuse shrug and a lime-green plaid maxi skirt. It's a casual shot: I'm seated, holding my knees, smiling. Beaming, really. But my eyes looked small.

I sent a copy to my mother in Michigan. She called me as soon as the package arrived. "Oh, Selma," she said. "You look so unimportant. When are you going to come home and get a real job?"

Hollywood

IN MANY WAYS, my time in Hollywood felt to me like an extension of my Cranbrook days, in that I've taken a liking to almost everyone I've met. I was genuinely friendly and old enough to be damn grateful. As a supporting player, I didn't feel competitive. I've met everyone, it seems. I will have some story, some personal anecdote to share about them. While I like Six Degrees of Kevin Bacon, I'd bet if the game were changed to Two Degrees of Selma Blair, it would have even more wings. (By the way, Kyra Sedgwick and I get our hair done by the same colorist and talked just last week. See what I mean?)

I've met so many great people here among the shits. People I like to run into at the grocery store. The truth is, I don't know that

I would fit in elsewhere. It's much easier here, in this setting where people need a bit of a label to be understood. I don't know if they talk behind my back; I'm sure there are a few. But for the most part, I love the women in this town. I love them like my sisters. We talk, we text. We share stories and advice and support one another. I could rattle off big names. I won't. But I did spend a recent big holiday at Sharon Stone's house. Gorgeous place.

The first working actress friend I made was Amy Hargreaves. She was a commercial actress in New York while I lived there, and we moved out to L.A. at the same time. We were with the same agency, and we had been cast in the same first show, *Matt Waters*, back in New York. She was the star. Upon arrival in L.A., we went to a showcase and to dinner after at Jones on Formosa. It was dark inside, with red booths and poodle paintings over the tables. Decidedly Hollywood. Lo and behold, Matt Dillon strolled in. He saw us by the door, stopped by to say hi, and asked Amy if she was having any luck. Then he left. Amy moved back to New York and kept on as I did out West.

Early in my friendship with Reese, she invited me to a Billy Blanks workout class in Woodland Hills. I was so looking forward to spending time with her. Historically, I am never late. I thought I'd given myself enough time, but this was before GPS, I was coming from work at Warner Bros., and the drive took longer than expected. As it got closer to the start time, I began to panic. I saw a parking spot and decided to grab it. Little did I know that it was still two miles away. Wearing a full face of TV makeup, I walked and ran and sprinted. After around a mile and a half, all I could do was sprint. I am not a sprinter. This might very well be the only time I've sprinted a mile in my life. But I did it, fueled by the rage at my own incompetence.

I finally made it to the class, but I was late, sweaty, and wiped out. And now I had to slog my way through a Tae Bo class, a totally new concept. I was lost, totally inept. Halfway through, I thought I was going to die. Reese, on the other hand, sailed effortlessly through it. I had no doubt that if the roles were reversed and she'd somehow made the same idiot blunder I did, she could have run those miles and still made it on time, prepared for class.

After class we went out to dinner at Teru Sushi on Ventura and talked and laughed, Reese putting me at ease as she always does. Her world of work was so beyond my own, and I was fascinated. We chatted and caught up; she mentioned she had just worked on *Friends* or was about to and we both marveled at Jennifer Aniston's incredible physique.

I have a recurring nightmare that I'm meeting Reese again, but I parked too far away and only my legs can take me to her on time. I start running but my legs won't keep at it. So I allow myself too much room for error if I'm going to meet her for lunch. Invariably, I dawdle and fuck up. I always wind up late. And she always waits for me and greets me with a hug after texting back: "Just be safe."

In the early days of *Mad Men,* Bottega Veneta threw a party that January Jones and I both attended. I'd been feeling sick that day, slurring my words. I took a couple of shots and a nap, but I still felt off before the party. I figured it was because I hadn't eaten and the alcohol amplified everything. Now I see it was the MS. I was so out of it that I fell asleep mid-sentence during hair and makeup, and then threw up.

When I arrived at the party, I laid eyes on January, center stage, who looked stunning as ever. "January!" I called, making my way through the crowd. "You're Betty Draper!" I exclaimed, once I reached her. "Betty Draper! Betty Draper!" I kept repeating myself, aware of what was happening but powerless to stop it. January very calmly put her lovely hand on my shoulder, and said, "You do know I'm not Betty Draper."

It was one of those awkward social encounters, confirmation that I shouldn't have let myself out that day. "I should have more champagne!" I said, before backtracking. "Wait, no I shouldn't."

She gently took my hand and reassured me. "We should all, always, have more champagne," she said, smiling, before returning to the party. We were already good acquaintances, and it wasn't exactly as strange as it appeared. But I spent the night disoriented and sick and then resigned myself to more champagne. People noticed.

Another favorite, Amanda Anka, has a few stories like that about me too. One took place at the kickoff party for *The Sweetest Thing*. Amanda was a familiar face to me at a party, always amiable and inclusive, but I didn't know her well. "Have you seen Jason Bateman?" I asked her, gesturing across the room. "He is so hot. I love him. He's going to be my husband."

"That's so amazing!" Amanda said. "He's my fiancé." She was genuinely pleased and amused I made such a gaffe. That is an easygoing betrothed girl.

My closest friend is Claire Danes, whom I met at a Sunday night dinner party with my boyfriend, Jason Schwartzman. I remember thinking her skin was so clear. I watched her from across the table, her blond hair falling over her face as she leaned forward and pushed her hair behind her ears to listen to the conversation. I'd never seen her in person before, and I told her, on that first meeting, right as we were leaving, that I had bacne. And she, very nonjudgmentally, told me I should try Proactiv. No one was using it—no one had even heard of it—back then. She was totally unfazed *and* offered advice, so I thought, "Well, there's a practical friend." I decided never to let her go. She remains sacred to me.

In a crowded room, I also tend to keep an eye out for Kirsten Dunst, a longtime favorite actress as well. I have always been a bona fide fan. You see, I came to Hollywood late in the game. I'd already gone through college and spent a few years in New York, and by the time I arrived, I didn't feel like a young starlet. It felt strange that one minute I could've been in college in the Midwest, then suddenly find myself across from that actress from *Interview with the Vampire,* a movie that meant so much to me in my previous life. I always appreciated that.

In 2002, I saw Kirsten at a show for Jason's band Phantom Planet at the Standard in L.A. We arranged to meet for breakfast the next day. As we walked back to my house, I spotted a paparazzo with a long lens. "What do you do about those paparazzi?" I asked her, assuming such a major young star must have to confront them all the time. It had been a problem for me for years, though I was always photographed by default—by virtue of my neighborhood or the more famous people in the frame. Even so, it always left me feeling ambushed and worried.

"Oh, they never photograph me," she answered.

"What do you mean? There's one right there!" I pointed at the photographer crouching in the bushes. In that moment, I witnessed loss of innocence. She was genuinely surprised and befuddled, and in the ensuing years the paparazzi presence would only grow with the quick multiplication of invaders. I didn't realize how bad their monitoring of young female celebrities would become, nor what an issue it would pose for so many people.

Jake Gyllenhaal and I had become friends from *Highway,* a film we shot in Seattle, in which I'd played a hooker on the run, her only shoes a sparkly red pair, like Dorothy's. When he was shooting *Donnie Darko,* I stopped by his trailer to visit him. In recent days, he'd seen so many of his school friends having these big successes. "I wonder when it'll be my time," he said.

"It *is* your time," I said. History soon proved me right.

When all the pieces line up, Hollywood is captivating. I got to live through another golden age of Hollywood. I have been a witness to the new greats making their mark. Claire invited me to her Hollywood Walk of Fame induction years later, which I attended while my child napped at home.

⟟⟟⟟

I have a manager. He was my publicist in those early days. We are a team now. Our first meeting was arranged by David Weber, who was my boyfriend (and lawyer) at the time. My first impression of Troy was that he was trim and handsome in a black shirt, black pants, and good shoes. The three of us sat in a big conference room overlooking Wilshire Boulevard, and at one point he leaned over to David and said something like "Just tell this one she's pretty." I was miffed. It felt condescending, dismissive. Invalidating of any talent or intelligence. I didn't say much.

"He was adorable, but I'm not sure he got me," I recapped with David at the elevator as we were leaving.

I may have misunderstood Troy's remark. In any event, I was wrong. He got me. Over the years, I'd had agents and managers I liked and admired. But I struggled to find a true focus or ambition. Troy saw me light up in the hands of a great artist. He knew this world, and he saw something in me. We've been inseparable ever since.

We are, in many ways, of brother and sister makeup. We play and annoy, we egg each other on. We call each other "monkey." We agree it reads a bit pathetic to have my main gay and cohort a commissioned employee. We are Elizabeth Taylor and Jason Winters, we joke, so fundamental to my life is he.

Troy is better than anyone at pushing what he believes in. For years, I thought he was the boss. For years, he thought I was. It was only this past year that we realized we are partners. (An epiphany that made us cry.) I have never had anyone stand by my side like this man.

Troy told me I was America's last great beauty, although he doesn't remember saying this (or I misunderstood the remark— again). He had me meet Krista Smith at *Vanity Fair,* another person with an incredible eye as well as a brain. The two became like parents to me, even if peers in age. Over the years, I appeared on the cover of *Vanity Fair* two times, for the Young Hollywood issue. For the first time, after a long day of *Zoe,* I flew to Miami for the cover shoot and got a horrible bloody nose on the plane. It wouldn't stop, so I called Troy for help. I was up all night, got my nose quickly cauterized, and showed up on set an hour later, still wiping blood from a spot under my chin, dazed by the greatness of Annie Leibovitz.

I was so looking forward to having my hair and makeup done for this shoot, to be made glamorous for *Vanity Fair.* I had studied the Hollywood covers and knew there was no skimp on gowns or glam. When I entered the room where Annie was setting up for the garden shot, she took one look at me and said, "Don't touch her." At the time, I was shocked. But now I see. She *saw* me. She saw me, exactly as I arrived, and thought I was the cool girl for that moment. "Don't do anything," she said. They wiped my face, added a dab of concealer, a swipe of mascara, and that was it.

It got better. "This is what you're wearing," she said, and handed me a polka-dot leather bikini, still on a hanger.

A voice trilled, excited, "Oh my gosh, you finally got someone to wear the bikini!"

Already feeling a little long in the tooth, there I was barefoot, in a leather bikini, void of major hair and makeup, and sitting next to my crush Wes Bentley and new friends Jordana Brewster and Paul Walker. When they turned the fan on, my self-consciousness blew away and I enjoyed the scene.

At one point, Annie was studying me, scrutinizing. She squinted. She whispered something to Sally Hershberger, who threw up her hands and comb. "What can I do if she has a bad haircut and a bald spot?" I think Sally dabbed a little eyeshadow in the widest spot of my part. Troy and I still laugh at this comment, a familiar one by now. From that point on, my bald spots became a short-lived obsession; for a while after that I carried around a Bobbi Brown eye shadow to touch up my scalp before auditions.

The second time, Annie shot me again, this time for the Young Women in Hollywood issue. Older and wiser, I came armed with a haircut by Chris McMillan. I thought for sure I would be put in a gown, lengthened and made stunning.

I waltzed on set in a black turtleneck and a pair of jeans, lean and fresh-faced. Annie glanced up, hugged me briefly, and called out, "Oh, Selma. Perfect! Nobody touch her." That was my blessing and my curse.

With some photographers, they saw me, and there was an instant connection. Tired, dark circles, jeans, whatever. That's Selma; she is who she is. My look didn't translate into the greatness I needed for Hollywood. It didn't align with what it takes to be a leading woman. But it still led me to this incredible life.

Troy stayed away on those days. To let me be. To honor the reputation of these masters. And when he popped in, freshly buzzed hair, new Prada pants, we always laughed. And made others laugh, too. (Possibly at us.) But we all had an all right time.

My greediest, happiest moments were spent in front of a camera. The glory of my life was that I became the first actress ever to grace the cover of Italian *Vogue*. In those days, Italian *Vogue* was everything in fashion. When I got the cover, that was my Oscar. I was Edie Sedgwick in Warhol's house. Steven Meisel waited with his huge brown eyes, long eyelashes, the bandanna over his head, and in those days a cigarette. He processed the pictures in a little tent I couldn't see, and then he emerged to show me. "There. That is the lighting test." He laid them out, right there, in a spread. I looked like the cover.

If only I could have Steven Meisel's eye and light frame me forever. That superseded everything. I didn't celebrate this moment. I couldn't fully contemplate it. I was so grateful for it I didn't know how to put it into words. That was my glory. My dream alongside my mother's.

Looking down the lens at Michael Thompson or Peter Lindbergh or Steven or Annie and having them see me and approve, that's the stuff. Lindbergh and I sent postcards after he shot me—just once, for the Pirelli Calendar, on the Sony lot. He was charmingly old-fashioned and old-school in the way he created a whole environment, with the cold and the fog. Because I am not tall, I am often given underwear to wear, since it does not require alterations. On this Pirelli shoot, I was in underwear and heels, and I was chilly in the manufactured rain and fog, so wardrobe gave me a tuxedo jacket to wear, and I walked toward Peter. "I love this energy," he called. That became the shot. The makeup artist Gucci Westman gave me a red lip, which I loved. She was the first to pull that off on me. I couldn't wait for my mother to approve. I was finally playing the part she wanted me to. I'm not sure she ever even saw it.

My mother always wanted a full report. "What were the compliments, Selma?" Like when Michael Thompson confided to Joe Zee that I moved better than most models, up there with Kate Moss. I didn't allow the sublime glee I felt to get out. Not to anyone, not even to Troy. I was afraid. Afraid I would attract attention. Afraid Elliot would somehow ruin it, or me. So I became private about my successes.

And then there were the duds. As soon as a photographer says, "Relax," I know it's all over. All he sees is a short Jewish girl from the Midwest whom he needs to make into a star. "Relax" makes me feel inadequate and stiff. I never knew how to behave in those moments when I knew someone couldn't see me. Inwardly, I would disappear.

These days, I see myself everywhere, quite literally. As I write this, I am surrounded by large, framed portraits of yours truly that hang all over my home, relics of these indelible gifts. I'm a *Saturday Night Live* sketch of a Hollywood actress. A house wearing its owner on its sleeve.

⌐⌐

Then there were the powerful, magnificent cheerleaders, the prophets of some great promise I am still waiting to fulfill. The writer, editor, and cultural figure Ingrid Sischy was that person for me. From our first meeting, at a *Vanity Fair* dinner, she saw a glimmer of something in me. She saw me, in all my awkwardness, and believed in me fully.

Ingrid was born in South Africa and became a fixture in the

New York media scene as the editor in chief of *Artforum* and later
Interview. She invested in it all—art, celebrity culture, music, and
fashion, especially. With her big warm questions and welcoming
face, she was a tastemaker who set people in motion. She was so
encouraging of others. Of people with talent. Miraculously, she
became my mentor.

She would tell me about the people I should know—really
know. Miuccia Prada and Karl Lagerfeld. And I would tell her
whom she should: Amy Adams and Kate Bosworth and Scarlett
Johansson. One day long before Kanye West was famous, Ingrid
and I were sitting in an upstairs Japanese restaurant sharing one
of our first lunches. "Kanye. You gotta know him," she said. "He
has an album coming out soon and he's brilliant! Brilliant!" She
connected me to everyone and everything that was fabulous, and
she did it single-handedly, because her influence was that big. She
created this energy around artists and interactions, and for some
reason she really saw me as a star, or a fellow changemaker.

Soon after we met, I became guest West Coast editor of *Interview*. Because Ingrid's two closest friends in fashion were Karl and
Miuccia, she made sure I was part of something. A muse. I was
doing campaigns for Prada and Miu Miu and Chanel. Ingrid did
know I was prone to severe depression, and she gave me places to
go, things to do. She gave me work and assignments and a direction. She kept me afloat.

I lived a dream in the fashion world largely thanks to Ingrid,
under Troy's approval. She was an incredible woman to have in
your corner. When she died of cancer on July 24, 2015, at the age
of sixty-three, the media world was shaken. I was shocked.

From Graydon Carter's obituary: "Ingrid was a great friend and
therefore she had a lot of friends. And they will be utterly bereft
for the next little while, so be kind to them. They will be the ones

wandering the streets, or just staring off into the middle distances, lost in the knowledge that a beloved original in an age of generics has gone somewhere else and left them behind."

Now I really see how much she did for me, and I wish I'd known how to run with it then. But I was quiet. God, how I wish Ingrid were here. I would do anything now—anything she asked, without hesitation. For so much time, I was breathless with appreciation, and I didn't even know how to address it. *One day,* I thought, *I'll be able to tell her.* I figured that eventually she would teach me enough so I could finally find the right actions to say thank you, to make her proud to have found me and believed in me.

It was through Ingrid that I found my way to Karl. He actually came to my house on Cynthia Street to shoot me for *Interview* magazine. Ingrid came in from New York, as well as L'Wren Scott, who was the stylist that day. Before Karl arrived, L'Wren and I decided it would be fun to dress me up as him. This was right when he'd lost the weight and was in the sexy libertine, rocker chic look, with the cravat and the tight jeans. His were so tight, so pegged, with the balls to the right. I made a comment about the crotch area. Again, the audacity of me!

When he saw me dressed as Karl, he gave a smile. We embraced. I wanted to do more. More theatrics! More drama! But instead, he had me take it all off, keeping only my own tank top on. Just a touch of mascara and gel in my spiky hair.

It was swelteringly hot that day. I spent most of it trying to look serene in the skylight of my very small house. Karl looked around, aiming for the best light. He pointed to the skylight and asked if I would get up there, go right up to the light. I climbed on the shoulders of his muscular companion, a gorgeous young man, naturally. I balanced there, like a young girl playing chicken fight in a pool, looking down at Karl. "Good. Good. This is you," he said. And we were done.

On our lunch break, Karl's only request was a Diet Coke. I didn't have a Diet Coke in the house, and that was his only request. Forevermore, I keep a Diet Coke on hand, in honor of him. (For years afterward, Ingrid raved about the lunch I provided that day. Which was and still is hilarious to me, because I'm pretty sure she provided it. I am many things, but I am no hostess.)

From that very first meeting, I loved Karl and felt at home with him. Karl and I became friends, actually. He was obviously the most brilliant man I have ever met. He was spotless. He even smelled clean. His hands were like a mechanic's—handsome worker hands. Not rough, just big and capable. He was incredible. He was the revered one. Everything about him was otherworldly—his shape, his presence, his style. I don't think there will ever be another figure in fashion so suited for greatness.

Karl always sent pink peonies when we shot together, a sumptuous bounty of pale full blooms. Heavenly. I remember opening the door to my hotel room in Paris and discovering the entire space was infused with the scent of these arrangements. Oh, to have a small, perfect room on the Left Bank, filled with peonies sent by Karl. I mourned having to leave them so soon, still fresh. I hope someone at the Hotel Montalembert saved them after I'd gone. Sometimes I look back and I still don't know how I got there. I don't know how Karl shot me, and loved me, and put me up in a hotel filled with such glorious petals that my hair and clothes still held the scent even after I got home.

Throughout my years of being a still life, I have only one regret. I wish I had picked up my own camera more often. I regret not having stood on the other side of the lens. I was exposed to so many phenomenal artists, but I never shot them. I worried I'd be seen as an intruder. An outsider.

At the *Vanity Fair* shoot in Miami, I had gathered that Penélope Cruz brought a camera everywhere she went. She'd just bring the camera to her beautiful face and—click—took photos of everyone else. She had such a lovely European way about her, it never looked invasive. I felt like a clunky American girl, so I rarely brought my own lens. Now I wish I had. Regrets, I have a few!

On Cynthia Street, Karl posed with me before leaving. It was the one time I dared to pick up my little vintage ecru camera. "Let's have a shot!" I ventured. He accepted. "Yes! Here is good?" he asked. We stood on the edge of a fountain, the sunlight slicing our heads. The snap is framed on my desk, unflattering to both of us in the harsh glare. But the only shot I have.

I lived well in those years. Paris and shows, diamonds and gowns with provenance. Dresses from the archives. In the moments when I dared to consider it, it felt wonderful. I've had an enchanted life. I still consider myself one of the luckiest girls in Hollywood.

The Man and the Muse

*D*URING A LIGHTING SETUP on *Cruel Intentions,* I went searching for Reese. I found her next to Ryan, talking to a handsome man I didn't know. He had height and bore a resemblance to JFK Jr. He looked good, and I'd learn he looked even better on paper.

Roger, the director, brought me over and said, "This is Ryan's lawyer, David Weber. He'll probably try to sign you—don't do it." I shook his hand and said it was nice to meet him. He looked bored. *Well, then,* I thought, *I'll be off!* I left him with the two cherubs and went on to craft services.

I was surprised when after our meet-cute, which was not very cute, he asked me out. After running into each other at a function where he gave me a wave hello—barely an acknowledgment—he called and asked if I would like to go to Roger's birthday dinner with him.

"I will come get you," he said. And I said, "Sure."

He picked me up in his long silver Volvo station wagon, which felt very lawyerly. I was still living at my first apartment then and felt intimidated by his professional air. Over the course of the next few weeks, David came to really like me, and I came to like him, too.

∾

David was solid, adult, steady. And gorgeous. We fell in love. The adults in my life celebrated our relationship. I felt, based on some vague societal standard, that I was supposed to be moving forward, toward something, in a direction. I was an adult and adults were meant to find a person to commit to. David represented exactly what I thought that was.

Our relationship progressed, and he bought us a Spanish 1920s house. It was idyllic, right down to our neighbors, Reese and Ryan, who lived in a charming bungalow up the street. Across the street from them was Winona's house, with big, incredible yellow trumpet flowering trees that smelled heavenly, like jasmine, but are in fact very toxic. Crazy-making if brewed or eaten.

David planned to propose to me, one ill-fated weekend at a Cranbrook Kingswood reunion in 2000. I was afraid he was going to ask. When we arrived in Michigan, I became very ill with a fever and headache. He had told my mom his plan, and had even bought the ring, but once he saw how sick I was, he put a pin in it.

He did eventually ask me, the morning after a *CosmoGirl* photo shoot. He presented me with an elegant, emerald cut diamond. Bravo, David Weber. It was so flawlessly beautiful that I tried to hide it when out, worried what people would think of someone so young and inexperienced with such a perfect ring.

So, I was engaged. But it was not so simple.

David was my ideal. But I was about to meet my muse.

The first time I saw Jason Schwartzman on-screen in Wes Anderson's charming *Rushmore,* David in the theater seat beside me, he took my breath away. I'd never seen anyone like him—not Dustin Hoffman, not Tom Cruise. He was charming and captivating and pure. The prep school where *Rushmore* took place reminded me so much of Cranbrook, and Jason's character's love for his school reminded me of my own commitment to my school. He had such charisma. I was enamored. When the movie was over, I turned to David and said, "Wow, he was great." And he said, "You know, that's Talia Shire's son."

I kept returning to Jason in my thoughts. When *Cruel Intentions* premiered, I went on *Total Request Live* on MTV, where I was asked, "Do you have a celebrity crush?" And I answered, "Jason Schwartzman, from *Rushmore.*" As if I could will him to me. I had no bones about making my infatuation with him public, because in no universe did I ever imagine that we would wind up together.

Months later, at a photo shoot, I learned that the photographer shooting me knew Jason. I persuaded Jazzy to get Jason to come to the shoot as a special request. "I'll stay longer if you can get him to come," I begged. Then, there he was.

His eyes were unreal in person, the color of a passionate storm sky. I was smitten. I was in a black tuxedo and skirt. He handed me a daisy he'd picked from the grass and gently kissed me on the lips. The moment was captured in a tiny contact sheet frame that I still have on my shelf. He was a boy, only nineteen. I was twenty-five or so. I thought of him as a child, and myself as a much older woman.

I was madly in love from the moment I met him. It felt like a homecoming of spirit, as if I'd known him forever. Destined. A simultaneous heartbreak and joy.

Much later, he came to my house—the home I shared with David, who was at his office in Beverly Hills. Jason looked around, taking in all the trappings of adulthood. "You really are a grown-up," he said. When we got to the part where I showed him the view and the balcony, he sat on the edge of the tub, looked around, and said, "Wow. This is a lot."

We already knew we loved each other. I looked at him, knowing full well that we would have some future together. "If we fall in love, this will end badly," I whispered. I was immediately angry at myself. It sounded just like something my mother would say. Sabotaging it before anything had even taken hold. Jason looked at me and rested his chin in the heel of my hand. And that was that.

In many ways, a relationship with Jason felt like an impossibility. I was living with another man. I loved David very much, but I felt too big a pull toward Jason. I was immediately in love with him in that emotional, overpowering teenage way. I knew it wasn't possible to move forward with both of them. My heart chose Jason.

My breakup with David was murky and sad. I remember listening to *Play,* the Moby album, on repeat as I packed up the home we'd shared. Sadly, I gave back the perfect ring when I called off the engagement. Though we never did tie the knot, I remained married to David, in a way, for decades, because he continued to be my lawyer.

A few months later, Jason and I became a couple.

Once, after he bought a new Prius, Jason drove us all the way up to Yosemite to visit my mom, who was visiting her cousin Stella and her husband and son at their home there. Jason played guitar, made us laugh, talked about spirits and horse ghosts rumored to roam the property. My mom got a little bit tipsy and ordered us to take off our shoes. We studied our feet. He had Fred Flintstone feet, he joked—big, thick, comical, and adorable. I loved them. Stella said they were a sign of a passionate character.

We stayed together, off and on, for several years. His mother called me beloved. But I never publicly embraced the relationship as much as I wanted to, because I was ashamed. Not of Jason or my feelings for him, but because I thought I should be getting married, and I didn't want to drag Jason toward that. I didn't necessarily *want* to get married. I calibrated my expectations based on what I read in magazines, or other people's experiences, or the pervasive cultural attitude about what someone my age should be doing. I couldn't fully own how I felt about him, worrying that our eight-year age difference must be inappropriate, that my mother wouldn't approve of this match, snatching such a young boy. I imagined I was way more grown up than I was. But I believed, at the time, that I was already too old for such things like infatuation.

I loved the abandon and purity of youth that he represented. But I didn't know how to let myself be a young girl in love. Instead, I kept him somewhat hidden. Afraid he would be ruined by Elliot.

He was young. But we both were. We got jealous. Things happened. I flirted, as was my habit; he made out with supermodels. Hearts were broken, repaired, broken again. I was hurt by his actions, though they were more age appropriate than the relationship we were destroying. By the time we were finally "ready" to be a real couple, we had broken each other apart.

⁓

We went to see an astrologist. Jason's mother, Talia, was very into astrology, to the point where she consulted the stars as a road map to her life. She conferred with the cosmos before making plans. If one of us was going out of town, she would look to the stars to see if it was a good time.

She sent the two of us to a highly gifted and reputable adviser, who printed out a whole series of charts. As he explained their meanings, I circled the things I found exciting. At the time, all I wanted to know was if Jason and I would weather our age difference and be together forever. The astrologer considered this from every angle. The stars all agreed we would end up heartbroken.

⁓

Time away working on a film allowed me to focus, offering a respite from the cycle of self-flagellation, doubt, loneliness, and neuralgia. But when I was in Prague filming *Hellboy,* I floundered in my solitude. On my weeks off in the Czech Republic, I resembled a pinball careening from wall to floor to wall to hallway and finally gripping pillars holding arches carved out of stone. From catacombs to car to bar to bed to bathroom, crying to myself out loud on the floor. Sometimes I lost myself in the comfort of memories of my time with Jason. We had a rocky farewell. After time apart, I knew we were done, but I couldn't let him go.

Late one night, as I sat in my trailer smoking countless cigarettes and grieving my loss while playing "Under Pressure" by Queen and David Bowie, I called Jason for what must have been the fortieth time that week. It always went to voice mail, the dreaded click-to-beep. But that night, he picked up. His voice. Both my heart and my gut froze.

"Oh, finally," I said.

"I love you, I forgive you, I will never see you again, I will never be with you again," he declared calmly. "Do not call me. Do not call me." And then he hung up.

I wanted to die. I was airless. Flaccid. Destroyed. He was resolute. He would save himself, from me.

I had never felt more sure my whole future would be a loss now.

Heartsick, I flooded myself with champagne and vodka, fresh mojitos in dark bars in the old part of town. I drank, surrounded by girls made up like prostitutes. Pale, skinny. Tacky, glamorous. Faded already and not even twenty. Men in square-toed loafers stepped on my feet, sliding past. These were the bars I left every night, out onto the Charles Bridge as the beggars cried on their knees, shrouded in black robes, silent and bowed.

In the morning, I'd report to set and perform in a big movie. I was crushed. Silenced. I didn't see the miracle that was my life. I didn't see the wins, the fabulous directors, the famous friends. I saw only heartbreak. I didn't believe I would recover.

⁕

July 29 - 30   2:15 a.m.
Wrap later today.
This journey is almost
over. A memory.
The pain and growing d
Reive gone through in Prague
as immense,

Love

Shooting *Hellboy II,* several years later and still grieving, I called him one more time. That's when I accepted it was over for good. We spoke. He told me he was in a great relationship, with the woman who would later become his wife, Brady. He was happy. He was so clear in his devotion to her that my heart found grace and was healed. I loved him enough, I realized, that I actually felt relief. He forgave me and wished me well, he said. Then we said goodbye.

Not too long ago, my son, Arthur, and I ran into Jason at the drugstore. He was carrying a big box of diapers. Arthur asked, "What's that?" To which Jason replied, "Pillows! I come here to get my pillows!" My son laughed. And I thought, *Wow. This did not end badly after all. This ended perfectly.* Finally.

Even as my acting career continued, as lovers came and went, as friendships deepened or trickled off and time marched on, I would return to drinking. To be clear, I did not drink on set. When I worked, I was totally sober. Those were sacred moments, where I was given a job and I did it. But left to my own devices, I let sleep, sadness, and drink take over. I'd go for periods when I didn't drink at all or didn't drink as much, and then I'd go all in again, crippled with pain and fatigue, bingeing until I passed out, welcoming oblivion.

Before shooting *Storytelling* in New York, I wound up going back to rehab for a second time. I wanted to go, it was my idea— I didn't feel safe with myself. I was worried about my overall health. I entered the Sierra Tucson center for treatment of my alcohol addiction and depression. The intake nurse reviewed my form and assigned me to the eating disorder unit. I told them I didn't have an actual eating disorder, which I thought true. While I knew I wasn't one to nourish myself adequately, I did not feel I had an eating disorder. Though I did mind my weight, I didn't count calories, I didn't starve myself (my middle school years were another story), I didn't follow any of the patterns that accompany disordered eating. But I doth protest too much.

Ironically, the experience gave me a full-blown eating disorder for a long time. I substituted an eating disorder for drinking. The people I met there taught me how. Everyone sat around obsessing about calories, competitive with weighing and measuring and packets of artificial sweeteners. I became embarrassed to gain weight there, and I was given less to eat than I normally would have, because they didn't want to trigger me. I see now that it was always in me. Latent, waiting. I just needed someone to prompt me to be better at it. To compete.

Once I left the program, regulating my own starvation became a bigger theme in my life. I read the book *Stick Figure,* not as a cautionary tale about the danger of eating disorders, but as a how-to guide. It was like encountering Sarah T. all over again, trading out shots of vodka for withholding food.

On the other hand, I did stay sober for a while. But it would not be for good.

Alcohol had been the salve, the relief, the warmth. I thought I found a way to stay on this planet with my wine. But the electric anxiety and loneliness found a friend to creep around with in the dark halls. Alone in my bedroom, I was like Alice, sampling what the order "drink me" could bring. Nothing good.

Wink

THERE ARE DAPPLES of light in my story, all along the way. Wink was one of them.

When I was still with Jason, I suffered a bout of despair and chronic trigeminal neuralgia that had me searching for a distraction. So I took a volunteer job walking dogs at a local animal shelter, the Lange Foundation. There was this mutt, a forgotten one-eyed corgi mix named Wink. She could not stop jumping whenever I walked past. She reminded me of a Hanna-Barbera cartoon doggy on a pogo stick. At night, alone in my house, I couldn't stop thinking about her delightful, boundless joy; she bounced around in my head, even in my dreams.

One bright morning over buckwheat pancakes at Quality, I asked Jason what he thought about taking Wink home for a night. "And then I'll write a glowing personal report to pin on her crate at the shelter, to help charm a potential forever-home adopter," I said. When we went to collect her for the overnight evaluation, I had little intention of keeping her. I'd never taken care of a dog on my own before, and besides, I didn't want the added responsibility as I tried to build a career and stay awake, really.

On our way home in his Prius, with Wink snuggled happily next to me in the front seat, we stopped by Jason's mother's house. Talia wanted to meet her and Wink replied in kind. "This is a great dog!" Talia shouted as her three pugs and Wink chased one another around the lawn. "You have to keep this dog, Selma," she insisted, before she adjourned inside to read more Pirandello, still grieving her beloved late husband, Jack.

I took Wink home that night and with me she stayed. It was a miracle to have found her. She was my Steinbeck companion. My *Travels with Wink.* Everybody loved Wink. Wink, who once ate an entire pumpkin pancake from my plate at La Conversation with such swiftness I never even saw her do it. She sat contentedly on my lap through so many meals, eyeing my steak frites, ever hopeful. She sat quietly in my lap, still while makeup artists readied me for camera, away on location. She accompanied me on every trip and to every movie set, for every sleep and every waking.

When I was overwhelmed by melancholy and wiped out for weeks, she brought me mice and rats and even a possum. Loyal little dog was she, staying tucked beside me when I retreated to my bed, or howled in pain, whether from a broken heart or the pain in my face, or from missing my mother. She was a dear witness to all of it, the happiest dog I've ever known, fearful only in thunderstorms. One spring night in Budapest while I was filming *Hellboy II,* the sky cracked with lightning and driving rain. As Wink trembled in my arms, I hummed deeply into her heart, the vibration soothing her to sleep. Guillermo del Toro honored her in the film by naming a character after her. I cared for her as tenderly as I would a human child, cherished her above all else, every night and every morning gently kissing her and thanking my angels for her company. I could not imagine a life without her.

Carrie

MEETING CARRIE FISHER was another bright spot. As soon as she found me, life grew softer. My world felt kinder and more exciting with her in it.

Now, I should preface this by saying: I was not a Princess Leia fangirl. I'd seen *Star Wars* in the theater, when it was first released—Lizzie, Katie, Mom, Dad, and me. I enjoyed it. The famous font scrolling by, accompanied by the dramatic, sweeping building orchestra. C-3PO lost in the blurry haze of the desert. Katie liked C-3PO best; he was skinny like her. Lizzie was Chewbacca, cute and strong. I was relegated to being R2-D2 because we were both the smallest. I was not amused by this. My parents bought me a shirt with an R2-D2 decal on it, and I was so upset that I screamed and screamed until my mother locked me in my room. That was the only time I can recall her doing that, although Katie would trap me often.

But the Force! I missed the whole point. "May the Force be with you" became my rosary, my mantra, my wish. In my young eyes, Darth was the real star. The cape, the breathing, the mask. A presence. Dramatic. Frightening. Imperious. Who wanted to be R2-D2 when you could be Darth? That, to me, was the true meaning of the Force. He reminded me of my mother.

⁓

Fast-forward to 2001, at a Women in Hollywood luncheon. *Cruel Intentions* and *Legally Blonde* had put me on the map. I was dating Jason Schwartzman, deeply in love. I was riding high and thin from late 1990s fame, thinking the world would only keep getting better. I was wearing a gray Jane Mayle dress that Jason had purchased for me on the advice of his cousin Sofia Coppola, Gucci boots, a vintage Hermès Kelly bag on my arm.

The parking lot of the Beverly Hills Four Seasons swarmed with gorgeous, important women. One of them came running up to me from across the way. I didn't recognize her at first. She was middle-aged, attractive. Her long scarf trailed behind her, where it latched onto the back of her shoe like toilet paper. She was comical—dropping things, carrying on, adorable. As she got closer, I realized the woman was Carrie Fisher. She looked right into my eyes, grabbed my arm, and said, "It's my birthday, please come to my party!" Bruce Wagner, her tall, handsome sidekick, wearing a boilersuit, took my number for her and promised to call me with her address. The citizens of Los Angeles can be flaky, so I was pleased when he actually did.

Jason was a huge *Star Wars* aficionado, so we went. We drove out to her home, a sprawling estate off Coldwater Canyon. It had once been owned by Bette Davis, followed by the Academy Award–winning costume designer Edith Head. Carrie had it redone in a colorful, kitschy way, filling every inch with London flea market finds and folk art. As we drove up the driveway, signs pleaded, "Please Do Not Enter." They looked as if they were written by charming trolls. A chandelier glimmered from a tree, and tiny bulbs twinkled in all the lace-boughed branches. There was a swimming pool with an old-fashioned slide way up on the hill. The whole place was whimsical, marvelous. Every corner of the house told a story of her life.

Jason and I walked into the party arm in arm. Carrie greeted us, so genuine and friendly. "Don't stand too close to each other; you'll look like garden gnomes," she quipped, in a good-natured joke about our short stature. She reminded me she was once married to Paul Simon and together they reminded her of salt and pepper shakers.

The people whose work I admired on-screen were suddenly mingling about. George Lucas waited in line for the bathroom. Michael Keaton at the bar. Robert Downey Jr. on the bar, but not drinking any longer. Meg Ryan, looking like Meg Ryan, dressed in her combat boots and tights. Tracey Ullman and Téa Leoni and David Duchovny. It was like the Mad Hatter's tea party come to life. A who's who of the old guard.

After that party, Carrie was in my life as though she'd been there all along. We'd smoke cigarettes in her bed and watch Turner Classic Movies as she wrote on her yellow pad. She always kept one by her side, as my mother used to do. (Now I do, too.) Carrie was very skilled at her trade; she knew she had to fucking write, so she sat on her bed and she wrote. Every now and then she'd look up and go on these riffs. I'd roar! She was so enthusiastic. Sometimes she'd get dark in her writing. She'd read a passage aloud and I'd suggest edits. "You're right, you have to leave room for laughter," she'd say, nodding, trying to build up my confidence. Sometimes, like with my mother, she'd admire one of my quips. Always, she wanted to help me, knowing I was not yet ready in life.

We'd have long dinners, her stained-glass light boxes of saints glowing behind us. She knew a little about every subject under the sun. The most brilliant wit. One night, while talking about the filmmaker Buñuel, she stopped mid-sentence and said, "Let's go down to Mom's house and scare her!" Her mother, Debbie Reynolds, lived on the property.

Once Carrie got an idea in her head, she ran with it, full steam. We'd slink around and play ding-dong ditch and dress up in her Leia costume, drinking Diet Coke. One of the best parts of Carrie's world was that you didn't have to be polite. You could just be you. Messy and raw. I felt compelled to fill the silence. But Carrie justified everything. She would wave her hands and say, "Who cares?"

At Carrie's house, you could wander around. You could say what popped up. You could go deep, talk about something for twenty minutes, have a Diet Coke and maybe a cigarette outside, while she dropped glitter on my head, and then leave. Or you could stay forever. She didn't have expectations. Carrie took the responsibility off things. She knew how to make people comfortable. She was the kind of friend I could handle.

Plus, she sent a good email. No one sends a good email anymore. She signed them all to me "Leia."

We would talk about being misunderstood. "I know," she'd say. "It's all a misunderstanding. And all of it is true."

After attending a couple of Carrie's gatherings, I noticed that she often made her way to bed even before the party was over. She really did try to live each day, but she struggled. Sometimes she'd disappear into the bathroom and come back talking gibberish. I never asked a question, never brought up the pills. I respected her too much, and I didn't feel it was my place.

We never once drank together. We never once took a pill together. Only once ever did Carrie see me drunk. It happened to be the last real time I saw her.

Arthur was a toddler. I'd checked us into Shutters on the Beach in Santa Monica for a night of relaxation. The front desk sent up a bottle of champagne. I wasn't drinking much then, but that day I was sobbing uncontrollably about some child-proofing issue I was nervous about. I would fall into spasms of sobs unprovoked, and it could all be too much. I couldn't stop crying, so I poured a glass. I decided, why not? (This was the first of only two times in my life when I drank in front of my son.) At one point, I stumbled down the hall, already exhausted again, a champagne flute in one hand, Arthur balanced on my hip, and there was Carrie, walking with Bruce Wagner. We screamed and squealed and hugged. She was such a hugger. Unlike my mother, she loved human touch. We couldn't believe it! We couldn't believe it. We hugged again and again. I didn't want to let her go.

She invited me to come up to her room. "Bring Arthur!" she said. But all I wanted to do was hide in my room and cry and drink. So we hugged once more, swaying back and forth in each other's arms, and that was it. We walked away, promising I would make it to her room. I did not.

❧

A couple weeks before she died, I was at Barnes & Noble in L.A. with Arthur, my beau, Ron, and his daughter, Chloe, when I noticed all the characters from *Star Wars* wandering around the store. I went up to a guy dressed as Boba Fett and asked him, "What is this? What's going on?" In a voice muffled by his armor, he said, "It's for Carrie Fisher's book party." I squealed. "Carrie's book party!"

It was a huge crowd. There were so many costumes. So many Carrie Fisher admirers. I gave Boba Fett's female companion a message. "If you get a chance to meet Carrie, please tell her I was here, but I have to get my son home."

Later that night, Boba Fett's friend found me on social media and sent me a note. "I gave Carrie your message and she said, 'Goddammit where is that bitch?' And then she called out looking for you. 'Bitch! Bitch!!! Where are you?'" I laughed and wrote back, "I hope you told her this bitch had already gone." I pictured her standing on a chair, searching the rows and rows of books, trying to find me in the crowd, just as she had years before.

I was home alone when I found out she'd gone into cardiac arrest on a plane and was in a coma. It was Christmastime, and I'd just put up our tree. I sat next to it and sobbed. She died four days later, on December 27, 2016. When I heard the news, I couldn't breathe.

Someone once told me that grief is love you can no longer express, and that's certainly how I feel about the loss of Carrie. I loved her. I did take Carrie for granted. I thought she would always be there. She was larger than my life. I didn't think she would ever go—I didn't think.

I really, really miss her. We were true loners, Carrie and I. Real recluses. But because of her, I learned how to listen. Because of her, I learned that it's good to idolize the people who are here now, the ones who really mean something. Because of her, I try to always say "I love you" to those I take for granted. Because of her I keep a tree lit and decorated with ornaments all year round, as she did. Her Leia figure hidden in the plastic branches.

⁓

I didn't go to her funeral. The only person who would have invited me to it was Carrie herself, and she was dead. We'd never worked together. I wasn't on anyone's list. I was only on Carrie's list. They'd put her ashes in a Prozac bottle, a kitschy object from an old pharma display. She would've laughed.

The loss was so huge. When there was an auction of some of her things, I bought her dollhouse, her trinkets, the molded modern furniture, her light-up Saint Francis, her hanging Lucite chair. I couldn't bear the thought of her things going to anyone else. I wanted to hold on to her. I spent too much money on it all, just as she did. "It's expensive being Carrie Fisher," she lamented once.

I did talk to Carrie on the night before her funeral. I told her I wanted to leave a rock on her grave site. (We both had Jewish fathers, and that's what Jews do.) "I have to bring a rock," I said out loud. "I need a heart-shaped crystal." And I swear I heard her voice reply, "Please don't leave a heart-shaped crystal! Just write something, you lazy asshole!"

"I don't own any yellow legal pads," I said to her. "And I don't have anything to say."

Missing her voice, I started to reread her memoir *Shockaholic,* but it was too fucking painful. I put the book down, thinking I'd get to it later. I placed it on the far side of the room, right next to a lamp she'd given me. And then I forgot about it.

A few days later, I went back over to the book. Right on top of it, there was a big, amorphous crystal. It was a smoky quartz, and if you look at it just so, you can see it's in the shape of a jagged heart. As soon as I saw it, I started shaking. A feeling of warmth washed over me. I felt her presence.

I screamed, "Oh my God! Carrie Fisher! You're real!"

A voice back: "Fuck you, I'm real."

"This is so special," I responded. "I'll never tell anyone about this."

(I have told anyone who will listen.)

After Carrie died, I met with the clairvoyant medium Tyler Henry. I felt unmoored after losing her, and I wanted to talk to her. I needed a bedtime story. I was so intent on meeting him that at one point I actually called E!, the network that airs his show, *Hollywood Medium,* and said, "I'm going to go on the show, if that's the only way to get a reading." And that is exactly what happened.

I do believe that some people can see spirits, the same way I can see lint on other people's jackets that they don't seem to notice. Personally, I've never seen a spirit. And aside from the day I found Carrie's rock, I've never *felt* a spirit. But I am open to it.

The reading took place in my home. I brought Tyler three objects connected to loved ones: Bradley Bluestone's photo, the crystal Carrie left me, and a picture of Wink. I set them down in front of him, with the photos turned over so he could see only the backs.

The first thing we discussed was my career. "I'm ready to get back," I told him. I'd been feeling stalled, sick, weak for years, and I needed good news.

"I don't really see you acting," he said. "You're going to be more of an advocate." This was not what I wanted to hear.

"Oh, fuck no." I laughed. "I'm not a giver like that. I am a privileged, miserable white woman who struggles with depression, so I can't even offer a self-help spin. Advocate for what?" This was before my MS diagnosis, and I could never have predicted what was coming. (He was right, of course, just as he was with Alan Thicke's impending heart attack.)

We started with the objects. Tyler picked up on everything from Brad. He felt Wink come through loud and clear. "Wink!" he said, without any prompting. He said he'd never had such a big energy between dog and person. He told me Wink was so glad I made a memorial for her, and I began to cry.

I thought, out of everything, Carrie's rock would explode, but Tyler held it, and nothing happened. He shook his head. "I don't see anything. I'm not getting anything from it at all."

To this day, I have no accounting for that crystal and its appearance. It is the only instance in my life, aside from making a baby, that was my one real account of magic. When I saw it, I picked it up and felt such warmth in my chest. It was so tangible. The rock is still here, but it doesn't have the magic anymore. Almost like an expired birthday wish. I let time dissipate my belief it was really from her.

"You know," Tyler said, putting the rock back down, "this reminds me of the time Beverly D'Angelo wanted to talk to Carrie Fisher. She wouldn't come through. She just didn't want to be public anymore." Oh, Carrie. I apologize.

The Julies

WHEN I LOOK BACK through my childhood diaries, it's mostly about boys. Boy after boy after boy. And misery. And body pains. *What did I do wrong? How can I get him to like me? What could I do to keep him?* And *My face burns. I can't take this pain.* I had it all backward. I was looking for help, love. I wasn't even looking for attention or approval. I was looking for a Julie—a soul mate, a confidante. Someone who sees me for who I am and loves me in spite of it all.

I collect Julies. Everyone needs a Julie, but preferably a handful.

A Julie is one of those stable, well-adjusted, loving, and utterly grounded women who comes into your life and makes it better in every way. I owe the major steps of my life to the Julies of the world. As much as is humanly possible, I surround myself with their love.

I met my first Julie on the first day of Cranbrook Kingswood. (This Julie was actually Sue.) She was everything I wasn't—blond, tall, good to the bone, properly ambitious in life. After high school, my friends Kelly and Fran and Chip and I revered her so much that whenever we found a good person, we'd call her a Sue. When I moved to Los Angeles, I met another Sue, but her name was Lisa. And she stayed by my side, sharing my adventures over a glass of wine. Then I met Julie when I moved to my first house. Now, whenever I meet a good person, I call her a Julie.

The house on Cynthia Street was a charming little bungalow, once a pied-à-terre for Groucho Marx's mistress. The day I moved, in the summer of 2001, a little girl, a precious sprite with long brown hair named Anna, came over to say hello. She bounded up the driveway, trailed by her mother, to give me a welcome hug. The affection from that girl has never wavered, but the greatest gift was the woman standing behind her, her mother, Julie De Santo, whose three other kids and husband, Elio, were waiting at home, next door.

Julie brought out home-cooked Italian meals, welcomed me into her family, became my confidante and my cheerleader. She and Elio owned a restaurant in L.A. for years, and she was a devoted mother who ran what was basically a day care out of her house so she could be with her four children. After her kids were grown, she followed her calling to become a trauma therapist. I watched in awe as she transformed her family, and her life, through her understanding of how trauma and pain are held in the body and how we can recover from them.

In December 2015, I met another Julie. I had just started working on a film called *Mothers and Daughters,* and my life was in a desperate place. I had been experiencing aggravated, unidentified MS symptoms for years, and I was really in bad shape. I probably weighed eighty-five pounds, if that, and was in constant pain, with tight, burning, inflamed skin. My financial situation wasn't much better. I hadn't worked since 2013, when I was fired from *Anger Management* after I called Charlie Sheen a "menace to work with"—at least that's what I read. I was broke—my funds had dwindled so much, I shouldn't even have splurged on going out to dinner. This job offered me three paid weeks in L.A.

On the first day of work, the car showed up with a young, pretty woman at the wheel, ready to transport me. She wore a big parka and sensible running shoes. Her name was Bonny. During the next few weeks, she cheerfully and skillfully managed my life on that shoot, taking everything in stride. She made sure a constant supply of nourishing snacks was eaten by me. She was extremely capable and grounded; in other words, she was a Julie. I learned she'd been a Montessori teacher for five years but had burned out and, like me, she was looking for a change. In the car home one evening, we discussed life plans. She came on as my assistant and stayed by my side through it all. She was and is a beautiful and reliable woman. It was as if she'd been sent to me by some benevolent force in the universe. I don't know what I would have done without her at this time.

So now everyone who knows me calls the good people in their lives a Julie. Another piece of advice: Find yourself a Julie—those guardian angels who walk among us. And then hold on to her.

☙

I first saw the ethereal brand of Julie known as Jaime King on a magazine cover in 1996 with a story by Jennifer Egan titled "James Is a Girl." I fell in love. I'm a sucker for beauty, and she has one of those faces that made me grateful and envious. Grateful that such a face exists, anxious it wasn't mine.

Later, in California, Jaime and I auditioned for the same role in the movie *Slackers*—Angela, the pretty girl—and she got the part. Jason Schwartzman was also cast, and suddenly, instead of admiration, I felt jealousy. Not only did I think Jaime was heartbreakingly gorgeous, but certainly my boyfriend would, too.

I'll never forget the name Angela, because Jason had to shave an *A* into his chest hair as part of the movie. Now I saw the *A* in the shower and when we were intimate. A constant reminder of this girl who was now playing the girl who steals my love's heart.

I drove to Riverside to visit him on set, but I accidentally passed the exit, driving hours out of my way. By the time I arrived, I was hungry and dehydrated. When I saw Jaime in person, I couldn't believe there was a creature so beautiful. She was Grace Kelly, a young Brooke Shields, perfection magnified. It was otherworldly. She wore Birkenstocks, and all I could think was, "Of course they look good on her." When I wore mine, I looked very Seattle coffee bean, or as my mother said, like a potato picker, but they looked stylish on her. *Alors.* When I saw how perfectly she presented even in a Birkenstock, I excused myself from set.

If ever she and Jason had dinner in his room together, I became paranoid. "Don't trust her," I told him. "Don't be alone with her." I'd never seen her act inappropriately toward him, but she was friendly, flirty. "What's her deal?" I grilled him. "Why does she want to be alone with you?" Whenever I went to set, I grew silent and judgmental. Eventually, I saw she'd done nothing. I'd been making her into something she wasn't.

A couple months later, I called her from the bathtub, where I went to think. "You know, I'm really jealous of you," I admitted. I apologized for being cold and distrustful. And Jaime was true. "Thank you so much," she said, with so much grace. She offered me a lot of grace. From there, we fell in love, as young close friends do.

I had a dream the world was ending. Gravity had disappeared and everyone was slipping into space. In this dreamworld, as I tried to hang on, I noticed that I was holding Jaime's hand. In the morning, Jaime called me. "I had a dream about you," she said. "I dreamed that I was holding your hand." Ever since, it's been understood that we are sisters of a sort.

I love her. She pulls through for everything. She's generous beyond. She's a real seeker of things. She's a long hugger—maybe a little too long. Julie always said everyone should hug for nine seconds to really feel it, but nine seconds is a long time. Still, as with most things, Jaime easily gets away with it. Minutes. Hours. Years. Holding on to me, please.

Ahmet

I did get married once. It happened, in part, because of a horoscope.

I was thirty-two at the time, a rag doll, way too depressed and exhausted, still living in the aftermath of my ruined relationship with Jason Schwartzman, the love of my young life.

One day, my friend Amanda Anka asked me, "Who are you dating?"

I was very much not dating anyone.

"I think I have your husband," she said.

"Really? Who?" I asked.

"Ahmet Zappa." She waited for my reaction.

"The bald guy who was on MTV?" Not the reaction she was hoping for.

"He has a crush on you!" she said. "He just asked me, 'When are you going to introduce me to my wife?'"

So, I met Ahmet for breakfast at Hugo's in West Hollywood. His first impression of me was that I looked like, as he put it, "a brown clown." Like my mother before me, I am heavy-handed with a blush brush, which I believe is the sign of either an insane woman or a great artist. I was trying to look sun kissed, but instead I showed up caked in bronzer.

"Hello, brown clown!" he said when I sat down.

We got engaged eight days later.

Ahmet was sweet. He had a kind face and big, warm eyes with lashes like a Snuffleupagus. When he blinked, I felt like Beyoncé, with my very own wind machine. He was tall and cuddly, inappropriate with a remark, and fun. With his friends, we made up stories that we told in silly accents. I played a woman named Donatella who made hoopskirts for ponies. "Dis hoopskirt is the height of fashion for the pony who wants more girth!" Ahmet laughed and laughed.

The week after we met, I took him to my Julie's house. She approved and we all cozied up in her daughters' room as the girls got ready for bed, laughing together, which made me happy. Deeply entrenched in that new-couple glow, we picked up a book—a zodiac book on astrological love matches. It was one of those tomes you find for $1.99 on the bargain shelf at Barnes & Noble. The book told us that Taurus and Cancer were the ideal match. He was a Taurus. I was a Cancer. Clearly, I was someone who had trouble straying from a forecast. Whatever the prophecy was, I felt I had an obligation to fulfill it.

When we got in the car, Ahmet asked, "Will you marry me?"

I laughed and said, "What?" A moment passed. I could see he was serious, so I giggled again and said, "Well, where's the offering?" He fumbled in the glove box, found a yellow highlighter pen, and repeated, "Will you marry me?"

It was so Zappa. Very impulsive. I thought, *This is what I need. Someone spontaneous. Someone who is going to jump off the edge for me, because I'm pretty far down.*

I was happy that it was written in the stars. With Ahmet, I could wipe off my brown clown and be myself. So, I accepted the highlighter. And just like that, we were engaged.

After I said yes, Ahmet remembered how his father, Frank, had proposed to his mother, Gail, with a ballpoint pen. It was another sign: this match was meant to be. Why I thought either of these stories was romantic, instead of hasty and impulsive, I do not know. We were two loving people who hadn't yet found their person. We walked in blindfolded but holding hands.

⌒◦◦

When I called my mother to tell her the "big" news, she sighed loudly. "Oh, Selma." Then she asked, "Who are his people?"

"He's a Zappa," I said. Still, she was indignant. "Well, I'm not going to throw you a wedding when you're only going to get divorced. You're like me; you're not meant to be married." Ever the rebel, I did it anyway. Though her words haunted me.

The whole wedding was somewhat wonderfully ridiculous, as many of these things are. I was shooting a John Waters movie with Tracey Ullman at the time, and when I announced to her that we were engaged, she immediately called Carrie Fisher, with whom she was close. On speakerphone, she screamed, "Carrie! Carrie! Carrie, are you there? I have Selma here! Don't you want her to get married at your house?" And that's exactly what happened. Carrie Fisher generously offered to host my wedding at her home—when she was strong-armed into it by a trio of celebrants.

Karl offered to make my wedding gown, which *Vogue,* under Anna Wintour, covered in a piece by Plum Sykes. I went to his studio in Paris for the fitting. He drew a simple column in a very pale pink, with rhinestones on the satin ribbons wrapping around my neck and down my back. At first, I protested. "No, no! This is my wedding! I want a big giant fairy princess ball gown!" But Karl said, without skipping a beat, "Darling, the ball gown will be for your next wedding." He made an identical dress in black, for the party, so I could drink red wine without concern.

Our rehearsal dinner was held at the Chateau Marmont. Everyone in attendance had a copy of Carrie Fisher's latest book, *The Best Awful,* which had just come out. It was dusk, and we were about to play drag queen bingo, with prizes donated by Carrie, from her eclectic personal collection. My mother appeared at the door of the bungalow, backlit by the evening sun. She looked very, very shaken. "Helmut Newton just dropped dead," my mother announced. "Here. Right in front of me." Soon after, the food arrived, and the meat in the burgers was still frozen because the kitchen had gone into a tailspin after Newton's heart attack. He was a resident, and they were horrified. (And boom. This is the part where the fortune-tellers weigh in, and the signs are clear. The universe was telling me to run.)

Nothing felt right. I felt sick. I wanted to go home, back to Michigan, with my mother and Sue, Kelly, and Frances, my Fab Four group from high school. Instead, I picked up a glass. I found someone's abandoned red wine and drank what was left. I sorted my fishtail linen skirt, which I'd bought in Milan with Lizzie and her husband while on a break from shooting *Hellboy* in Prague, and tightened my ponytail. Well, I thought. At least my mother will go home having witnessed something memorable: Helmut Newton's death.

The wedding itself was small, around forty guests. I didn't invite many people, because I don't think I actually believed I was getting married. The entire guest list was made up of my closest friends from Cranbrook, my sisters, Reese, Troy, Julie, Jaime. My heart wasn't in any of it. (Apparently, neither was Carrie's; she forgot all about the wedding time and showed up at her own home after the ceremony was over, after having a fresh salon cut.)

Our engagement might have been written in the stars, but believe you me, a year into that marriage I went to see another intuitive. But in the end, I couldn't really get answers. How was I supposed to know if I should get out of the marriage when I barely understood how I'd gotten into it?

After the wedding, Ahmet and I traveled around Europe and Japan for the *Hellboy* press tour. In the Frankfurt airport, Ahmet bought me a brown stuffed rabbit he named Snoobles. We got along well on that trip, relishing the company and the music and the food, the smell of chocolate in Zurich, the clean air. We were young and hopeful, and we really did love each other. But there was no deep sexual attraction between us. It wasn't totally foolish, but it wasn't built for the long term. We should have been goofy friends who saw each other for dinner every two years, joking about what a fun couple we'd make, then going on our merry way.

We might have done that if we were not so impulsive, so wanting, so wounded.

Our relationship did not provide the comfort I needed. Once I married Ahmet, the emptiness came back. I lost hope and drive. I didn't know what I wanted to do, how I could secure another good job on-screen. I felt sad and terrified. Claustrophobic. I had trouble sleeping. I would sob and laugh at the same time, or wake myself in paroxysms of grief. It felt as if I were falling apart. It felt like a slow treading of water, of things falling away. I couldn't keep up mentally or physically. I didn't recognize myself. I was in bed. Under cover. Literally and figuratively. Swollen, wet with constant tears.

I started drinking, and I wanted to drink alone. I didn't recognize how fragile I'd become. Or that it would ever change. My spirit couldn't get comfortable in my shell-shocked, love-torn, glass-near-empty mindset. And I couldn't wake up. By the end of the marriage, I was drinking at lunch, drunk by dinner.

I wanted a divorce, I told him seriously. We had just come home from Julie's grad school graduation and reception. She was going to be a trauma specialist. It was evident she was living the life she wanted. And it made me realize, in stark relief, that I *wasn't* living the life I wanted. I still didn't know what the fuck I wanted. All I knew was that I wanted to be drunk and be done with this marriage.

Ahmet and I did try. Together, we went to therapy. Eventually, he gave in to my request for a divorce. In the end, we had an important, short relationship that wasn't meant to be.

When I called my mother to tell her that Ahmet and I were divorcing, I made sure to lead with the part where she was correct. "You were right, Mom," I said. "I shouldn't have gotten married. I'm not capable of so much compromise."

"That's okay," she said. "At least I didn't pay for that wedding. And my *God,* your hair was *awful.* Good thing you didn't invite anybody. Now that's over. Like Karl said, 'The next one!' Maybe you will fix your hair next time. Do you have to pay him alimony? I hope you had a prenup. Silly. Just silly. I still love you."

After we split, I decided that was it. My mother was right. I wasn't meant to be married. I would *never* make that mistake again.

I hadn't changed my name to Zappa, so I didn't need to give it back. The responsibility of being a Zappa, with my personality, hit too close. I did get stationery with my married name, though—*Selma James Blair Zappa.* Sometimes I still use it. Every now and then, I'll write to someone giving them that unexpected gift of history.

Bite Me

WITH THE EXCEPTION of high school or spring break, where everyone does stupid things, I hardly ever drank around other people. I was not a social drinker. "How much did you drink?" a friend would ask. "Nothing," I would shrug. I didn't get publicly sloppy from booze very often. I didn't want to make mistakes. I already felt bizarre and uncomfortable, and I didn't need alcohol to exacerbate those qualities for all to worry or judge. For me, the act of drinking was only ever a last resort (more like a common resort), a way to pass out and go into the void.

One night after my divorce, I was at the Chateau Marmont, drink in hand, and lo and behold, there was Sienna Miller. Everyone had told me how much I would love Sienna, and she didn't disappoint. She had such a great smile, with a dimple and white teeth. I couldn't begrudge her for any part she was winning over me.

So, I grabbed her arm and bit it, playfully, as if it were an apple.

Even as I held her forearm in my mouth I was aghast at myself. I thought, *What have I gotten myself into? Or her? This is horrible behavior.* Followed closely by, *Please, Selma. Please don't leave the house again.* I have very sharp canines. But Sienna couldn't have been more charming. She kind of screamed, "Opa!" as I do whenever someone breaks a plate. "You bit me, didn't you? You really did!" she said, in her charming accent. She didn't shame me. For this, in my book, she will forever be the belle of the ball.

There was another such incident that did not go as well. The thought of it still makes me redden. Scarlett Johansson and I had met while working on the movie *In Good Company* and were on our way to becoming friends. When she invited me on a trip to Las Vegas with a group of her friends, I didn't hesitate to accept.

It started out well enough. We got to fly on a private plane. I liked her friends. The room was great.

On our first night there, we all went downstairs for great sushi. Because I wasn't good at social drinking, I did not realize how drunk one can get while seated at a table, eating. (In fact, it's quite possible the last time I'd done it was that Passover seder all those years ago.) One minute, I was sitting there feeling fine, the next, I stood up and I was right back at Pete's Tavern. I was the kind of drunk where you're crawling off the stool and the room is spinning and finding your way to the bathroom feels like circumnavigating the globe.

After dinner, we needed to make an appearance at some very loud club. I did my best to work it out, dancing halfheartedly, Paris Hilton–style. I was wearing a dress and cape by The Row, and I remember reminding myself how Ashley Olsen would advise I go to bed. This didn't have to be.

My friend the actor Seth Green was at the club that night, and he came up to me and said, "I want you to meet my friend." He proceeded to introduce me to Seth MacFarlane. I love Seth Mac-Farlane! I was starstruck. What do I do in public situations where I admire someone, but feel as if I don't bring anything to the party? I bit him on the hand.

"Whoa!" he yelled. "That really hurt." It wasn't a disaster; I didn't break skin. But I soon hated myself.

The following week, there was a story in the *Enquirer* about how I met Seth McFarlane and how shocked he was when I bit him. The story did not die there. Seth was the voice of Johann in *Hellboy II,* and he told Guillermo del Toro the same story. ("Did you really bite him, monkey brain?" Guillermo later asked me. Monkey brain was a nickname he gave me because my eyes cross when sleepy.) By the time of this telling, I had been sober for a while. But the story lived on. Anytime I met anyone connected with Seth, which is not a small number of people, I would ask, "Do you know I bit him?" And invariably, they would say, "Yeah."

Scarlett has never invited me anywhere since.

The truth is, I am a person who is meant to stay home and read books, maybe have a nice dinner, and then put myself to bed. That is the life I'm built for. It's all about the setting. When I'm out in public, it's as if my system gets overwhelmed and instantaneously short-circuits. I turned the phoenix into ashes, by accident, in small ways, all the time.

In my life, social interactions have been cumbersome. I worried about my mental state for a long time, because I didn't yet understand that the MS symptoms accruing over the years were something real. I just thought, *My God, I'm a fucking mess!* Falling and dramatic, affable or ridiculous in public.

To my family, I'm brooding and quiet. To the world, I'm like Phyllis Diller in drag—attention seeking and big. I'm a loner, but when I talk to people, I overcompensate and try to give them their money's worth (even if no one asked and no one paid). But it doesn't always have the intended effect. I get overstimulated, unreadable.

Thank goodness there are the Sienna Millers of the world. Those who are willing to play. Those who are willing to see. Once a person has patience for me, I calm down. But first I throw everything at the wall trying to see what sticks, trying to connect. I'm a slow burn. Someone has to really like me in order to be with me. It's just one of the reasons I love the friends I have so much—the ones who understood me and loved me just the same.

The first and only person to bite me back was Kate Moss.

Kate and I were friends of a sort, through Robert Rich. In the heyday of Marc Jacobs, he was the PR director and celebrity liaison for the brand, and he held court from his basement office on Mercer Street. Some of my best days were spent in that basement, taking Polaroids, drinking rosé out of a can. An inner circle.

"You're Kate Moss," I said, when I first met her. But my intimidation melted quickly, because she was so fucking funny and cool. For a stretch of time, whenever she came to New York, or whenever I went to London, we would hang out.

After a Marc Jacobs show, a bunch of us were lounging around in a big suite at Claridge's London. I had just started taking Adderall again, which I was prescribed for depression. It worked, in a way, because it got me out of bed. It also made me able to drink more. That night, and well into the morning, Kate and I were having a great time, taking Polaroids with Robert. And then I bit her finger. She laughed. And because she laughed, I did it again.

The second time, she did not laugh. With annoyance, she took her other hand, the one I hadn't bitten, and punched me on my back.

"That really fucking hurt!" she said.

Then she bit me back. She grabbed my thumb and crunched right into it. This was the first time I had any inkling of how much I might hurt people when I bit them. Immediately, I transformed into a shamed nursery school kid.

"Oh my gosh," I whispered, "I am so sorry."

I looked down at the little bit of blood on my thumb, and thought, "Oh my God. This could scar." (No. It couldn't.) I felt so happy. I hoped it would. I'd have a scar forever—a scar that came from Kate Moss. (Sadly, it didn't leave a mark.) I loved how she bit me back, 'cause that put an end to that.

Personality-wise, Kate and I exist on very different planes. One night, we were standing on a balcony at the Chateau, when she said, "I want to stay up tonight! Give me a number."

"Eight?" I guessed. I had no idea where she was going with this game. She looked at me, expecting me to continue.

"Four?" I supplied. This went on for longer than it should have.

Of course, she wanted a phone number for a person. A low-key, high-end connection. Weed, or whatever. I was just a run-of-the-mill drunk. I had no such number. Robert and I still crack up about that. Every time I see him, that's the joke. "Give me a number!"

The idea of someone asking me for a number is particularly funny if you consider the fact that I had never done cocaine and didn't enjoy pot. The one time I tried snorting, it was nothing short of a disaster. It was the night before the Met Gala in 2009, and I was staying at the Carlyle. In the room above mine, there was a gathering. A spring breeze floated through the open balcony doors. At one point, I went in the bathroom, where someone had laid out a single line of white powder. I'd never tried cocaine, or any recreational drugs for that matter, for the simple reason that if I acted as weirdly as I did when I drank, best to abstain from hard-core drugs. But it was a small, wealthy group of icons, and it wasn't a huge amount. So I figured this was the time to do it.

It tasted horrible—unspeakably awful. It was so bad that I had to remove myself from all festivities for the rest of the evening. *How do people do this?* I wondered. It was easily the worst thing, other than a Tic Tac in my youth, I put in my nose. It cut a burning trail of bitterness all the way down my throat. My sinuses were on fire.

As I made my way back to my hotel room, I didn't feel any type of stoned. Not a lift, not a buzz, nothing at all. I went into my bathroom and opened a tiny bottle of champagne. I drank it, then inexplicably passed out on my bathroom floor.

The next thing I knew, I woke up hungover. But this wasn't a typical hangover. It was the lowest I've ever felt in my life. I'm talking teeth-chattering, body-shaking illness coupled with over-whelming nausea. It turns out that what I'd taken probably wasn't cocaine at all. It was probably crystal meth. But by this point, it was far too late to do anything about it.

Chris McMillan came to nurse me to health but I was sicker than I'd ever been. I spent the day vomiting, wondering how I would possibly make it through. My face was puffy from throwing up all day. To make matters worse, I had lost most of my hair due to an autoimmune issue, but thankfully the hair genius Teddy Charles put a long fall, like my mother would have worn, on me to disguise it.

I pieced myself together enough to make it to the gala, where I gave Anna Wintour a hug in the receiving line. (You do *not* give Anna Wintour a hug.) I might even have kissed her on the cheek. It was a serious gaffe. I knew better. But I loved her with deep admiration. I'm expressive. Maybe it's because I was so out of it, or maybe because Ingrid and Karl liked me, I had a momentary lapse in judgment, where I thought I could get away with such behavior. But I am fully aware this is not how it's done with Anna Wintour. (Thank you, Anna, for being so gracious.)

I wore a black Marc Jacobs minidress with Louboutin Kate stiletto heels that had me in pain. No one took my picture at the event. I was confused. Later, I realized that no one recognized me with fake hair and a swollen face, or maybe illness rendered me invisible.

Luckily, I kept it together. No drunk shenanigans, no further embarrassments. In fact, nothing horrible happened to me that night, except that the only man who spoke to me was Donald Trump.

While everyone dispersed to their various cool spots, I was standing, floating where I had sat, lingering at the end. I was next to Carine Roitfeld, and she said, "Don't worry, I'll take you home." Just then, Donald Trump sidled up to us.

The first thing he said to me was, "Wow. Amazing hair." I could tell it was *genuine.* "That hair. You have beautiful hair. Really. That is sensational hair. Don't you think so, Melania?" Melania was back three paces. She took a step forward, holding her expensive clutch, and politely agreed.

Carine was talking again about rides home, and Donald said, "You need a ride? I'll take you!" But I turned him down. I preferred to go with Carine, of course, because she was the coolest.

My brief conversation with Donald Trump is funny to me now, for a couple reasons. The first is that it was a very positive exchange. He really liked my hair! The second is that I was wearing fake hair that night. Of course I didn't tell him.

⁓

A bad thing happened. I took up with a new guy, hereafter known as the Monster, who turned out to be toxic in every sense of the word. (I actually met him at the Chateau the same night I bit Sienna Miller.) From the moment he pushed into my scene, everything fell apart.

The Monster barged in when I was particularly vulnerable. I was making a real effort to go out and make friends again, but unfortunately that often went hand in hand with drinking. The MS hit me really hard at this point, but I didn't yet understand what it was. I let go of my nutrition, too shut down to digest; I was smoking, I was drinking, and all of it was affecting my looks. My personal life was disintegrating.

Emotionally, I was in the perfect position to fall for a toxic person, a fact he instantly got. I wasn't even into him, but he was persistent. Quite possibly the most persistent suitor I've ever encountered.

People warned me about this guy. My dear Quinn, a newly made close friend, warned me he was a con man, not to be trusted. He was just after the spotlight, he only wanted his picture taken. But he wormed his way into my life. He was, quite literally, all about appearances. He hung around the Chateau, leaving a trail of heavy cologne in his wake. He wore colored contact lenses but denied it. His self-tanner left brown spots on the white bathroom walls. As soon as we started seeing each other, paparazzi appeared in places they had never been. They kept turning up—at the dog park, not on Robertson Boulevard, where it's expected. It became apparent afterward that he was the one calling them.

When I went away to work, he set up camp at my house unin-vited. He looked through my journals, read my private thoughts. When he found something, some fact that he could use to his advantage, he stayed silent. He never divulged that he knew. He uncovered every weakness, cataloging them for later use, to bribe and extort me. As if that weren't bad enough, he remained in my home, living there while I was gone. I was on the other side of the world, and I couldn't get him out.

He became vicious. If we disagreed, he would turn on a dime. He spouted nonsensical things, telling stories that never happened and saying things that weren't true about people I happened to know. At first, I thought he was gaslighting me, but it seemed as though he truly believed them himself. I didn't know how much a person could scare me until I met him. When it became clearer, I tried to extricate myself.

This was that time—that Juicy Couture track suit moment—when the internet exploded. Gossip websites like Perez Hilton and PopSugar were hugely popular, and they began posting awful things about me, prompted by his insider machinations. One site, the Evil Beet, was the worst of all. I was late to the internet gossip thing, but while I was shooting *Hellboy II,* I became acquainted with a computer and discovered that you could search for your own name and a slew of information would pop up. That was the first time I ever googled myself, and it just about undid me. I was already not in a great place, and that put me firmly over the edge.

Back in L.A., the Monster posted lies all over the internet—that I was crazy, that I did drugs. He changed my Wikipedia page to include his vicious untruths. I tried to defend myself, taking it upon myself to call these bloggers and explain the situation. But there was only so much I could do. It's not that I was some highly credible character; there were already stories out there about me biting people.

It continued this way for a year. Eventually, investigators I hired went to his home and told him how the evidence was traced to his router in L.A., as well as to his parents' home in the Midwest. I had already blocked him. But so much damage had been done.

☙

The first few years I spent regaining my balance after the divorce were an awful, awful time, a fun-house mirror of bad experiences. I felt totally lost. I would stay in my house, trying to will myself not to drink. My life was messy, ugly, unfocused. I was lonely, I was puffy and hot, and I was tired. Always, always tired. I couldn't keep it together. In my attempts to self-medicate, my drinking grew heavier as my mind grew less and less focused.

After another bad binge, Troy contacted a rehab specialist who got me into Promises in Malibu. I didn't trust that I could get better being alone in my home. Though my insurance would have covered it, I paid for it in cash, too afraid someone might find out. As with all my stints in rehab, I tried as best as I could to keep it to myself. I didn't want to be labeled, as either an addict or a depressive, because I worried the stigma could impact my ability to get work. It was all a humiliating weakness. I didn't tell anyone—only Troy and a couple close friends.

I was in a state of constant terror.

As it turned out, the biggest star in the universe, Britney Spears, was also recuperating there. I loved her right away, recognizing she was incredibly dear.

At the time, she had a shaved head and wore a cheap platinum bob wig. After we became friends, I suggested she ditch it. I took her wig and told her that she couldn't wear it anymore. It was associated with the "crazy" label, this tumultuous time in her life, and she was ready for the next chapter, I thought. And told her. May the record stand, I did not steal it—though I did ask her for it, and she gave it to me. I held on to Britney's wig because I wanted to protect her. I told her she was beautiful, and she really, really was. She was so gamine and young, but in a horrible situation.

She also wore wedged flip-flops; you could hear her coming

and going from rooms away. Since she asked me what I bought, what I wore, how I knew what to do, I felt she wanted advice. So I secretly dropped the worn sandals in the trash, hoping it might inspire her to get some real shoes. Instead, she found them in the garbage minutes later and was hurt. "Who threw away my flip-flops?" she cried. I never told her it was me. I thought I was being helpful. I've since come to feel terrible about this. Here was the biggest pop star in the world, in the middle of managing her own public and personal crisis, which her family trapped her in, and I'm throwing away her flip-flops. I meant well. I was just being a girl (not yet a woman).

(Britney, I want you to know I'm sorry I threw your flip-flops in the trash.)

She was an angel, with wisdom and sweetness in equal measure.

I had no real idea of the extent of her suffering. I still have her blond wig. It lives in my closet, in its own little time capsule. A relic of a bygone era. I truly love that girl.

We didn't keep in touch; her number changed a week after she left.

Family

After my trip to hell with the Monster, I resigned myself to being alone. I was working long hours on the set of *Kath & Kim,* weary and bloated from eating Doritos and Cinnabon rolls on film as my lazy, snack-driven character. I was juggling both a TV show and press for *Hellboy II,* which made it easier to distract myself with work and promotion. We traveled through Mexico with Guillermo and the main cast for a pampered while. My makeup artist, Rachel Goodwin, and I sampled mezcal worm tacos at the Four Seasons in Mexico City with Guillermo explaining how he dreamed about these tacos, soft white worms delicately seasoned. I couldn't swallow the bite, my American brain stubborn as ever. There were long, jubilant nights at candlelit tables in Berlin and Madrid, laughter and stories from our cherished director himself, well-deserved hangovers along with somber and reverential visits to the Holocaust and Anne Frank museums. My best friend at the time, my dear Quinn, traveled with us and delighted in it as much as I did, even finishing a shallow dish of soup with a baby bird presented in the center. At the chicest, gastronomically superior, six-table restaurant in the Spanish city. When pressed, Quinn appreciatively told the table that the bird was soft. The beak and bones only slightly crunchy. I closed my eyes and had a sip of cold water. And we smiled as we strolled the streets after-ward, all spiffy and high-heeled was I.

When the festivities ended, I headed back to L.A. Months passed. In short order, a girlfriend set me up on a date with Jason Bleick, the designer of a clothing brand I admired called Ever. I had a sweatshirt, the logo of a leaf on the right arm. Jason was quiet and reserved, muscular and gentle, with piercing eyes that were impossibly clear and blue, like a Siberian husky's. I thought he was handsome and sexy, but we didn't connect instantly.

He lived in a giant teepee in Topanga, where we had our first date. When I arrived at his little compound, he had candles lit. They twinkled in the tiny tiled bathroom in his studio there, and a beautiful hinoki-scented one danced in its flame atop a large stack of Rizzoli art books. The effect was lovely. The smell of a familiar fig candle Victoria Beckham had been burning on a few visits to her stunning house was gently wafting among his sketch pads and leather samples. I also noticed he was nervous. I actually tried to cancel the date because I'd crushed my left hand earlier that day from a forceful horse kick while out galloping in the hills of Sun-land with another friend. But instead, Jason sent a car for me. I was charmed by his thoughtfulness. We walked to dinner at the Inn of the Seventh Ray. And as we ate in relative quiet outdoors that evening, with twinkle lights all around, he cut my food because I couldn't use my knife. I noticed he was strong, with good taste, a good eye. A special kind of man. But he was reserved. Also intrigu-ing. I couldn't get a real read on him.

After dinner, we went back to the teepee with its wood-burning stove in the center. We casually lay down on the bed, each staring up, nestled among the fur blankets. It wasn't romantic as much as it was . . . just being present. At one point, a spider quickly spun down from a beam of the teepee, heading for my face! I rolled over, pressing into his side. It was just a reaction. But he rolled away. I was sensitive and it hurt my feelings.

"Well," I said, "I guess it's time to go."

The car arrived. We said goodbye. We shared an awkward hug. The whole interaction felt platonic, confusing. I left, bemused and fine. I didn't expect to hear from him again.

A week later, he sent a text: "When can I see you again?"

It was funny to me. And now I was curious. Why would he want to spend more time in my company? I didn't know him, how reserved he was in new situations especially, though I would come to understand he is a man of few words.

He arranged to pick me up to go to an art gallery. M+S was the name of it. A small, cool space with an exhibit by a great artist who does pool photos. And oceans. Not Slim. Someone else. But someone great. He was visibly nervous; he didn't speak much in the car. His speech seemed kinda clipped. Quiet. So I talked a lot. As I do. "I like this song. [It was Jay-Z and Alicia Keys. "Empire State of Mind."] You know, I stopped listening to anything. But I like that you do. Listen. To music." Silence. He smiled and got us to the space. I was amused. I didn't know what to make of it. When we pulled up to the gallery, it was closed. He had the date wrong. He was stricken, mortified. Stunned. I laughed and said, "Don't worry! Let's get a coffee." Coffee turned into dinner at Pace in Laurel Canyon. We sat in a cozy booth in the farthest corner. At some point, he took my hand and held it. I held his hand back. When he dropped me off at home, I went inside and cried. I felt inexplicably forlorn. And I kept thinking of his hand holding mine at the table. I knew. I just knew we were connected until the end. And I felt hard times in it.

On our first day date, he took me paddleboarding at Topanga Beach. He drove us to the Malibu Country Mart on a rich-looking customized black BMW bike. We wound around the late after-noon canyon sun to get there, both wearing Ever leather jackets. We held hands, already in love. For the first time in my adult life, I felt I had a man on my arm who was suitable for me. I smiled and leaned in as the ever-present paparazzi snapped a few pho-tos as we strolled. Earlier, I took a picture of him unstrapping the boards from the top of his Mercedes G wagon. I sent it to Troy, who approved. And so, we were a couple.

My heart grew full and in love. I found him fascinating and specific. Passionate about Dan Eldon and his family, about fonts and branding. His hands were handsome and strong with long nail beds, which my mother and I always favored. We were mad about each other. He thoughtfully customized my riding helmets, mak-ing leather bands to go around the sun-soaked velvet, complete with my initials embossed by him. Loving gestures . . . to say the least. I gave him my soft cotton hankie to use for his allergies when we drove up to ride my horse, Dark. I loved the way he slowly walked with a coffee in his hand. Pleased to be doing just that. He liked real cinnamon sticks in his coffee. (He once told me that was all he needed from me—cinnamon sticks in his coffee. It turns out that wasn't true. Or maybe it was, and I was the one who was after something more.) I still have jars of cinnamon sticks, waiting to be plunked in his dark brew.

Soon after, he left to go on a trek with his best friend, Scooter, visiting ancient monasteries in Tibet, while I flew to New York to shoot another movie, *Dark Horse,* with Todd Solondz. The film was a major win for me, an honor. Todd being my favorite director to work with, and knowing my mother would be pleased.

"*Happiness* is pitch-perfect," my mother would announce. "PERFECT!" We were in wholehearted agreement that Todd Solondz was our personal story hero. Mom couldn't make it in the winter to visit, but Jason came to visit me twice. Todd liked him. He was likable, a good man.

Like a hopeful teenage girl, I scrawled Jason's name all over my notebooks. I wrote his name over and over on the soles of my Converse, along with the word "ever." I was smitten.

On October 13, 2010, he flew from Nepal to New York to be with me. It was the first time we'd been together in several months. I was staying at the Standard Hotel in the Meatpacking District, my friend André's hotel, and ran downstairs to greet him. We had the most healing and enduring hug that I've ever had in my life. I was so overwhelmed with gratitude and love I could barely catch my breath. In love. In hope. Miraculous. A fellow guest at the hotel, laying eyes on the two of us, reunited, and in the elevator, going back up to our room, said, "You're both so beautiful. Look at that happiness." It was truth.

That night, our son Arthur came into existence. It was a perfect night. I wasn't impulsive or lost. I was there, fully present. Everything about that moment was very loving. We were safe and didn't have any idea a baby was in the cards. When I found out I was pregnant, six weeks later, all I could think was how desperately I wanted this baby to be safe. I wanted him with all my heart. Whatever that meant.

The tide of my life was turning toward a new north star. Every decision I made, every stumble and success, brought me to this moment. Arthur was growing inside me. A miracle, a reason. Oceans upon oceans upon oceans of love swelled inside me even before I saw his face.

PART III

ANSWERS

Motherhood

THROUGH ALL THE MESSAGES and predictions I'd heard in my life, from all the mystics and healers and energy workers, there was always a common refrain. They all noted I had a darkness around me.

Early in my pregnancy, I drove to Woodland Hills to see a man named Kit. He had more of a pedigree than I was used to; apparently, he read for presidents. I hoped this time might be different.

"You'll have a hard time with the baby's father," he told me. "You won't stay together." I didn't have any intention of being a single mother. But I also think Jason and I knew that it probably wouldn't last. "You and your son will be inseparable until he's three, at which point he'll be closer to his dad also." He paused before continuing. "You will go through a very hard time. You've gone through a hard time already, and you will be tested for the next ten years."

He called it all.

Another seer, Bobby, said, "This kid's going to take everything from you. You will live in that moment between the lightning and the thunderstorm. And in the end you will not be afraid." He told me I needed to keep the circulation going in the spot where my brain stem meets my neck. As it turns out, that is my problem area—the place where I have the most damage.

Right before Arthur was born, I went to see Kit again. He told me that in Arthur's last life, he was an Irish fisherman with an anchor tattoo. Maybe it's pure coincidence, but now Arthur's biggest passions in life are deep-sea fishing and swearing like a sailor.

The truth is, I was scared to death to have a child. I knew I had love to give. But otherwise I felt ill-equipped.

I was afraid of how much help would cost.

I was afraid of how I'd adjust, because I'm such a loner.

Other pregnant people would touch their bellies and smile, proclaiming, "I don't care if it's a boy or a girl, I just hope it's healthy!"

My version of that was, "I don't care if it's a boy or a girl, just let it be a puppy!" Until I got pregnant, I was never someone who dreamed of having a child, so I thought maybe, just maybe, the doctor would pronounce it a puppy. My only dependent up to that point had been Wink, my precious rescue dog.

Even my mother was skeptical of this unexpected turn in my life story. "This is awful, Selma," she moaned when I told her the news over the phone. "How will you work?" She was afraid for my career. I'm sure it also brought up memories of the hardships she had experienced during her own single motherhood and how strong she had to be, going to law school in the midst of it.

My pregnancy was bookended by destabilizing pain and bladder and kidney infections. But the rest of it was magical. The truth was, I'd never felt better. What I know now is that pregnancy can put MS into remission. It was amazing. I had energy, clarity, hope. I ate well. I didn't touch alcohol. It was, for many reasons, the happiest time I'd ever experienced up to that point.

All my life I'd always felt most comfortable dressed in black—

it was my wardrobe staple—but now I was so blissed out that I started wearing pastels. (In multiple magazine interviews about my pregnancy, I'm quoted as saying, "I am just too happy to wear black!") I was photographed looking healthy in white sundresses and wedge heels.

Jason and I went down to Mexico for a babymoon. It was such a joy to be sober, back in the water, and to feel safe, bobbing up and down like a seal, feeling the large waves lift me up and down. I was photographed in a tiny bikini, my belly a watermelon, my entire face a smile.

I loved my obstetrician, but I'd watched Ricki Lake's documentary *The Business of Being Born* and felt inspired to have a home birth with a midwife and a doula. I wanted my son to work his way here. I wanted him to come in comfortable, prepared. More than anything, I didn't want to repeat my mother's scheduled C-sections, her rigid birth schedule. For me, childbirth would not be a chore. I wanted this baby with every ounce of myself.

When I was in the second trimester of my pregnancy, at what was otherwise one of the healthiest and happiest times of my life, Wink suddenly fell ill. She lay on the floor at the foot of the bed all morning and didn't move, her spirit subdued. "This is the end," I said to Jason. He said she would be okay, try not to worry. But I was worried. That afternoon I took her to the vet, and they decided to keep her for observation.

A few days later, the vet called to say she'd blown a clot. They were keeping her alive so I could come and say goodbye. "You need to come now," they said. When they gave her the shot to end her suffering, I held her against my pregnant belly and willed her back to me. I prayed harder than I ever had. But she was gone. A wall of pain surrounded me as they wrapped her up so I could take her home. Other than Bradley, losing Wink was my biggest loss up to that point. I could barely breathe. They'd even died on the same day: February 7. I still feel a bone-deep pang on that date every year, my body remembering.

Jason dug a hole in our backyard. I wrapped her in my forest-green monogrammed towel, a graduation gift from Cranbrook. I set her little head against the embroidered letters of my name and gently placed her in the ground, cursing and blessing God for taking her from me now when I still needed her.

⁊

A month past my due date, Arthur showed no signs of budging. The midwife had no choice but to let me go. When I went for that last scan, my obstetrician said I'd gone too long and needed to be induced right away. It was evening by that point, and I hadn't slept in days.

The Pitocin took a terrible toll on me, but still I refused a cesarean, or even an epidural. Thirty-seven hours of labor later, Julie rushed home early from a vacation to sit with me. She rubbed my head and encouraged me to get an epidural.

"I'm scared. I don't know how to be a good mother," I said.

"It doesn't matter if you don't know how to be a good mother," she told me, over and over. "You just have to want to be good enough."

Finally, she persuaded me to get the epidural, which only worked on half my body. I'd never felt such asymmetrical pain. Another epidural followed. I wasn't dilating enough. The baby was in distress.

And then I pushed. His head came out. My body finally realized he was ready and let him go. I reached down and pulled him from me and placed him on my pelvis.

When Jason first caught sight of him, he yelled, "Wow! He looks exactly like you! This is crazy!"

I placed my handsome baby on my stomach because I wanted him to find his own way to me. Everyone in the hospital room watched as he slowly started his army crawl to my right breast. I'd heard of this phenomenon, but I couldn't believe it until I saw it happen with my own eyes. I couldn't believe my damaged body, my enemy for so much of my life, had done this one good, heroic thing. I still can't believe it. Giving birth to a baby even in the best of circumstances is nothing short of miraculous.

He latched onto my breast, where he drew out the colostrum and fell asleep. Even Julie, who'd given birth four times by then, had never witnessed a baby do this. From his first moments on earth, we were all very impressed with Arthur Saint Bleick. As I held him to me, I thought of Wink and thanked her over and over again. Thank you for getting me to this place, sweet girl. I wouldn't be here without you.

❧

That first night in the hospital, Arthur slept. "What an easy baby!" I thought. Once again, he had other plans.

Arthur was anything but an easy baby, and I was not at ease. I was stiff and weak. Everyone assured me this was normal, it was my body normalizing, this was all normal normal normal. But I felt as if something were terribly wrong.

From the first instant I saw him, I loved Arthur more than I could ever dream of loving anyone. But when I got home from the hospital, everything hit me at once. I was not well, and I would not be well for many years to come. I was broken.

I was exhausted to the point where I couldn't see straight. I'd gone through periods like this before, but now I had a child to care for, and it just felt completely overwhelming. I'd never planned on having a baby of my own, and now, at home with this tiny creature, the buyer's remorse was brutal. I was woefully unequipped.

Early on, I called a cranial-sacral postpartum specialist. I explained through sobs that my pain was too "impractical." Tears led to further exhaustion and dehydration, but I was too deep in it to care. I couldn't stop crying. "I don't like any of it," I said. "Eating my encapsulated freeze-dried placenta hasn't helped for shit." She worked on me; she was patient. She listened. She advised healthy fats and restorative rest.

Before I had a baby, I had been able to check out whenever my body betrayed me or made things hard. Back then, I had solitude. I had Tanqueray. I knew how to numb the pain and disappear out of myself. Suddenly I was hit with a terrible realization: now that I was a mother, I would never be able to check out again.

The nanny I hired for Arthur had worked for me for only two weeks when I decided I had to let her go. I needed a live-in. She didn't want to be a live-in.

I paid her severance. We agreed to part ways amicably. Or so I thought.

A few days later, *Star* magazine called Troy to say that a former nanny was calling to sell a story about me. Of course I knew who it was. I paid five thousand dollars to quash the story. A year later, when she had a child of her own, she sent me an email saying her boyfriend at the time persuaded her to do it as revenge for firing her. She said she was so sorry. "We figured you were rich. I am so, so sorry." I wrote back, "I understand."

⁓

From the moment I gave birth, pain blossomed throughout my body in ways that were both familiar and entirely new to me. Every joint, every muscle grew stiff and brittle. My neck and shoulders spasmed. I couldn't walk to the bathroom; I couldn't get out of bed. The doctor explained how every woman who gives birth feels this. The ligaments just needed time to adjust, I was told. I believed this, I accepted it.

My eyes were red and irritated. My skin broke out. My mind broke down. It was hellish and it felt as if there were no way out. All I could feel was exhaustion. Arthur cried and cried and cried. No matter what we did, he cried. Unless he got exactly what he wanted, he cried. I was flailing and felt like a failure.

I wanted to die, but I couldn't die, because I didn't want to leave Arthur motherless. I went into survival mode. I had room in my life for only one other person and that was Arthur. I didn't have room for Jason. I lacked life force, so I prioritized, I thought.

My sense of smell was still so extreme, I couldn't stand myself if left unshowered for a day. Needless to say, Jason took the brunt of this because I couldn't take his smell either. Which is undetectable to other noses. Jason drifted, and I did, too. Our love vanished, replaced with a new feeling that was just as overwhelming. I wished a city bus would run him over. He felt the same way about me. So afraid were we both we would lose precious time with baby.

Jason had his house. It didn't make sense for both of us to go unrested, I said.

He started sleeping at his house more and came every morning before work to have coffee and son time.

We said goodbye, both of us knowing that though we would no longer be together, we would both raise Arthur. Somehow.

∽

When Arthur was born, I prayed he'd latch on to nurse right away, and a big part of my job would be done. I'd be a mother. To this I warn: be careful what you wish for. From the moment Arthur arrived, he only wanted to nurse. He was relentless. He nursed as he slept. He wanted everything, sucking the marrow from my bones. He once nursed for twelve hours straight on a flight to Venice. I was drowning. When I nursed, I never felt the oxytocin sense of calm that some women experience. I could never sleep, knowing he was going to wake up and need me.

When Arthur was a toddler, I hired a woman to help me be a better parent. She asked him what his favorite food was, and he said, "Boob soup."

The woman turned to me and said, "You've got a great kid. He's cool. He'll be fine."

Then she taught me about boundaries.

I told him, "I don't want you to have a girlfriend while you still recall nursing!"

Without missing a beat, he replied, "Why you always gotta be so stressy?"

He no longer latches on. He's ten, though.

Once, in an effort to establish said boundaries, I went into the bathroom to change.

"Mama, what are you doing?" Arthur said.

"I just need some privacy, Arthur. Sometimes I need time to myself."

He replied, without missing a beat: "Mama, don't be embarrassed of your itty-witty boobies. I think they're cute."

                        ❦

My son looked like an angel. But his lion child tendencies were strong. His roar was not characteristic of our family laugh. It was, and still is, deafening, demanding.

Once, I told him he would have to wait. His heel indented in the stairway wall. A kick of rage because he was not immediately placated. Waiting for him to calm down, I scrambled him eggs. He smiled and placed the buttery cooked yolks in my morning coffee, with a shit-eating grin. "In Mama's coffee?" he asked. Sweetly. Curiously. I roared and kissed him. My very own to love. My little "Saint."

                        ❦

I decided I needed to break some of my bad habits in order to give Arthur a shot at a happy, normal life. First and foremost, I wanted him to have a healthy relationship with food. It's taken me until writing this book to realize how malnourished I've always been. I don't have a goal weight, I don't get on the scale, I don't limit myself, I don't have an active eating disorder. But clinically, I have anorexia. Because for years and years I didn't eat.

My mother was the same way. For her, thin was the only way. On a weekend, if we were home, she would say, "Cut yourself an apple and a piece of cheese." And that was enough. Even though it was never enough.

When I was younger, I didn't eat, because I had a nervous stomach, or I wanted to disappear or stave off puberty. Now I don't eat because my MS makes it both too hard to cut things and too easy to choke on them after I do. In some ways, learning to feed myself has been my greatest teacher, because I needed to see that the way to get the most out of life, out of this body I've been given, is through real nourishment. I never had the patience to make something for myself. On some level I believed I was not worth the effort. Plus, every time I turned on the oven, I thought of Sylvia Plath. I have lived a whole lifetime not feeding myself properly. There's no secret here. I write it because I need to admit it to myself.

I wanted Arthur to have the opposite experience. I wanted him to associate his mother with nourishment. Shortly after I bought our house in Studio City, I planted rows and rows of leafy greens. They grew wild and spicy in the sun-soaked garden. When Arthur was just a year old and exploring the backyard, I would wander to the greens—romaine, chard, butter, and arugula—and snap off what the earth had made. Exhausted from nursing through the night, I would whimper as I brought a jagged piece of arugula to my mouth. With bees hovering by the flowers, I stood hunched and ate. Slowly chewing until I had no choice but to swallow. When I brought Arthur over to try some, he screwed up his face and announced, "Too spicy." I thought so, too. Hot and peppery. I shoved leaf after leaf into my mouth. It was all I could eat that first year. I was like that character from *Into the Woods*. Greens, greens, nothing but greens. Bitter greens, mustardy and hot.

At the table, when I set down Arthur's much preferred butter lettuce with olive oil and lemon juice drizzled throughout, I gently told him it was okay to eat with his little hands. I didn't mind. "Eat, eat!" I said. I only wanted him to eat some food. Natural, wholesome food. I pureed yams and peas, butternut squash and strawberries mixed with sour cream and honey. Macerated into a

delicious kind of sweet stew. Meatballs made from bison in a mari-
nara sauce his godmother Julie always made. Eggs in butter, warm
croissants from the local bakery owned by two Russian women.
He shook his head and walked to me, his toddler arms out like
Frankenstein's monster: "Nurse." That is all he wanted.

He wanted every vitamin and mineral from my own bones, and
I gave it to him, the only thing my body did well all on its own.
His needy body groped until it settled into the soft flesh of my full
breasts. The plates full of tiny portions, cut up for a tiny mouth,
sat in the sink while we nursed upstairs, tears falling from my swollen eyes.

One weekend his dad took him for visitation. Seeing Arthur
go always left me empty and in terror. I nagged his father about a
toy knife or a screwdriver I saw in my son's grip in a photo text he
sent. Nervous, I asked him to be careful. He was too young to hold
such a weapon. He was too young to sleep away from his mother,
I thought but could not say. I could only pick apart safety hazards.

One Sunday, his father reported how Arthur ate his salad with
his fingers.

"I think he got that from you," he said. I could see he was embarrassed. He was right. I eat salad with my hands, dipping each piece
into just the right amount of olive oil.

At least he eats, I wanted to say. But I bit my tongue.

❧

Back at home, I watched as Arthur picked up each damp green
leaf of lettuce from the garden and dipped it into the small bowl
of Wish-Bone Italian dressing he favors, which I had carefully
placed next to him. He took a whole folded leaf and stuffed it

into his perfect little mouth. Some oil smeared on his chin. He went in for another, his bitten nails just skimming the flavored oil when he dipped. He was eating. He was happy. This small boy was so different from the fearful, sensitive girl I was, trying to impress my family, trying to understand the rules, hiding under the bed in shame. He was the complete opposite of me, in fact. Arthur didn't care. He made his own rules. He doesn't fit under any of the beds in this house. And he would never try to. Unless to scare you. Naturally.

☙

When Arthur was six months old, I knew I needed to bring in an income, so I "landed" a job. But he had no intention of giving up nursing. One night during a terrible thunderstorm, I tried to make him wait, and he started what I thought was breath holding. After a few moments, he turned the color of the kitchen counter when the lights were off: rigid and unresponsive and gray.

I ran to the door, Arthur cradled in my arms, not knowing what to do. The phones were down from the lightning. I couldn't call anyone. I couldn't reach out for help. The thought that kept repeating in my mind was, what will I tell his father?

I put him down on the ground, his body so gray on the glossy white floor, and started CPR as I'd learned in infant CPR class. *Thirty pushes, two breaths, thirty pushes, two breaths.* His body was as stiff and rubbery as the dummy I'd learned on. It wasn't working. He wasn't coming back.

I held him with my right hand, trying to keep his head down so his brain wouldn't lose what oxygen was there. I swung open the bedroom door and raced outside. I ripped his clothes off, hoping the cold would shock him. Nothing. I placed him carefully on the ground and started CPR again. I screamed to God, so loud that there wasn't even any sound. *Please save him.*

The rain landed on his eyes. He didn't flinch. I started CPR again, and this time he brought his eyes back to me and smiled. I brought him to my breast, and he latched and nursed. He drank almost as if he were unconscious. Back inside, I held him all night long, praying he would be okay.

In the morning, the sun came out. I called Jason and told him what had happened. As I said the words, it felt almost as if it hadn't been real.

Six months later, it happened again. This time, Jason witnessed it. Anytime I tried to make him wait to nurse, or to pry something out of his little baby hands, he would hold his breath and turn gray and collapse. I would do CPR, and he'd come back.

With each month that he got older, it happened again and again.

I devoted all my time to trying to heal him. By the time he was three and a half, his pediatrician was out of possible answers. No one could find what was wrong.

Finally, a diagnosis: reflex asystolic syncope, a nervous system issue.

When the human body goes into fight or flight, it releases adrenaline. The nervous system is what regulates that adrenaline. But Arthur's nervous system didn't regulate; instead, it shut down all the adrenaline, which in turn shut down his heart. His heart actually stopped beating. He really took playing possum too far.

When he was little and had these episodes, I nursed him. Even after he stopped breast-feeding, I needed to feel his body close to mine. It was the thing that seemed to regulate him the most. The attacks continued until he was six.

It happened at a mall in Topanga, with dozens of terrified parents looking on. It happened when Arthur was doing ninja moves in the living room, while I sat near him making stencils. That time, his whole body sucked in like a paper bag. He looked so different. It was the most violent episode he'd ever had. In between doing CPR, I called Jason and said, "Get over here. I don't think Arthur's going to live." I called 911. By the time they arrived, I had gotten him breathing again. I threw the stencils away.

I recently started taking him on roller-coaster rides so if it happened then, with me, I could help him. I'm terrified it will happen when he's alone, or with a friend who can't help him. I've done everything I can to expose him to adrenaline, like immersion therapy.

Once, I showed him a snake on Animal Planet. I was curious if it would trigger him when the snake bit a man on-screen. "Do we need to turn it off?" I asked. We were lying down. "No." He continued watching this grisly scene, while I kept watch over him, studying him. He looked weird. He went gray. I got him down off the bed and did CPR until he came to. We've never watched Animal Planet again.

❧

Anyone who cares for Arthur now knows that he needs to keep his head down. The doctor said he'll grow out of it. He should be able to recover on his own. The last time it happened, my assistant, Bonny, was in the kitchen and Arthur was going to the door to wave goodbye. He must have hit his hip. There was no blood. He came up to me, pale and clammy, and reached for my hand. As he held it, he said, "Mom, it's happening." It was the first time he'd ever identified it himself.

I had a fire going. I laid him down by the warm flames. I started CPR. The area around his mouth was already tinged with dark blue. I heard a gurgling, but I also felt how hot he was. I screamed for Bonny to help me. She stayed calm because she's a pro in all situations. "Keep his head down, grab his feet." I did CPR again, and he came to.

I once read about a girl who had this condition who died at age fifteen. She was hit in the head with a softball, but she didn't die of the injury; she died from the seizure that followed. I think of her all the time.

Split/Screen

WHEN I LOOK BACK on Arthur's early years, I see the images play out on a split screen. On the one side there's me with my gorgeous, sparkly-eyed, adventurous, and curious boy, exploring the bright world together in an Instagram filter of pure joy. And that is all true. We had many, many happy times. Every day with him has a bit of magic to it. He's such a vibrant kid. Being with him requires me to be so present I almost can't focus on my own body.

But on the other side there's me in a filter of gray. I am stumbling. Throughout Arthur's early childhood, I was off more often than I was on. I now know these were MS flares. I'd fall down our carpeted stairs. My legs would give way for no reason. I felt confused much of the time. Exhausted. I would make a pot of coffee, and instead of pouring it into a mug, I'd pour it down the drain. My face grew puffy; I had boils. I'd wake up on weekends with a new cut on my back not remembering how I'd gotten it. I had to pee constantly. I thought I was stressed, battle scarred. I thought I'd brought this on myself.

Jason thought I was drinking again. I promised him I wasn't. I swore I wasn't. I was sober then, mostly. Occasionally, when Arthur was with Jason, I'd allow myself an airplane-sized bottle of tequila, dipping my toe back into the pleasures of disappearing for only a little while, of erasing the pain and numbing the discombobulation. But I wasn't drinking the way I had when I was younger. I was trying so very hard to be a good mother. Something else was going on inside me. I could feel it growing and spreading, but I had no idea what it was.

Elliot Again

WHEN ARTHUR was a year and a half, I decided I needed to make amends with my father and introduce him to my son. It felt wrong to me that he'd never met his grandfather; I hoped seeing my beautiful son would help us start anew. Elliot had been trying to reconcile; he had sent me some money, for which I was grateful. He was trying. I wanted to reciprocate. He was in his early eighties by then, and in poor health, with a failing heart. I made plans to visit him in Michigan for Thanksgiving.

A few days before my trip, Katie called to tell me Elliot had died. When she told me the news, I felt so sad. I felt sad for the relationship we never had, and more than anything for the pain I knew Katie was in; she was Elliot's favorite, and her grief was profound. He'd called Katie from a hotel suite to tell her he wasn't feeling well, and that he was scared, and by the time she arrived to try to bring him to the hospital, he was gone. She lay next to him, wiped his brow, dressed him one last time.

Arthur and I flew to Michigan for the funeral, using the tickets I'd bought weeks earlier in hopes of a reconciliation, never guessing I'd be going to bury him instead. I wanted to see him one last time, so when Arthur and I arrived at the funeral home, I went straight to the room where Elliot lay in his coffin. He looked the same. Young for his age, full head of thick black hair. He was still with that awful woman. He still played tennis. He had never met my son. I touched his cold forehead and whispered a prayer of mourning. And then I took Arthur outside to the car. He was restless and fidgeting and wanting to nurse.

Rock Bottom

In June 2016, Jason, Arthur, and I traveled to Cancún as a family. We stayed in the Presidential Suite at the Hard Rock Cafe, as part of a Father's Day promotion.

Here is what Arthur, who was almost five at the time, remembers:

He remembers seeing me eat toast with butter and a piece of fish.

He remembers seeing an iguana.

That's all he remembers. For this I am eternally grateful.

Here is what I remember:

I was falling apart. The exhaustion and anxiety were destroying me. I couldn't hold it together even for Arthur. I lost control and spent every stolen minute I could alone in our hotel room, drinking. The last night of our trip, I fell over the sink and vomited three times, then lifted my head and searched for my eyes. My eyes, my eyes, my eyes. They were floating around the mirror, detached from my face.

"Why do you hate me so much?" I said to my own reflection. "You're fucking up, Blair. You're fucking up, you fuckup, you fuckup, you stupid fucking fuckup." And then I fell into the closet and reached for the bottle of tequila—the big gallon bottle I'd brought in from the huge bar in the living room—that I'd hidden in my room. I unscrewed the metal cap and spilled the tequila on my face and down my throat. Then I collapsed on the bed and cried myself somewhere into oblivion.

I don't remember much else from that week, except constant vomiting, running into walls, and bruising myself from going to get more alcohol from the other room. It was a place I had never before been in my life. Thus far. With responsibilities. A child! The pain I felt in Mexico—I could've been dead, and I wouldn't have known the difference. It was four days. It was the longest, most destructive binge I'd ever had.

When we got to the airport to fly home, I was exhausted, dehydrated, hungover. I thought, if I can just get some rest, I'll be able to function as a mother again. I figured I would get some sleep en route, wake up alive again, and everything would be okay. Ish.

We boarded the plane, took our seats in first class. Jason, holding Arthur, was seated one row ahead of me. The man next to me ordered me a glass of wine. When it arrived, I drank it very fast, eager to get on with it, back to feeling livable. Then he asked me if I needed to sleep. I said I did. He offered me an Ambien, which I don't normally take, but I thought, "Oh, what's the difference?" So, I took it.

I remember feeling agitated, kicking the seat in front of me, trying to irritate Jason.

The next thing I remember is waking up in a hospital, with an IV in my arm.

Later, I found out there were nurses tending to me for the entire flight.

Later, I found out I nearly died from dehydration and elevated blood pressure.

Now I know I had MS symptoms that I was trying to self-medicate with booze, but at the time I thought I was losing my mind.

As all this was unfolding, Jason, petrified, continued holding Arthur, who miraculously was asleep with headphones on. (He has never slept on a plane, before or since.) Jason didn't move, didn't react to the commotion, so as not to wake our sleeping child. Arthur slept through the entire flight. I will forever be grateful.

The story was all over the news. CNN, the *Daily Mail, People, TMZ,* Refinery29. A blurry photo of me, taken by another passenger, appeared in all the papers. Quotes from a witness popped up overnight. When I got out of the hospital, the paparazzi were all over the house, wildcats bored and hungry to humiliate.

There is something unexpectedly freeing about public humiliation of this magnitude. It can't get any worse until it gets worse. It wasn't until Cancún that I saw how I had zero concept of how to take care of myself. Now I understood. I needed to make a change. (With all things, we see, this must come from within.)

I had never fully saturated myself in personal responsibility, but now I had Arthur. I had gotten drunk—beyond all control—in front of my son. The worst feeling of all was that he had witnessed it. I felt, for a mother, that was a lockup offense. My mother had taught me as much. Throughout my life, she remained a fearsome, strong figure, with full conviction that a child needed to have a sense of fear and boundaries in order to feel safe.

Now I was putting fear in my son, but it was the opposite fear—the worry that I wouldn't be able to care for myself. Even as a drunk who had done dangerous things to my own self, I would never put my son in danger. Knowing that my son, the person I created, that I am now responsible for, was present at a time when I lost all sense of myself—the clarity of that shook me to my core.

Nothing truly tragic happened on that trip. It could have. And that was enough. That was the wake-up call. It knocked me out of Selma. It knocked me out of my own discomfort long enough to say, I won't do this anymore.

I am so sorry to everyone I disturbed on that plane. Even if one of the passengers was cruel and recorded it, or exploited it, I was the one in the wrong. It was reckless. It was sad. I was the one who put myself in that position, and I saw it for just how pitiful it was.

After the flight, a doctor was tending to me in the hospital, and I asked, "Can I get up and go home?" This doctor, this woman, could not have been clearer. She shook her head, looked me in the eyes, and said, "Girl. If this ever happens again, you will be dead. So, if you make the choice to walk out of here, please know that."

It was a mental switch. I finally got it.

Get out of your own way.

You have to treat yourself as you would want your mother to treat you.

You have to treat yourself the way you would treat your son.

You've got a kid.

This isn't just about you anymore.

You cannot let this get you down so hard you won't recover.

You will not kill yourself over this.

You will not kill yourself.
You must break the shame.

I saw, suddenly, in a new light. I understood that I needed to love this person, this human being whose body I was in, broken as it was. Otherwise, it would be a total waste.

I stood up. And that changed me forever.

⁓

The episode needed an explanation. Troy offered to send out a press release on my behalf, but I told him not to. I wanted to write something myself, in my own words. I apologized in a statement to *Vanity Fair:*

> I made a big mistake yesterday. After a lovely trip with my son and his dad, I mixed alcohol with medication. That caused me to black out. It caused me to say and do things that I deeply regret . . . I take this very seriously and I apologize to all of the passengers and crew that I disturbed and am thankful to all of the people who helped me in the aftermath. I am a flawed human being who makes mistakes and am filled with shame over this incident. I am truly very sorry.

I saw that not only could I not do this to myself anymore, but I also couldn't do this to the people I loved.

My friends were incredible. Troy and Bonny were so supportive. Reese wrote to me immediately: "You're going to be OK, kid." She said the best course of action was to be honest and move on.

When Carrie found out what happened, she called me. I told

her how ashamed I was to nearly die on a plane. She said, "You're not doing that! You can't die on a plane. You know if anyone dies on a plane, it's going to be me." She was joking, trying to make light of it by saying she'd do it better. Her words haunt me every single day.

❧

A note from Bonny after Cancún:

The jig is up. You need
1. Detox.
2. Treatment.
3. Therapist.
4. Daily Schedule.
5. Accountability.
6. No more bullshit.

The hangover lasted two weeks.

I returned home. I wept and wept. The sadness poured out of me. I realized I had something that was even more out of control than my addiction. I needed to fix my emotions.

I vowed I was going to break this cycle. But how was I going to go about changing everything I'd built my whole life? How was I going to rewrite an existence that relied on alcohol as the only fire door when my body needed soothing?

I immediately set to work. I started with food. For the first time in my life, I was really nourishing myself. Detoxing. Replacing alcohol with what my body needed: meat, strawberries, gluten-free muffins, tempeh, squash, all sorts of greens.

Within two days, I started to feel like a grown-up. I felt as though I were taking responsibility. There was a shift in my brain. It was my first real step in saying, "I will do whatever I must to learn to be a healthy person."

From there, my entire relationship with alcohol truly changed. I had hit my rock bottom and I fully surrendered. Years of AA only amplified my gratitude, humility, and commitment to sobriety. I abandoned all old patterns and ways of thinking. I opened myself up, and it was transformational.

Throughout the process, I told myself: *Go basic. Your brain is like an analytical maze from childhood. So, let's start from the beginning.* I looked into my genetics, which proved insightful. I discovered I had the *MTHFR* mutation, as well as the *CBS* mutation, which was causing my body to produce too much sulfur and ammonia—real, measurable toxicities that were activated and severe.

I needed to move more. I thought back on my experiences with Outward Bound and how those wilderness trips had helped me through rough times. When I was in motion, the depression lifted, was replaced with a task.

When I look back on my recovery process, I recognize that one of the main pieces was Jason. Before the Mexico trip, our relationship had been plagued by a contentious custody battle and an air of sadness and mistrust. After that trip, we dropped it, but now we were standing together, on the same page, trying to solve it.

When we got home, Jason returned my son to me, under the condition that he would help ensure that it was safe. We had a long discussion about what we could do, how we could work together, to make things all right with my drinking. As part of this, he gave me examples of behaviors that concerned him—emotional outbursts and events where he thought I was drunk. I'd trip and fall and I didn't know how to explain it. I told him, truthfully, that I hadn't been drinking on any of those occasions. The Mexico trip notwithstanding, I never, ever drank around Arthur. I was just being who I was at that time; we didn't yet know that MS was stalking me.

Still, I couldn't believe Jason could trust in me after such an extreme, public breakdown. For Jason to continue to have faith in my ability to be a good mother, even after seeing the very worst I could pull out of a hat, was an enormous act of generosity on his part. I'll always love him for that. Always. Jason stood by me and helped me get better, and my family gave me the will to never drink again.

I believe that once you've become an addict, of any sort, to anything, it changes you. I think it changes your brain, your personality, your drive. I think it changes your character, and as such will always need to be maintained. I know firsthand: It's a relief you will chase forever. That first feeling of warmth. That first moment of comfort.

But seeking that comfort in the old ways is not a possibility for me. It really hit home this time. Before, I would leave myself a bread crumb, a way to get back to myself. Now I saw that I needed to start over.

I stayed sober. I have had vices. But I haven't had a drink since that day.

Every day, there are prayers. There is work. There is acknowledgment. If I ever have a drink again, I will have the accountability. (Though I plan on never doing that.)

The truth was, this epic humiliation was the wake-up call I'd been waiting for. I imploded publicly, in the ugliest way possible, but miraculously I didn't hurt anyone. Throughout my years of searching, that's all I ever prayed for. I was lost and I wanted hope, and that was such a clear, final warning. I will forever say, "Thank you. Thank you for allowing me to hit that bottom without really harming somebody."

꿈

My mother's mind was already slipping when the *Daily Mail* called her for a quote. "Selma was my last daughter and she's really quite difficult! She gets me upset when these things happen." (Let's be honest: my mother herself was probably a bit pickled when she gave this sneak-attack interview.) "She took an Ativan and had a glass of wine and went crazy! She's a lovely girl! She's never had any problems with airplanes or flying before!"

꿈

I wish I could see what I would have been like without alcohol. I would truly love to know.

My mom was a big drinker, but she wasn't a drunk. Molly was functioning. Molly was responsible. She was always—always—on top of it, just as she was on top of everything. She never fell apart the way I did. She kept her shit together.

But is it any wonder? All my life, I saw a stunning, capable woman who was able to smoke and drink. I idolized her, in all ways. Of course, I was going to copy that.

I watch Arthur like a hawk now. I don't even want him to try it. I don't want to project my thought patterns, my own experiences, onto him. I don't want him to relate to the side of me that's not as capable as I want to be.

His memory of my drinking years is minimal at best. He

remembers once getting in a fight with me in Mexico, one of the two times I drank in front of him, over the game Chutes and Ladders. (A sloppy moment. Did I throw a Chutes and Ladders piece at my kid? Was I that pathetic?) Thankfully, he doesn't even recall a drink in my hand. He doesn't question it. He doesn't know me as a drinker. It's not something his mom does.

I hope some good has come of my failing. I hope that I've broken the cycle.

Ducky Manor

I WANTED TO CREATE a safe space for Arthur. In 2012, I bought an old Cape Cod–style house built in 1950, a hodgepodge of small rooms. I loved that it was cozy and dark, with windows that were bright but dirty, more Cambridge than Studio City. I gave it a tailored ambience—walls painted in shades of hunter green and "Polo blue" and lined with bookshelves. It's intentionally reminiscent of a prep school. I wanted it to feel like Cranbrook, the place that changed me. I filled it with things from people I've loved, reminders of the places I've been. My home tells the story of my life.

There are lemon and lime trees in the backyard, and a swimming pool built into the slant of the Laurel Canyon hill. I planted jasmine on our terrace, and every April it blooms wild, its fragrance synonymous with springtime.

Our home has been our cocoon. Arthur feels safe in this house. I feel safe in this house. It has held us through the nights. In the time that we've lived here, our home has seen so much. It has seen death and loss. But oh, my Lord, it has also seen resilience.

Arthur and I named the house Ducky Manor after our first dog together. Ducky was a rescue we brought home on a hot, sunny late summer evening. I was trying to fill the hole left by Wink, who had been my soul mate before Arthur was born. I still missed her terribly.

Arthur and I had stopped at every adoption stall, but no luck. No little dogs captured our attention. As we resigned ourselves to leaving empty-handed, I spotted a small white dog whose eyes were so big I later joked that I could only see Maggie Smith in her expression. "What about her?" I asked the woman from the rescue. She gently coaxed the dog out of her cage. Arthur looked at me pleadingly. I told him to sit down crisscross applesauce, and she walked right into Arthur's lap. She settled there, already home. She was perfect. We named her Ducky.

One evening when Arthur was four, I let Ducky out to pee in the backyard, and a moment later she was gone. It happened so fast, in an instant. I barely had a chance to make sense of what had happened. One moment, Arthur was playing in his tree house, and the next he was screaming and crying for help. "Ducky!" he yelled as he climbed down the ladder, his little boy voice ringing out in the evening air. "Ducky!"

I ran up the rocks by the pool to help her. I thought perhaps she had fallen, broken a leg. But then I saw her, lying on a rock in the blue-and-white sweater she always wore. There were puncture wounds in her abdomen, as if she'd been attacked by something. An owl maybe, or a coyote. I had no clue what had happened, only that I'd failed to protect her. Ducky was shaken. I did my best to stay calm, but I could tell her breathing was shallow. We rushed her to the animal hospital, where the vets tried everything to save her, but her injuries were too severe. Sweet Ducky died in my arms.

I was immediately overcome with that same familiar feeling. I'd let us all down. I had tried to create a place for Arthur and me, a safe life anchored around this home. And yet I let something horrible happen to our family.

And then I had to tell my son that Ducky was gone.

For years animals have appeared in my home as warnings, signs, gifts. The possum Wink brought me during a years-long depression. A gift just as vulnerable as I was. The owl who perched in the backyard in the early years of Arthur's life, standing guard. The scorpions, exotic and dangerous, raising their white bodies in the brush on our hill. I keep a clean house, but the animals don't care. Nature finds a way.

Once, there was a drowning deer in our black-bottom pool. She had fallen in and couldn't find her way out. She thrashed, bleeding, on the edge, my own heart caught in her twig legs. She was more frightened of me than I was of her, so I corralled her to the shallow end. She looked at me for four long seconds, before regaining her senses. Like thunder, she flew up the hill. Like the dreams I had that have come to seem like premonitions, I remember her.

Sometimes the warnings are gentle, and sometimes they are not.

The day Ducky died, when I saw her sprawled on that rock like a dead rabbit, my first thought was that a great horned owl got her. But the vet said no, a bird wouldn't lift a dog with a sweater on. They were certain, very certain, it was a coyote.

Looking back, that violence should have been a sign of some of the losses ahead. How fragile and vulnerable we are. The way life can change instantaneously. As with most great losses, it was also a reminder of how life does go on.

☙

After some time, we adopted our dog, Pippa. Before she came home, I did everything one could possibly do in order to coyote-proof the yard. Still, out of an abundance of caution, we never leave her alone.

The other day, I was sitting under an umbrella in our bricked backyard when I heard a crash. My adrenaline picked up, and I raced into the grass to discover a red-tailed hawk swooping down at 120 miles an hour near the rock at the top of the hill. I immediately covered Pip, thinking, *I will die before I let another bad thing happen to my son.*

"This is what happened to Ducky," my boyfriend said. In an instant I realized he was right. A hawk tried to pick her up, then left her on that rock. For years, I'd been on high alert, looking for this coyote. But it wasn't a coyote at all.

That's life. It'll blindside you, that thing you didn't know about. Especially when it's been there all along.

Diagnosis

THAT THING you didn't know about. It had been there all along.

The pieces started falling into place.

I'd suffered from symptoms that would come and go ever since childhood. Fevers, urinary tract infections, nerve pain and numbness, depression. Symptoms I tried to dull with alcohol, but the effect was temporary. Symptoms that only grew stronger over time.

Right around the time I met Jason Bleick, I began to lose feeling in my legs in a way I never had before. They started to give up, inexplicably. I'd been riding again, which I loved. One day, I was walking down a hill with my horse, when out of nowhere I fell. The ground just slipped out from under me.

I wasn't binge drinking then. In fact, I felt I was in a good place: Jason and I were happy, I was active, I had work. I decided, since I wasn't drinking, it must be diet related. I hired a chef to make macrobiotic, mostly vegetarian meals, inspired by Alicia Silverstone's *Kind Life*. I ate tempura and fish in special sauces, made pots of green soups. I went to chiropractors, energy workers, every kind of healer. (What's ironic to me now is that I spent so much of my life consulting experts, looking for signs, when all along there were signs right in front of me.)

Then I got shingles. Intense nerve pain, unlike anything I'd ever experienced, shot up and down my leg, up into my hips. The shingles cleared up thanks to antivirals and rest, but I still felt unwell. My leg still gave out. Doctors told me it was postherpetic neuralgia—the body's memory of the shingles virus.

This continued, off and on, for several years. Some episodes were petrifying. When Arthur was about three and a half, we took a trip to Palm Springs for the weekend. In the car, my legs began shaking uncontrollably. There was nothing I could do to stop it. I was scared to drive, so I pulled over and told Arthur I was okay, I just needed a minute. I got back on the highway and drove for five miles before having to get off again. It took us hours to go just a few miles. Arriving at our hotel felt like summiting Mount Everest. When we finally pulled in, I practically fell out of the car. I told the concierge, "You have to help me. Something is seriously wrong."

In all my medical journal snooping, as I dug into depressive symptoms and alcoholism, searching for a link, I never once looked up movement disorders. It was unthinkable.

Over the next three years, there were more and more episodes like that one. It would come and go. The symptoms grew worse. I saw every doctor under the sun. They blamed hormones, depression, anxiety, exhaustion, malnutrition, my "neurasthenic" nature. One doctor went so far as to tell me I might feel better if I had a boyfriend. Through all the symptoms, all the visits, I never once had an MRI. The only doctor who had ever mentioned MS as a possibility was my eye doctor who saw me for eye pain when I was twenty-two. I see now that most of those doctors, well intentioned as they were, truly believed this was mostly in my head.

In early August 2018, I went to Miami alone to visit friends. I was shooting a movie in Atlanta and dragging from fatigue. I hoped the Florida sun and warm ocean water would invigorate me. It was a trip made for Instagram. I bought a tiny Eres bikini and Hermès shoes. Our friend wanted to enjoy the ocean on his new yacht. When we were out on the water, no land in sight, I walked to the edge of the boat and leaped high in the air. As soon as I hit the water, I knew something was terribly wrong. I couldn't swim. The act of jumping had taken everything I had out of me.

I knew then that the body I lived in had dramatically changed. I found my legs and with all my might kicked my way to the surface. Unsure of what to do, I floated on my back. For a long time, I stared up at the clouds, keeping what had just happened to myself. I didn't want to alert anyone. I turned it into a meditative moment. When I finally floated back to the boat, my friend Amy had to help me back onto the stern. I felt cradled by love and concern. She showed me the photo she had taken of my final leap into the air. I'm flying and it is glorious. My hands are outstretched ballerina-style, my

legs are tucked under, my toes pointed. My mother would be so proud of my perfect form, thin in my bikini, tanned with blond highlights. I looked great.

If you didn't know, you wouldn't know. But I knew. That's when I really, truly knew.

It was right after this trip that I finally got the diagnosis. It happened so randomly that it's a miracle it happened at all. I had posted on Instagram:

Monday. So, I am in pretty intense pain. Whiplash a few times on my horse and sitting on planes . . . and now I am in a real musculoskeletal bind. Hanging in though. Hoping I can rehab it and get back to riding and writing again soon. #chronicpain is a real challenge. Love to all of us.

My friend the actress Elizabeth Berkley, whom I actually knew from Cranbrook, saw it and sent me a message. "Are you ok?" she asked. I told her all my symptoms; I would tell anyone who would listen at that point. "You need to see my brother right away," she told me. "He's a spinal neurologist. Maybe he can help. I'll call him now. Stand by."

That's how I came to Jason Berkley's office in Beverly Hills. Social media can be noxious, but it can also be miraculous. On that day, it saved me.

He performed the Romberg's test, a simple examination where you put your feet together and close your eyes. My legs gave out beneath me. I fell backward, dropping like a plank onto the exam room floor. He ordered an MRI on the spot.

With my eyes shut, I had no sense of where I was, but gravity did. And then, finally, answers.

The scan was my new fortune-teller. The only one I needed. It revealed a number of midsized MS-related lesions on my brain, six of which were problematic because they were active. Little fires burning from canyon to canyon on the synapses. The connection between my brain and my body demyelinated. It all made so much sense now. Dr. Berkley saw it first, then referred me to an MS specialist, Dr. Silver, who confirmed what Dr. Berkley suspected. He gave the news to Dr. Berkley, who then called me.

When Dr. Berkley said the words "You have MS," I felt an adrenaline rush of emotion. It felt like giving birth. The release of it. The catharsis of it. But more than anything, I was overwhelmed by a sense of relief, like the way you feel when an ocean wave breaks right at the shore before taking you under. For years, my symptoms were dismissed as "anxiety" and "emotional." It was all in my head, perhaps. It's psychosomatic, they suggested. For years I'd known they were wrong (and right—it was in my head, only not in the way they thought). And now I had a map to follow. I had information. A label. This time, one that fit.

There are words that explain what is wrong with me.
It's not my fault. At least . . . I hope it's not my fault.
I can work with this.
I can learn how to cope with this.
It can't get any worse than this. Or it can.
I will teach myself how to be okay.

I thought back to the time when my mother cried with relief upon learning I was an alcoholic and suddenly understood why she felt comforted. There is great power in words. In an answer. In a diagnosis. To make sense of a plot you could hardly keep up with any longer.

In the moments after I received the diagnosis, and in the days that followed, I stayed surprisingly composed. I was so tired. I was too tired to be sad, I think. Too tired to be angry at all the time I'd lost. When Dr. Berkley first gave me the news, I did cry. Loud, choking sobs poured out of me for exactly two minutes. And then I was done. I was supposed to return to Atlanta to finish filming *After* the next day; the film was my first foray back to work after a long hiatus. I didn't want to let the director down.

"I'm getting on that plane. The show must go on," I said dramatically.

"You can't go to Atlanta," Dr. Berkley warned. "You're in an MS flare. You cannot get on a plane. You have to cancel your trip."

I didn't understand. "This disease is incurable, right?"

He didn't understand either. "You must cancel it."

"But it's chronic, right? It will still be there, will still be incurable, when I finish. It will always be there."

"Yes. Always."

"Okay, then. So it's possible for me to work."

"It's possible," he finally admitted. "But you have to understand, it will be hard."

(Truer words have never been spoken.)

I didn't cancel my trip. The show did go on. But right before I saw Dr. Berkley, I'd made the mistake of getting a steroid injection in my neck to stop the spasms, not knowing at the time that I had MS and that the shot would exacerbate my symptoms. My body raged. I was in a bigger flare than normal, and at the same time I was trying to resurrect my career. On the plane to Atlanta, shuddering in pain, I googled my disease for the first time and was shocked to find Joan Didion had MS. My idol. I couldn't believe it! Joan Didion! If Joan had it, then I must be in really good company. There was a certain dignity about it.

I learned that Joan was diagnosed in 1968 after suffering from periods of intermittent blindness and extreme vertigo. When I got back from Atlanta, I pulled her essay collection down from my shelf and reread "The White Album," in which she describes receiving the news in a doctor's office in Beverly Hills, perhaps not far from where I had received my own diagnosis, and the way hearing this news slammed her face right into her own mortality. It was a jarring experience for her. As she wrote, "I had, at this time, a sharp apprehension not of what it was like to be old but of what it was like to open the door to the stranger and find that the stranger did indeed have the knife . . . I could be struck by lightning, could dare to eat a peach and be poisoned by the cyanide in the stone."

I felt so grateful to Joan for giving us this essay. She gave coherence to what I felt. It was the realization of possible limitations, grief, and fear. She so elegantly offered me a reference point. I no longer felt alone.

In many ways, I related to her initial reaction. It's life changing to be given a diagnosis of MS, or any other chronic disease. Even if you've lived with the symptoms for years, the story now has a name. It has a label. There is language for your experience. The future you imagined for yourself begins to morph before your very eyes. Your plans, even the ones you didn't realize you had, start to look radically different. In a moment, your life divides itself into the before and the after. You realize this body you've inhabited for so many years—this bizarre collection of cells—has turned against you. It's more than a betrayal. You feel trapped, a hostage inside your own skin. You are a stranger to you.

It was a long time coming. My whole life I felt lost and wanted an answer. I'd looked for truth anywhere I might find it. I'd asked sages, healers, the universe. Now, finally, here it was.

My diagnosis was the validation I'd been searching for—that I was human, and that it was okay.

I am so grateful that I was sober at that point in my life. When I progressed into a time lapse of MS, I did not go the way that Selma would've gone. The biggest realization is that I wasn't a victim. I was done with self-sabotage. Now it was time to use every resource I knew.

I saw with overwhelming clarity how every stage of my life has offered me incredible lessons. I had been given blessing upon blessing. My whole life I couldn't get my shit together. But now, from this new vantage point, I saw how there is a natural order, if only you slow down and listen. It's ugly and it's messy, until it's not anymore. This is how we progress.

⁊

I announced my MS diagnosis on Instagram on October 20, 2018. I was working on a new show for Netflix and wanted to thank my wardrobe designers, who had accommodated my symptoms and helped dress me with loving patience and care. The producers told me, "Everyone has something," as they held me through my tears. The entire Netflix team was so supportive.

My doctors urged me not to go public. They said people wouldn't understand my diagnosis. They worried I wouldn't get work. They said the disease might not progress beyond what I'd already experienced, so why share it? "You're an actress; your body, your voice, it's all you have."

But they were wrong; it wasn't.

I agreed to an interview and photo shoot with *Vanity Fair*, and when the magazine invited me to its annual Oscar party in April, I knew I wanted to be there. I wanted to wear high heels, but because my gait had grown increasingly unsteady, I'd need my cane. My stylist found the most gorgeous Ralph & Russo dress. It had a cape and a choker around the neck, which I appreciated because at the time I was having a lot of trouble with my voice. I felt cocooned in this dress. Protected. I wore my hair gelled up and back—no side part anymore. I've never felt more beautiful.

When I stepped out on the red carpet, with my beautiful dress and my cape and my bejeweled cane, and saw the cameras waiting for me, I broke down sobbing. Troy came over and helped me collect myself. I was just so astounded by it all. This act—this very public act—of being open about who I am overwhelmed me. There was no turning back.

To my utter amazement, when the photographers noticed I was crying, they put their cameras down and stopped shooting. They waited, quietly, as I dried my face and found my balance. "You look great, Selma!" a paparazzo shouted. "We love you!" I'd never seen anything like it. I smiled and readied myself to pose. And then they started up again.

The next morning, the headlines talked about how brave I was. They called me a warrior. In that moment I didn't feel like a warrior, or any kind of hero. But I did feel a new sense of peace and purpose. I felt, for maybe the first time in my life, fully and completely myself. I was doing what I'd done for much of my adult life—just trying to get through it all as best as I could.

Didion again: "There's a point where you go with what you've got. Or you don't go."

I made a decision. I would get up and go.

Years ago, when I was in high school, I saw a girl walking beside her mother at Sue's country club back home. She was young, maybe eight or nine, and her body lurched uncontrollably when she walked. It was a wonder; it was a terror; it was a shame. I'd never seen anyone like her.

Later, I described her to my mother. "What was wrong with that little girl?" I asked. I replayed the girl stepping jerkily over the concrete squares near our lounge chairs. Fragile, pathetic, awkward. My mom explained it was some kind of dyskinesia. "That poor girl," my mother said. "And her poor, poor mother."

When I play the scene now, I can still picture fat drops of pool water on the girl's thighs catching the sunlight on her skin like an ill-fitting sequin dress. She was indomitable. I see now how beautiful she was in that innocent determination. And then I realize something: My mom was wrong. So wrong. I wish I could go back and tell her how wrong she was. This girl was not to be pitied. She did not want our pity. Pitiable and determined are simply not companions.

> I wonder how many people I've looked
> at all my life and never seen.
>
> —JOHN STEINBECK,
> *THE WINTER OF OUR DISCONTENT*

Living

WHEN I WAS DIAGNOSED with MS, my life finally did markedly change. I became a kind of face for the disease. Just as Tyler Henry predicted, I am an advocate for something that matters to me. Though it's a role I never thought I would play, it has become who I am.

The community of people I've found, and who have found me, have comforted me. They see the real me and accept me as I am— weak, raw, humbled, dependent, free, honest, sensitive, scared, hopeful. The mean baby is still there, but her edges are softer, wiser, kinder.

I don't talk about MS as much as I craved someone talking about

MS when I was first diagnosed. Now I realize that the simple truth is I can't be a spokesperson for someone else when every person's experience is so unique. Joan Didion's MS is not my MS. As anyone who's had MS for long enough would tell me, "It'll be different for you." Our experience is ours alone, and I'll never know the extent of someone else's.

At the same time, I think it's important to talk about it. When it comes to chronic illnesses, there's a lot of shame in disclosing one's experiences. People judge. People dispute your symptoms. People say things can't be proven. Let me assure you, this stuff is real.

Living with MS is not as bad as I thought it would be. It's also way worse. My particular experience with this disease is that it has affected every inch of my body, from scalp to marrow.

If I stand up too quickly, I fall.

If I'm triggered by anything where I don't know the outcome, I can't speak.

I sweat through my clothes, but I'm freezing.

If I don't take my meds, I cannot feel my body. I don't know if I'm sopping wet or getting frostbite. Without my meds, I also lose the ability to speak.

When I'm in a flare, I sound like a tantrum-throwing toddler, distraught and gasping for breath. I sometimes choke when I eat. I am sometimes incontinent. Like. Enough!

The West Coast sun is impossible. The light is impossible. The weather is impossible. I no longer see all the way to the horizon.

There is no hanging out with my son and following the trajectory of our conversation. I will always be more disorganized and emotional than I want to be.

My gait will always be affected. I pay my toll in fatigue.

There is more—there's a lot more—that feels too complicated to share. In some ways, I'm doing amazingly well. I could dance for an hour if I wanted to! But the next day, I need a cane to get around. It's also hard to quantify, because it is ever-shifting. The shape of my experience changes from day to day, and conversation to conversation. It occupies a vast terrain between good and bad.

I don't have a lot of energy, and there are weeks when I sleep most of the day. That's a very common part of MS. But then I think, some people don't have the luxury of sleeping, and they have to get up and take their meds and go to their jobs and fight the fatigue.

Then there are times when the dog pees in the house, because I myself am busy trying to pee, but it takes too long for me to get there, and I wet my pants. I am one of the lucky ones. I will always have another pair of pants. I know this. I'm grateful for this.

I understand why people with MS spend a lot of time in their homes. Self-preservation. These small things add up. In my bedroom, on the floor that I'm used to, I can dance. But if I step off a curb wrong, I'm liable to injure myself.

When I announced my diagnosis, to the outside world it seemed as if "it hit so hard so fast." But they didn't see the constant fatigue or the years of inflammation or the signs that presented themselves all along. I'd gone through a lifetime of knowing. The only thing that changed was that I was given a name for it. I lived with so much self-hatred for so long. But now that I know what I've been living with—as best as we can determine, for at least twenty years—I can be gentler with myself. There is no "Why me?" anymore. There is just me.

This is part of my healing. I go easier. I try to be the best person I can be. I figure out small solutions to get by. I find moments of grace and I hold on to them.

On some level, MS is an adventure. It wasn't the one I wanted, but it was already there. So, I do my best to embrace it. Ironically,

I'm more comfortable in my skin now than I've ever been, even if my actual skin is uncomfortable. I love using my prop of a cane. I love my service dog. If I'm going to fall down, I want to look good while I'm doing it. I'm going to lean in. I'm going to embrace every perk I can, and I'm going to flaunt it.

In the end, I realize I'm just one of more than two million people on this earth who have MS. But I hope that because of my platform, I can do for others what Joan Didion did for me. I hope I can help erase the stigma attached to MS, bring increased awareness to those living with disabilities, and help people who are coping with chronic illnesses—or even just the painful experience of being human—to realize they are not alone.

Here's another realization I've come to as I write this book, now, at the age of forty-eight: every person on this earth needs just one person who sees them and roots for them. Deeply, truly. One person. It's what we all need to get through. The more the merrier, but let's start with one. Because of my illness, there are so many people I see now. And there are so many people who see me. But it wasn't always this way.

For years, I had a recurring nightmare that I was trapped in a burning house and couldn't get out. I'd wake up drenched in sweat, panicked and frightened. What I realize now is that the nightmare has become my reality: I'm trapped in a body that is often in rebellion against me. But I'm very much awake. I'm very present.

As Didion wrote, I've met the stranger with the knife. I've faced him head-on, but I still have the strength to push him aside and see all the good that exists behind him. I still have a chance to set my record straight.

I've always been a researcher, since I was a little girl. After I received my MS diagnosis, I had the chance to put that inclination to use. More than anything, getting the diagnosis was a wake-up call. *How can I continue to live?* It gave me a new outlook. Each time a challenge appeared, I would rise to meet it, instead of crawling under the bed. My diagnosis gave me a point of reference. It gave me tools.

Because I was diagnosed during a severe flare, I was able to begin a series of treatments to halt the progression of the disease. The onset of my worst symptoms was dramatic, so it made sense to me that the treatment needed to be similarly dramatic.

My sister Katie was the first one to mention HSCT—hematopoietic stem cell transplantation—as a possible therapy to slow the progression of my disease. I wasn't sure: the procedure was new and risky, and the idea of being immunosuppressed for several months while trying to raise a little boy struck me as foolhardy. But then, a few weeks later, again through the power of Instagram, the actress Jennifer Grey helped get this baby out of a corner. She messaged me about a friend whose own brother had undergone successful stem cell treatment at Northwestern and urged me to consider it.

Slowly, I warmed to the idea. The procedure appealed to me on two levels. Practically, it would use cells from my own blood, so I wouldn't need to match with a donor. And spiritually, it felt like the chance to reboot my whole system—to rid myself of all the darkness I carried in my genes and bring in more light. To be reborn.

In the spring of 2019, with my symptoms growing more severe and unmanageable by the day, I found out that I qualified for the program and that my insurance would cover the cost. I opted to move forward with it. I knew it was extreme, a Hail Mary pass. I knew there was a chance I wouldn't survive it. I knew it wasn't a cure. But if this treatment could improve my quality of life, and allow me to be here longer, for Arthur, then I decided it was worth it.

The treatment would quite literally suck the life out of me. Old cells purged. New cells from my own body pumped in.

I would spend two months in Chicago, followed by three weeks in isolation. I would need chemotherapy beforehand. It came with significant, terrifying risks, but on the other side was hope. I made a vow to focus on the hope.

In the days leading up to the procedure, I felt as if I were watching my funeral. All my Julies came out to Chicago to see me. My three sisters with their families. Jason. Troy. My lawyer, David. Bonny.

Arthur stayed by my side constantly, rolling around the city with me until I had to go into isolation. I was happy just to look at him. When he left for Los Angeles on July 9, I felt a sense of peace knowing that if something happened to me, he would be surrounded by so much love from all the people who had shown up for us. I knew that he would be safe.

I chose to do stem cell because I believed it would help me. It made sense to me at this point. It was the only treatment that offered rebirth. It was a sprint. My container was full. I had to take out the garbage, or the flies would still be there. I saw that I was where I was, my disease is progressing, and I'm not willing to go without a fight. If I fail, if I don't get to the end of the end, well, I tried. I wasn't scared. I was hopeful.

As plans were falling into place, I made another decision for which I'll be eternally grateful. One day, as Troy sat with me, I told him, "We need to shoot this. For Arthur. Plus, there are people like me who want to know about this." Cass Bird, who shot for *Vanity Fair,* introduced us to an extraordinary documentary filmmaker named Rachel Fleit, with whom I felt an immediate affinity, not least because one of her first films was a documentary short called *Gefilte,* about a Detroit family coming together to eat gefilte fish during Passover. It was *bashert*! I'd never pursued a starring role in anything, ever. A supporting role was my comfort zone. Playing the sidekick was who I was. But now I felt a calling. I wanted to do this for myself. I wanted to do this for Arthur. I wanted to do it for Troy, who stood by me through it all and always said I should have a one-woman show. I wanted to do this for everyone who suffers from physical pain, whether they know the label for it or not. I wanted to show the reality of life with chronic illness. I wanted to allow myself to be truly vulnerable.

When I was undergoing the process in my room, the film crew wasn't allowed inside, so I had to use my phone to capture footage. I was alone, with my blood whirring through the machines, receiving these gifts in the quiet wing of the hospital. It was during this time that I really looked at the unfinished puzzles in my life through new eyes. I thought of every snapshot I was ever shown. Riffled through every photo album in my mind. The rape in Florida that I never told anyone about. The Dean's hand tracing the small of my back while I froze, unable to run. All the wasted hours I spent looking into the bottom of a glass.

And then I brought in the happy images. I was determined to balance out the pain with joy. Heartbreak and beauty both. I summoned the sun-dappled beaches in Puerto Rico with my family where we could have ice cream from a cart. How my mom packed Christmas presents one year—an entire suitcase filled with gifts. All the charming people I had shared something with during my Hollywood life. All my friends. Bonny, who always made sure I got home. Arthur. Arthur telling people he loves boob soup. Arthur at the playground, running toward me. Bathing him in Julie's kitchen sink. Sometimes, she would take over with her strong, loving hands while I stood next to her and learned how to be a mother.

263

I promised myself that even lighting a candle would be appreciated after stem cell.

To have been so lucky.

Stem cell—and the diagnosis in general—were an extreme kind
of TED talk (for me) on growing up. And growing older. In real
time I felt and saw the generations I held in this body. I closed my
eyes and willed myself to let go of everything I held inside. To let
go of pain. To embrace a totally new life.

Bonny was at my side for the last couple of weeks and brought
me back to L.A. When we arrived at my house, I kissed Pippa, I
cried over my desk because I was still tired, and I knew a marathon
recovery awaited me. I was alone in the house with leaves filling
the pool. And then Arthur was there, Jason standing behind him. I

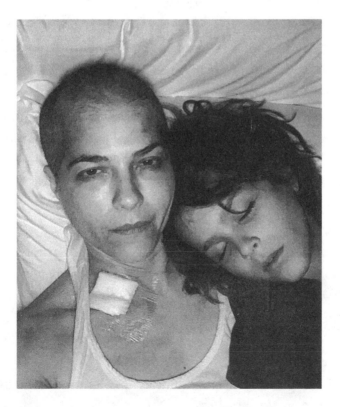

bent down to hug him, and I wrapped him in my arms and smelled him, and I was so grateful for that moment that I felt I could die happy.

Once I returned from Chicago, I felt worn down, weak, and vulnerable as my system worked to rebuild itself. Steroids coursed through my blood. My life became much smaller—occasional trips to the farmers market, visits from friends. It meant a lot of time at home, resting and healing, which my inner loner did not mind.

People called to see if they could stop by. They asked what they could bring for me, their offerings so L.A. I had to laugh. Celery juice? Acai bowls? Marijuana? "No, no, no," I answered, giggling. "Just bring logs." I'm sure they would've preferred celery juice. But it's logs I needed. Kindling for my fireplace.

I made a fire every day, no matter the weather. I tended it well. I curled up in front of it and watched the flames.

When you're quarantined, it feels as though there is nothing but time. Long, slow stretches of it. Time to confront the things you've been avoiding. Your consumerism. Your regrets. Your mistakes, dreams, desires. Everything gets clearer as the outside slips away. It's like being trapped at a casino in Las Vegas. Day? Night? Doesn't matter. The hours, days, weeks, bleed together.

I no longer felt tied to the mystery of death. We're all going to die. Not as a way to drama, but as a part of life. Before I accepted this fact as truth, I always felt either inspired or paralyzed. But now I feel as if I've exhausted it all. I want to be here now.

How can I continue to live?

I used to pray to the world, or to God or spirit or life force, whatever it is, that I would die knowing joy. Now I also wanted to live knowing joy.

This was going to be tough. But I was committed to trying.

By October 2019, my immune system was strong enough for me to get on a plane, so I went back to Cranbrook for homecoming weekend. In the weeks before that trip, I'd started feeling better. My new cells were agreeing with me. I could feel my body rebuilding itself, however shakily. But I was still struggling mightily with balance, my gait jerky and uneasy. As soon as I arrived on that campus, I was held in memories so strong it was as if I were turning my mind and body back in time. There was land, wide-open sky, no paparazzi. (The photographers do trip me up in Los Angeles. It's brutal when you are working through a challenge and you have cameras pointed in your face, recording your every slip and fall.)

It's the strangest thing. With MS, if I have new experiences, my body freezes. Each new eye line can cause a glitch in my brain. Demyelination of nerve fibers. I can't find the ground. I can't speak easily. I crave familiar terrain. Routine. But as I walked around that exquisite campus, I felt the support and freedom of my time at Cranbrook rushing back to me, lifting me up. I could transport myself. My body believed it was young again, without missing myelin sheaths.

I feel about Cranbrook the way a sports lover probably feels about a favorite team. Devoted, even when it fails me. Inspired, even when it disappoints me. I went walking into the same woods I'd journeyed through years before, with Chip. Once again, I went searching for the head of Zeus. As I made my way, I noticed I was really ambling along quite comfortably. For the first time in months, I hardly needed my cane.

That was when I knew, with total certainty, that the stem cell treatment was working. Later, my doctors would confirm that I was in remission.

After Cranbrook, I stopped in Plymouth to visit my mother, who had aged significantly since I'd last seen her. The cancer that she didn't know she had was taking a toll, and her mind was going. She didn't smoke anymore, but she still punctuated her sentences like Princess Anne with a cigarette, only now with a vape pen. Her nails were perfectly painted thanks to my sister Mimi, who took her for weekly manicures. She still had the same hacking cough she'd had since she was forty. She was in a wheelchair, tiny and frail. Perfectly dressed in Chanel ballet flats. Refined as always. This pleased me. I couldn't admit to anyone what was happening, but we all knew she was dying. But she didn't know. She wouldn't understand. As I was learning to understand my brain anew, she was losing hers.

She didn't recognize me at first. Maybe not at all. I was bald from the chemo, my face puffy from steroids. I used a cane. But

she didn't seem startled by my appearance or even my gait. Her wig was lopsided; mine was totally off. Nevertheless, she was in charge, regal. "Mom, it's me," I said. "It's Selma." I set my cane down and knelt beside her and took her hand. She said, "Selma, I saw the magazine," referring to the cover story about my MS journey in *People.* She looked around in her lap for the magazine, which was lying open on the table. (I do this, too. I'm always rummaging around for things that aren't there. Small things.) "It was good. It was good." She paused. And then I asked her for a kiss, and she gave it to me.

❧

I set other goals for myself after stem cell. To swim again. To break into a run again. To ride a horse again. My wonderful horse trainer, Kelly, is one of the biggest doctors I have right now. Four years ago, I confided in her that my dream was to become a successful amateur owner/rider. "I want to ride, I want to show, I want to be the best," I told her. At that point, I was pretty well established as an out-of-work actress, and by most measures buying a horse was not a good move. But I told myself, when I get down, I'm not going to drink; I'm going to go riding. This would help keep me together. This was an investment in myself.

The barn is out in Calabasas, in the Santa Monica Mountains, and whenever I go there, it brings back the feelings I had when I first came to California. I'm bowled over by the scenery, by the mountains and the air and the sky. I get caught up in the thrill of being in such a beautiful place, doing something I never thought I could.

There was a time when I felt as if I owed my life to horses. It was during that high point that I started to notice how broken my body was. I was doing something I loved, that brought me so much joy. Normally I could push through the fatigue, but I was passing out after every ride. When we went over fences and my horse took it a little long, the jarring action of his athleticism only amplified my deteriorating state. My neck would pinch. "Get into your hips," Kelly would say. And I'd say, "Where are my hips?" I truly didn't know. Once upon a time I was able to do a perfect backflip without a second thought. Now I couldn't get into my own hips. I blamed myself. Getting old is hard, I thought. You get older, and suddenly you can't feel your left leg.

I'm back in the saddle and that's a start. I don't have a lot of endurance to ride, but there is still nowhere else I'd rather be. Even though I'm not shiny, even though the fences I jump are more of a tiny crossrail.

I will ride in a show again; I'm not giving up on that dream. One day, I will wear a shadbelly coat, and I will win at least one class at the Thermal equestrian show. If I can manage to "relax" in my own way, if I can learn how to just feel him, the horse knows what to do. He'll take care of the going.

Memory

I have short-term memory loss. It's unclear whether it's caused by the MS itself or if it's a side effect from stem cell. I suspect a combination of the two. In practice, it means I can't always remember what I said ten minutes ago or what I ate for breakfast. But I have intricate, precise, and revealing thoughts.

My long-term memories are vivid, a high-def screen that plays inside my head. I sift through the images, as if searching for prisms of light. Pathways of glimmering, flickering candles guide my way as I work through my past.

I have no ability to organize. I can only choose one memory at a time, turning it over and over in my mind, like a stick of Juicy Fruit. I work on it until the flavor is gone. It never lasts as long as I hope. I do this over and over again, memory after memory, refreshing the old and dulling the new.

Focus is now my main problem. My brain is fatigued from the simple tasks I ask my body to perform: Getting out of bed. Making coffee. Brushing my teeth. Even just walking to my closet.

I stare at the rows of Chanel heels, the Isabel Marant sandals that are too complicated to fasten. Every movement I make now requires herculean effort. It takes so much out of me that my mouth is left unable to form words. Only grunts emerge. Twisted and spastic, I smile big to convey that I am okay. I smile so much these days.

～

On good days, I have a deal with my new brain. "Okay," I tell my brain. "Since you now seem intent on dissolving all my recent memories into particles of dust, how about this? I will give you a few irritating older ones to throw in the pyre." And so, we agree, my addled brain and me. We shake on it. I start tossing out unpleasant, needless memories like yellowed bills from 2001. The Winnie-the-Pooh cake topper goes into the fire, the colors melting into swirls of orange and red like an abstract painting.

For a while it works this way. I am fascinated! I summon a time I felt hurt or sad or betrayed, take a mental picture of it, and away it goes. I get cocky and toss in a random doozy of a memory. I can't even decide if it's gloomy or not. And poof! Fizzle fizzle, it's gone.

And then, suddenly, an image floats up, unbidden: Arthur as a toddler appears in the frame. He's at the beach in Santa Monica, waddling in and out of the waves, bending down to splash the water. He's at the playground, running up to me, play slapping me before he falls into my arms and collapses into me. Wait a minute, I say. Now wait just a minute. Arthur is not part of this game. This is a mistake. A terrible trade. Please, please give me back this one. I don't want to spare a single memory of my time with my son. I scream this in my head, as if I were yelling to an imaginary friend. But I can't control it. In my mind the image of a fire appears even though I try to resist it. I watch, helpless, as this photo gets tossed into the flames. I jump in to try to save it, but I'm too late, it's already gone.

I must be careful. Very careful. No more trades. Pain and joy together.

⁓

One night, I am alone in my house. I'm sitting near the fire, and it's heating my right side, my good side. I have a yellow legal pad next to me, and a black ballpoint pen. I have become my mother, always a yellow legal pad by her side. I am channeling Carrie, who wrote in bed. My head aches. I can't think. Black hole. Black sky. Maybe if I stay here, the fire warming my cheeks and my limbs, I won't start the chain reaction of pain. Maybe I can just *be* for a while. Curled into a woman ball, I wait for it to get dark. The flames make loud, satisfying pops and the wind chime sways and sings. I imagine my dog, Pippa, is already waiting for me under the covers in the spot on my bed where I usually sleep. I know I won't move for hours.

I think of my mother again. Every day, I think of her. I imagine her, at that same moment, across the country on a chair in her parlor in Plymouth, Michigan, an aide sitting nearby and with my oldest sister, Mimi, as her caretaker and only regular visitor. My mother. Her mind is going; she's sick. I picture her crying because she can't get home. "I missed the bus again," she moans to someone she can't see. She says this frequently. There is no bus. She is already home. She's not going anywhere. She almost never leaves the house anymore. Neither of us does.

I am so sorry I can't help you, Mom. I say this out loud into the dark. The sun is setting here in Los Angeles with its orange good night. I could go out now into the gloaming, with the sun beginning to sink into the earth. This is my golden hour. It's the daytime that is treacherous for me. The glare of the California sun is decimating to me and my condition. Another way to describe this feeling of disorientation: it's the physical equivalent of a tongue twister. Sally sells seashells by the seashore. That's the sensation. I try to breathe. The wind chimes are saying something.

I have to pee. I really, really have to pee. I'm not ready to get up yet, to shoulder the pain in my neck, the pain in my legs, my feet. I can't seem to care that I will wet the floor where I dropped myself when my son left. I am safe because he won't see this. I let it come, like a puppy marking her turf. I'll clean it up before he returns in the morning. I've given up on dignity. The only dignity I have left is to be kind. Kind to myself. Kind to others. The puddle sits on the floor. Another secret my house will keep. Well, until now.

❦

My mother always said, "When in doubt, get in the water." When I'm not sitting by the fire or watching Arthur swim in the pool, I'm in the bath. There are days when I'll bathe five times. It's the only place where my muscles don't spasm. It's the only place where I can lower my head, relax my breath, and hold time without interruption. I submerge myself and feel cool and young, permanent and formless.

My mother took a bath every day. Strangely, she liked to see proof that her tub was cleaned every week, so she always asked the housekeeper to leave a trail of Ajax at the bottom. I wondered if she bathed in the Ajax or simply liked the smell? Or did she just like to watch it run through the drain? I'll never know.

She once told me she was afraid of dying in the bath. This was particularly true during thunderstorms. Her tub was situated in a small bathroom near a window, framed by the lower boughs of elm trees. In her mind, the location practically invited a lightning strike. Sometimes she had me wait outside the room for her, my ear pressed to the door. I go back to this again and again. What a big job I had. If the water stopped swishing and I called to her and there was no answer, I would need to break down the door, get her dressed, put on her makeup, take off her turban, and fix her hair. All the things she never let me witness her do, but that I knew how to do all the same. I'd studied and prepared, whether she knew it or not.

I don't know who was waiting to save the other.

Later, when she was in a wheelchair with her hairdo on sideways, she would talk about her father, wailing and crying about how much she needed him. By this point I no longer knew if she took baths. Did an aide, or perhaps a nurse, give her one? She would have hated that. I wonder if she ever called out for me, the interloper, the last child she didn't want but learned to love. I was always waiting outside the bathroom door. That is my life: anticipating the lightning.

After losing my hair to chemo, my new mane grows in thick and gray, like a salt-and-pepper schnauzer. For a while, I shaved it, but now I think it's going to seriously protect my head. From me.

One day, I find myself reaching under the railing on the stairs to retrieve Pippa's damn pink-and-yellow fetch-until-you-trim-your-claws-to-nubs ball. Easy. But then I forget where I am and jolt to stand up. Impatient, quick, putting all my strength into a thrust up. Cracking into the oak rail. Fuck-shit-fuck-shit. I must be missing my spatial awareness more than I gathered.

I hold my head together as if it might split open. The pain causes drool to fall from my mouth, down onto the plaid runner. I am cracked open like a Babe Ruth fielder. Sparks. Wailing. Laughing. Fire behind my eyes. I don't feel the blood on my good right hand as I cradle my skull, which I had imagined as lambskin, like a football.

Wow. Turns out, I am actually okay. Not concussed, no stitches needed. I am whacked but I am fine. The lump on my head is five inches long and feels tender for days.

Still, I don't learn. I do this same thing all the time, sometimes six times a day. Like a Bugs Bunny cartoon on repeat. Major short-term memory loss causes bumps and bruises. I can see why people with MS are tempted to stay in bed, indefinitely.

Me? I won't, of course. I need to keep going. It's rooted in who I am.

Selma means battlefield.

Blair means Helmet of God.

I've been geared for battle my whole life. But I make a note to look into buying a helmet.

One day, I kept hearing parts of a concerto, the swell of violins and a piano. It was really lovely, but I couldn't tell where it was coming from. I searched everywhere. I kept checking my phone, but it was off. I got in my car and there it was again. I put the radio on and turned the dial up to high, until it drowned out the sound of the violins.

When I stopped the car, there it was again. That's when I realized the music was playing inside my ear. As it turns out, I have symphonic tinnitus, which is like a mellifluous version of ringing in the ears. Practically, this means that sometimes music plays inside my head.

Historically, I'm not a musical person, so this was exciting! How mind-blowing that at age forty-eight I finally had a musical ear.

When I got home, I listened to my ears for an hour. I tried to record it, because I wanted to remember. *Am I becoming Mozart?* I wondered. But the melody was pretty simple. I am an amateur musician at best.

I wrote a text to one of my best friends that said, "I can hear music! In my ear! It's really pleasant! I'm not worried."

"That sounds incredible!" she replied.

I wanted to tell my mom. I wanted to call her and say, "I have a song in my head, and I think I wrote it!" I'm finally composing the songs she told me to write in childhood. But I can't tell her.

I wish what I heard instead was her voice as she opened the basement door and called, "Selma! Dinner!"

Every night, when I say, "Arthur! Dinner!" I think of her.

The Moth

Mother's day, May 2020.

All day, I thought, *I need to call my mother.* But I never did.

We were well into COVID by then, accustomed to isolation. It had been two months of this. Days bled into days. I was in bed that week and felt nervous that if I called, she wouldn't know who I was. My sisters and I had been texting continuously about our mother's rapidly declining health. She was suffering and afraid; her mind was foggier than mine. It was as if our bodies were mirrors of each other. I didn't want to face what was happening to her.

For most of my adult life, I called her once a week. Even when I was younger, when her mind was all there, she would say, "Selma, you're boring me," and hang up. She had no tolerance for a shaggy-dog tale. You had to make her laugh and get out.

These days, she would trail off. She would go on tangents, talking about the baby in the next room, even though she knew I was no longer a baby. I was embarrassed on her behalf. I couldn't bear to witness her no longer being feared. And so I stayed away.

Arthur decided to go for a swim at sunset. I sat on a child's chaise near the deep end, holding Carrie's rock. Again, I thought, *It's Mother's Day. I should call my mother,* when, suddenly, a moth alighted on the stone in my hand. I have a mortal fear of moths. It was huge—bigger than a sparrow—with swirls of gray and brown and fuchsia covering its pretty wings. It looked almost like a Proenza Schouler print, or a blazer from the late 1970s. Two velvety black patches colored either side of its body, like a suede vest. It was both beautiful and terrifying, breathtaking and strange. I felt a moment of knowing, as though I had seen it in a dream.

Immediately, I thought of my closest dead loved one, Carrie. In my fortune-teller mind, where all the dots always connect to make up a story, I *knew* this moth was Carrie. It must be a sign. Perhaps she was trying to send me a message.

"Who are you?" I said to the moth. "And how lovely of you to come here so impeccably dressed!"

Later that night, I googled moths and discovered that this particular species, the sphinx moth, lives for only about a month or so. They're rarely found in Los Angeles and eat grape leaves. Ah, but of course. This moth was here to feast on the vines I'd planted and then die. Why else would it grace me with its presence? I invite death and loss like a magnet.

Maybe, I thought, my mind drifting again to Carrie, *this is my chance to say goodbye.*

The next day, I went out to the pool to discover that, improbably, the moth was still there. Still perched on Carrie's rock. I was so fascinated to see that it hung around that I went right up and touched it.

(My mother hated moths. They attacked our Burberry jackets and our Talbots blazers, ate our designer rugs. Like so many things handed down from her, I inherited this grudge.)

The moth kept me company, sleeping beside me all day. As I wrote on my legal pad, the moth tried to fly, but it was so weak it could only flutter its wings without ever leaving its perch. Its wingspan was huge—a flow of energy radiating from its epicenter. It took my breath away.

Day after day, the moth remained. It stayed with me, near me, sometimes even fluttering inside at night. We went for a swim together, the moth perched on my wrist. It fluttered up onto my shirt. Arthur and Bonny kept watch over it. "Wow," Bonny said. "It's been a week." The moth stayed, but as the days went by, I

couldn't help but notice it was getting smaller. I worried it was withering and would soon disappear.

A week later, on Memorial Day, my boyfriend came to my house. We sat outside, the moth still on its rock beside me. "That's crazy! How is that the same moth?" He put his hand out and the moth went to it, landing nimbly on his finger. It was fat with life. And then the moth flapped its wings and began to fly. It flew into the woods and was gone with such energy it left me speechless. And that's when I realized: It wasn't dying. It had only just been born.

The intensity of my error shocked me.

I clapped my hands with delight, like my mother whenever she thought I looked beautiful. "Brava, brava, brava!" Off it flew, into the woods, so high and so fast, off to greet its life.

After we bade the moth farewell, I went inside for my morning meditation, a COVID-inspired ritual. I had just settled in and closed my eyes when the phone rang. I glanced over and saw my sister Mimi's name, but I didn't answer.

When I was done, I listened to her message. Her voice sounded tight, as if she'd been crying. I replayed her message again. And again. And again. Until, at last, I understood.

My mother was gone.

When I was little and realized my mom would one day be dead, I cried into my worn pillowcase. I held the weight of it so tightly that I didn't sleep for weeks. I carried it with me, the truth of it too heavy to bear but too prescient to put down.

My whole life, I had been braced for it. And now it had happened.

My mother died.

My mother is gone.

We knew it was coming. And yet. And yet. When her firstborn, Mimi, called me, I knew. Her voice was composed as she said the words. She'd been my mother's only visitor during the pandemic. We shared group texts and FaceTimes. The last time we talked, Arthur had danced around adorably, alight with mischief. We all laughed, including my mom. I knew the next call would likely be the one to say she was dying. I didn't know it would be to say she was already gone.

I sobbed into the phone. Mimi asked if I needed to be alone. "Yes," I said. "Yes, thank you."

I wrote my mom a letter, the words flowing from pain. I begged her to come back and take care of me. I got out her crochet sweater and wrapped it around me. I closed my eyes and pictured her wearing it, back when I was a little girl. She looked like some kind of enchantress.

My sister Katie sent a picture of her. She doesn't have a stitch of makeup on. Her hairline is dotted with fine, silver strands. She looks both young and ancient. Pure. Her hands are elegant and thin. I put the picture away and wrap myself up in her warmth.

My mom's feet were beautiful to the end. Very bony, long, and pretty. She always took good care of them and they never aged. When she died, her toenails were painted red. This gives me some small amount of comfort.

⌒

We can't have a funeral or even a memorial service for now because of the virus. But my mom is not buried in the dirt, suffocating and cold. She is in a sprinkling vase on top of her hutch, waiting for us, her four girls, to reunite after the pandemic so we can put her back in the earth. (My mother would *hate* this urn. Black with gladiolus—she never had gladiolus.)

In the meantime, Mimi sends me things of hers, boxes and boxes of my mother's belongings. Unboxing Mom, I call it. Mimi is so sentimental that, left to her own devices, she wouldn't get rid of a single thing. So, I let her pay to ship it all to California, where I can be the one who decides what to send off to Goodwill.

I sit with my mother's possessions, unsure. What do I do with her dolls? Do I bury Skinny and Checkers? As soon as I see them, run my fingers across their filmy rag doll faces, I know that I can't.

For months, I comb through piles of my mother's precious shit. All of it is old. All of it smells like cigarettes and mothballs and a hint of Opium. Some boxes are a thrill, like the one with the turban from her second wedding. Others are just horrific.

This is our inheritance.

The truth is, I never dreamed of an Oscar. I've never given the pretend speech to the mirror, never even imagined it. That wasn't my thing. The lock of my mom's hair from her childhood—too precious for me to even open the envelope—that is what I treasure.

❧

I talk to my mother. Casually, as if she will answer me.

"Will you give it a rest, Selma?" I hear her say. Or, "How did you learn to be so funny, Selma?"

I miss her. I call her every day. Her answering machine is still set up, and I leave her messages.

A phrase I once read plays on a loop: grief is love you can no longer express.

I light cigarette after cigarette, hoping they will lead me to her.

Sometimes, I put on all her things so she can find me easily.

I love the way I sound like her sometimes. When I really cackle, I can hear her.

"Good night, Mom," I whisper every night. May all our dreams come true. Even the ones we haven't dreamed yet.

Arthur

I'M TRYING TO BREAK the cycle, but I'm facing a challenge. Arthur can be a mean baby!

It's true!

As an infant and later as a toddler, Arthur was not one to dole out a smile.

When he was about two, we went to a birthday party thrown by Rachel Zoe for her older son, who is Arthur's age. At one point, Jason Bateman came up to us with a big grin on his face and said, "Hey! Arthur!" Oh, the look Arthur gave him. As Jason so succinctly put it, "It just went dark." His words so perfectly encapsulated what I hadn't been able to describe. Then it hit me: what I observe in my son every day is exactly what people must have thought about me.

CRUD

At home, Arthur chases me around the house, attacking me with his Nerf gun until I spasm out. His constant assault of foam weaponry leaves me contorted and moaning, my posture rigid as I melt into the white wood floor.

My child sees me flopping around like a dying fish and keeps shooting, laughing. I grunt. Try to yell at him. But it's horrific. I get more rigid and weak. I drop. The demon child keeps pelting me. It stings now. My brain clutches. I'm furious.

And then I laugh. I laugh and howl and let go of the rage. I crawl to him and we laugh and smush and kiss. My body relaxes. He hugs and clings and punches gently, all over my body.

Eventually, I learn to set boundaries. The rule is, when I say, "Arthur, stop," he has to stop. Immediately. He understands that I am his playmate, but I am still, and most important, his mother. I may be fragile, but I am still in charge. Even if circumstances provide detours along the way.

Recently, for the first time in his life, I showed him one of my movies. On-screen, my character was smoking and drinking, looking weird and young and beautiful, and all he wanted to know was, "Is that *real* alcohol?"

"What do you think?" I asked him. "Do I look the same?"

"Yeah, on opposite day!" he yelled, pointing at the screen. "Because that girl is pretty, and you look nothing like her!" He roared with laughter. Before I had a chance to respond, he was already out of the room, grabbing his Nerf gun to shoot me with.

Jason tells me he did these things with his mom, whom he loves to no end. Luckily, Jason and I now have the best co-parenting relationship. It took a while to figure out—in the early days, letting my baby go for visitation was crippling to me—but now we are a proper family. For many reasons, I am glad that Jason is my father's son. Since both Jason and Arthur are babies, both wonderful boys that their mothers love, they're going to need each other. Honestly, I don't know who the hell is ever going to love them the way we do.

My favorite time is when Arthur is sleeping, and I can listen to him breathing. When he's asleep, I can pretend he's nice to me all the time. I spoon him. Sometimes he lets me; sometimes he pushes me away. But he has told me he loves me more than anything in the world, and that's going to have to do.

After all, mean babies like us have to stick together.

I am well aware that I am creating a horrible husband. I have made the person that I hope to never marry. For starters, I love carrying my son.

When Arthur was a toddler, he would yell, "I can't walk!"

"You *can* walk," I would say. "But if you want me to carry you, I will." And he would reply that yes, he wanted me to carry him.

"Mom! I want you to carry me to the bathroom!" he yells from his room. Because he is nine, many would argue that he is far too old to be carried. But I still carry him to the bathroom at night, practically dropping him along the way. But it benefits us both.

I find the only time I can walk, and walk well, without huge focus is when I'm holding Arthur. I have bad proprioception, from frontal cortex damage due to MS. But carrying my son always helps me to know where my body is in space. As soon as I drop him, I'm lost, which is both confounding and pretty tragic, because he's nine, and I'm forty-eight, and it's time to move on.

"God help me, un-koala yourself," I'll say, though I don't fully mean it.

I remember my own mom carrying me once in my whole life. It was such an anomaly that I wrote a poem about it. "Wow, my mom is strong enough to lift me," I thought. I truly had no idea. I knew she had other strengths, the kind involving high heels and going to work, but this one left me amazed.

Jason's mother, on the other hand, carried him all the time. This is how "horrible husbands" are made. Jason's mom is an angel woman (as I am now, ha), but in my book she was also a husband ruiner, and I once called to tell her so!

A bit of background: Arthur was a baby, and Jason and I were mid-breakup. We were walking together with the stroller, arguing about something that shouldn't have been such a huge deal, but custody and fear and fatigue and anxiety threw up their signs, and

I grabbed the stroller away from him and screamed, striking out at him, screeching in alarm and fear and stress that he didn't know anything.

I wasn't trying to hurt him, really. I was scared witless. It was the kind of episode where, if my friend recounted the story to me, I would have said, "It sounds like you had a bad day. Why don't you guys go take a breath, take some time apart." Instead, Jason called the police.

Holy shit, I thought, *I am dealing with a crazy person.*

"I've just been attacked," he said into the phone.

Meanwhile, I'm saying over and over again, "I didn't attack you, I didn't attack you, I didn't attack you."

In the end, he didn't file a complaint, because I was the mother of his child and because he wasn't at all hurt. But the whole ordeal served to cement that we were better off apart.

Later that day, I called his mother. I stood in my backyard, in tears, and said, "This is your fault. You raised your son to get everything he ever wanted. He's done this sort of thing to you for a million years, but I can't do the same to him, because you enabled this man-child!" That's how I felt. She was sad this was happening. I was on the brink of real self-harm, terrified Arthur would be taken from me.

I have since forgiven her (and she me—she is the sweetest person and the most loving, doting grandmother in the world), because I realize how hard it is to be the mom of a boy. I realize how hard it is to be a mother, in general.

I know that one day I might get a phone call similar to the one I gave Jason's mother. I won't be surprised. I am a husband ruiner, guilty as charged. But in my defense, Arthur does know how to cook. He does understand that women need naps. And I hear that outside the house he's very empathetic and wonderful. And Jason likes me well enough now. Besides the husband ruiner bit. And it's not even true anymore. Time heals.

Portland

AFTER I GOT SOBER, I went to Portland.

A group of us drove up to visit a psychic. A caravan of seekers, all in search of answers. We were nervous, anticipating. We acted as if it were a big deal. The psychic was pretty wardrobed up, but in practice she turned out to be terrible. Of all the working intuitives I've met in my time, she was the quickest to grab a buck, the quickest to say I was full of doom. I still took the bait for a while, gave her a couple phone calls on the credit card, because she picked up on my sadness. My vulnerability was palpable. You don't realize how much you're in it until you're not. Until you decide to change the story yourself.

❦

When you're a seeker, what you're really looking for is someone who speaks your language. You never give up hope of finding true connection. It's a little like hunting for a Birkin bag at an estate sale. There's always that glimmer of possibility. In a world full of fakes, maybe you'll find a *real* person who can give you the answer you've been after. Maybe you'll hear something that finally resonates. Maybe you'll stumble across the truth.

Here is what I've learned: you can make anything real.

I used to go looking for answers. I used to crave a warning, a map, a how-to manual, the secret code to hold myself together. I sought protection, largely from myself. I wanted permission to allow someone else to love me.

But this is new territory. In a way, MS has cured me. I've gotten enough advice from doctors to last me a lifetime. If a crystal ball fell in my lap, I would still gaze into it. I would listen to what it had to say. But now I take everything people tell me with a grain of salt. I no longer feel as if there were anyone who knows more than I do.

(I can be my own fortune-teller. Ready? I'm going to be the world's oldest supermodel.)

The truth is, I'm due for a visit to a psychic. But if I saw one today, what would I want to hear? I don't have the same fears I once did. I don't seek the same answers.

I want someone to tell me that my son is going to have a happy life. That I'm going to be okay. That I won't be a burden. That I'll see my loved ones again. I don't know that anyone else can tell me that. Or any of us.

⁓

Every night before bed, I get on my knees and pray. "What can I do," I ask, "for me, for my son, for other people?" (I've gotten a little lofty as I've gotten older.) Then I wait, listening for the answer.

The older I get, the more I see how interconnected things are. I think there must be something larger at play, that we exist to fulfill some teaching or some destiny. Otherwise, I can't explain the inexplicable love you feel for some people, or our inherent need for connection. It makes it better to think there are signs along the way. It feels more powerful if a message comes through. If something brings you comfort, I say, all the better for it.

There were times when I had to believe in fairy dust. Sometimes, I still do. I want to believe in magic, because I want to maintain there's more to it than *we're born, then we love, then we die*. But I also believe we make our fate. We can get in line and create a stronger story for ourselves. We can write it however we want. That is the wonderful, realistic part of magic.

I can't profess to understand the mysteries of the universe. All I know is that I desperately love a story. We all have one; I carry mine inside me. You carry yours inside you. I can hear mine now, in my own voice. Strong and clear. All it took was to stop listening to the stories everyone else told about me. I hope this helps you, too.

Dear Arthur

THIS BOOK IS DEDICATED to you and to my mother. But really, it's for you. Everything I do, even waking up, is all for you. I have loved it all—in its glorious, horrible, life-adjusting chiropractic-nightmare type of way.

You have heard all of this before, I know. But bear with me for just a little longer.

I am telling the old stories because I am learning a new way of living while we spend our time together on earth. I am undoing certain patterns of behavior. I am changing what I can.

Right now, I save the light I have to laugh with you. To feel the whole day and night with you. I will be with you as long as you need or want me to.

The other day, I watched you do a full flip in the pool, and I widened my bleak eyes in shock. *When did you get so brave?* I wanted to ask. The transformation was imperceptible. I missed the shift, and then you went and did it even as I was starting to say, "Hey, that might not be safe!"

You did it. And you survived it.

You you you. I have oceans of love for you, my baby boy. My eyes don't just light up when you walk into the room; they pool up when you leave that room in tatters. My God! You have a way of making it all seem wrecked in the most gorgeous way I could ever imagine. And you always help me tidy.

Always help to tidy up the messes, okay? We all make them. It's okay. Just clean up when you can. We have to help each other.

I hope you'll experience real joy. That you'll choose kindness over any alternative. That you'll surround yourself with people who see you for who you are. That you won't feel trapped, as I did. That you'll see people who might otherwise be invisible to the world. People who are broken, lonely, or sick. People who need someone to root for them.

Thank you for being someone who sees me.

I also want you to know that my disease is not a tragedy. Please don't forget this. For as long as I am here, I promise to live in a way that is an example for you and for myself. Because this is it. The only life we get. Let's make the most of it.

As for me, I will continue to be me for as long as that's possible. I will continue to love a good gown, or a suit, from Christian Siriano or Chanel. I will put in my mother's emerald earrings and show up. I will smile, but with my mouth closed. (My teeth, I feel, tell a story I am done telling. So I keep them hidden. I will explain this to you.)

I will always be happiest by a fire.

I will remember those I've loved and lost. Bradley, Chip, Jason, Jason, Jason. Ahmet. Ingrid. I will remember Carrie. I will yearn for my mother.

I will tend my wounds.

You are asleep in your room now. Happy, safe. I tucked you in. I watched you fall asleep. I laid out your school clothes and turned off the light.

Anchored,
Mother

Acknowledgments

I would very much like to acknowledge and thank my mother for allowing me to write anything about her. That's a lie. She's dead. But she was the first one to tell me I should write a book. I was seven. So I hope she understands how self-centered one's own stories can be. We could be a bit hard on each other. I'm sorry and miss having her here on earth so much it makes my teeth hurt. And, Wink, the three of us will meet again in the next imaginings. I like to picture our small pack walking together, contentedly in the shade, Wink chasing ducks along the shore.

To Elliot Sir, Daddy Sir! Thank you for some big-ticket school years. I wish you hadn't traded me in for lies. I wish it hadn't hurt us both so much. I hate hurt. Thank you for being the one to carry me on the escalator. I was really scared.

To my sisters, Mimi, Katie, and Lizzie. Thank you for supporting me in everything I do. KK, yes. *You* have been the most encouraging of my writing a book. Noted. With love. Rooting around in your room growing up, reading the candy section in *All in the Family* books, planning our trip to Sydney Bogg—with a whole dollar each!—or trading rainbow Spencers Gifts clear stickers on a short winter day, while Mom told you to "turn down the Victrola," are some of my most comforting memories. Now we are both published authors in the same book! Arthur and I love you very much.

Mimi, the best big sister with the shimmery pink lipstick I couldn't wait to apply every Saturday night between *Dance Fever* and *The Love Boat*. You are always so much fun and your summer visits with Jim meant the world to us and your care of Mom did, too.

Lizzie, my person. I know how you hate these group texts, so please just know I love you and can't wait for us to cuddle and play like puppies again soon.

Aunt Sally, for the love and attention and stories. Strangest thing to have become my mother but still have Little Blair with me now. Thanks for giving me acknowledgment all these years. Oceans. Arthur James Rubiner, you are wicked with a line. Beloved by all of us, even Molly. How she appreciated your Selma for turning her out so chicly, when her shithead husband left her and Mimi in Detroit. I love you, Uncle Jimmy, and all the cousins, Joey, Meg, Julia, and Matthew.

Jason Bleick. I love you. I love Arthur more. I know you feel the same.

Troy Nankin. We have been through almost all of it in our adult lives together. I can't wait to share the rest of it with you. What you did with *Introducing, Selma Blair* was the greatest gift. I thank you. I also thank you for rarely mentioning my neck and the pull of gravity in menopause. It's brutal for a team who admires the great beauty makers. You know where to find them, so we still have a few golden years left. I will always keep your mother's pendant of you with me. You are my partner and my family here, and I love you forever. Even when pulling over to rest and complain on the never-ending drive from Mary Vernieu's office. And thank you for the girls you love. For example:

Krista Smith, the most brilliant and solid woman in any room. Thank you for being my Dear Margot, my confidante and mentor, actually. Troy and I affectionately and solemnly recognize you as Mother. We defer. You have literally and metaphorically driven us to home and safety. A couple years out of college and new in town, meeting with you for that Vanities piece was potentially terrifying. I wore a Loro Piana black cashmere coat while you had on Chanel heels I admired. We sat in the burgundy-and-gold glow of the Four Seasons and became forever friends. Do not ever die. Or before me at least. Thanks.

Parker Posey! My word! You are as divine as everyone hopes. The support and love and friendship you have given me in this often brutal but incredible life is a major highlight. You are an amazing icon and I loved all our times together. I still have the journal where I glued a cutting of you from a *Fashion* magazine next to a list of seventy-nine auditions I had gone on with only two small jobs to show for them. I was a hostess with blisters on my feet, a student, and a salesgirl at the Gap, living in the Salvation Army when I discovered you on-screen. You take my breath away, and sentimental me can't believe legendary you is on my side on this earth. I am forever on yours and am hoping for a big-time *Columbo*-style show together in any event.

Mary-Louise Parker who over the years has been the incredible same-same sister I have looked to for light when the roads turned and grew over. Thank you for being the first to read this book and giving me your brilliant insight. Dazzling you.

Nothing would have kept *Mean Baby* moving without the love, support, encouragement, patience, and unbelievable care of my angel, Brettne Bloom. Nobody else could have accepted late-night text notes of lyrics to "November Rain" when I was crushed by remembering young love lost. Thank you for seeing silver linings in the hundreds of scraps of my heart. Some indecipherable, some just *chazerai,* and some simple truths I would not have found without your enduring belief in the value of our stories. I know how lucky I am to be embraced by the women of The Book Group. Julie Barer, your support and presence have been invaluable. Thank you for being another Julie in my life.

My editor, Jenny Jackson. You are a godsend and I am so proud to be with you and Knopf on this first leg of my journey, on this second act of my life. A dream come true. Thank you. Stories ahead! God willing. I can't wait to find them and write them under your eye. Since the day I warbled out "Big Spender" in Sonny's office, I was so grateful to have found my home with you. I'm also grateful to the entire team at Knopf for giving this mean baby a place on the shelf, most especially: the late, great Sonny Mehta. Reagan Arthur, Paul Bogaards, Jess Purcell, Sara Eagle, Maris Dyer, Nicole Pedersen, Anna Knighton, Janet Hansen, Erinn Hartman, I'm so grateful to all of you.

Caroline Cala Donofrio, your hours of attention and work on this book are so deeply appreciated. Your knowing and soul, I appreciate even more. Thank you for everything.

Hylda Queally. The strength and serenity of spirit you have given me by the power of your presence in my life has me thanking my lucky stars. I welcome this era of our days and hold it highest. Thank you, your Grace.

Kevin Huvane. From dinners with Ruthie and Weber twenty years ago, to graciously paying our bill when Ahmet and I took a stroll to dinner sans wallets, you covered it! To embracing me now as warmly as always. I kiss the ring with wholehearted thanks and love.

Berni Barta, Andrea Weintraub, Donovan Tatum, and my team

at CAA. I am honored to be on this leg of the journey with you all. Thank you so much.

Megan Moss Pachon. The perennially fresh-faced, wholesome beauty I first worked with almost twenty years ago is also the most capable, clear, protective, wise, efficient, incredible, and irreplaceable ally and publicist. Thank you for always being here and there. And Sloane Kessler who is remarkable and beloved. Thank you for making sure every *i* is dotted—metaphorically.

Elena Hansen. I thank whatever algorithm has put you in our lives. I would like to be like you when I grow up. You are great. Thank you. And Swim Social.

Bonny Burke, whom I believe angels sent to that funny set for me on a rainy winter morning. Oh, and you stayed and moved to L.A. to take care of us to help love me—and I fell in love with wonderful you. I am forever your family too and am convinced your path will be glorious. Karma owes you only the best. Now come back!! As if, rockstar.

Julie De Santo. How could I know you would become the foundation of my life? How could I know you merely thought Karl Lagerfeld looked familiar when you popped over with the girls as he stood before you? How could I know your love and faith would heal me? Please keep me forever. I couldn't love you more. And to you, Anna, Elena, Daniel, and Luca. Thank You. Understatement.

Ben Gaynor. Thank you for picking up the duties of the best older brother to King Arthur and for being my Boy Friday. If that can be a thing. You are a top mensch and I am so grateful for you.

Our entire documentary family: Mickey Liddell, Pete Shilaimon, and Troy again. Rachel Fleit, I hope this is just our first bird. Bird by bird. Cass Bird! Oh my! The miracle of Cass Bird joining up these birds. I love you both forever. And there are birds galore for us. See you tomorrow, Fleit, alopecia kisses and oceans of love.

Shane Sigler, Sloane Klevin, and Raphaelle Thibaut, who made the most extraordinary and heartbreaking soundtrack to my life. Igal Svet, for making sure everyone heard it.

Billie Lourd, we all loved your mom, and she loved you with all of her. Big love.

Sarah Michelle Gellar, you have been taking care of me since the day we met, feeding me from the get-go and showing me the ropes. I'm so happy the only real on-screen kiss of my career was with you, the great SMG! And to think Cecile and Kathryn have stood the test of time. I love who you are and how you live this life on-screen; your family is cherished over here and you are the gold standard of friends and stars.

Reese Witherspoon, the only person my beloved yet critical mother could find no flaw with. Your love of reading and even passing along favorite books to me since the early days was a wonderful thing. I am so in awe of what you have built from the true spirit of you. The most incredible woman. The world knows it, and I feel very cool loving your gorgeous brilliance in real life, too.

Clairus Danes, my truest and closest friend from this recluse existence. A little Blairus goes a long way. I think you do understand how much I cherish you. There is no better conversationalist and witness to go through this life with. Oceans of Love. Send a video right now.

Michelle Pfeiffer, I love you so much. For returning my texts and calls, for giving me the greatest encouragement to simply smell the scent of light and hope and to string a few words together and for you to pronounce them good. You are the brightest star in my orbit, and I'm floored by your grace. Thank you. And thank you, David E. Kelley, for giving me a great job once. Appreciated. The whole family.

Rajiv Joseph, Rebecca Taichman, Brad Fleischer, the horrible perfect greatness that is our *Gruesome Playground Injuries.*

Guillermo del Toro, the most astounding director and amazing friend, whose mere journals outrun everyone else in the race. My lord! You are an amazement and I am honored. Also, I do not have Liz's necklace. I wish I did. Some shit must have swiped it. But not this mean baby.

Todd Solondz who made my mother's favorite films. And mine. Thank you for the honor. The night is still young, buddy.

Roger Kumble, *mein Direktor.* We are a team somehow. What's next? Major love.

Ingrid Sischy. The way you lifted me up, put me to work at *Interview,* put me on the masthead, introduced me to Karl and Miuccia and Donatella. You gave me a table at Pastis. You gave me every single thing I would need to fly. And I got sick. I couldn't keep up with how wonderful the view was. But I have the images in my mind. Nothing will be lost on me now that I'm waking up, dear Ingrid. I wish you were here. Every day really. You were the most important woman I ever admired and loved. And to think you loved me unconditionally. You were truly the greatest witness of our time. Please come see me sometime. I'll set the table by the fire. You were exquisite, Ingrid Sischy. I see your kindness even more now. Just what I need.

Anna Wintour for making my first Chanel moment in Paris so perfect. André Leon Talley, how I have loved sitting on your lap, whether in custom Chanel or color blocks of Isaac Mizrahi. William Norwich, for documenting the date night at the Met Ball, when my plane had to be caught so soon into the night. *Quel dommage*. It was a resplendent evening and your words the tiara on top.

Applause for Karl Lagerfeld. You were sublime. I cannot believe what a puppy of a child I could be with you. I loved you so and will until I die. Wrap me in Chanel.

Steven Meisel, you are the answer, really, to every dark day. I wish to find myself in front of your lens again, Pat McGrath painting a perfect lip.

Inez and Vinoodh for seeing me. Laughing with me, being amazing people.

Joe Zee and Michael Thompson for the most striking and gorgeous *W* cover.

Peggy Sirota for the image on the cover of this book and for our day of shooting. It was one of the best days I can recall, along with meeting Chris McMillan at the end of it.

Christian Siriano, I love you. I never felt sexier than when next to you in a bathroom selfie in Toronto to celebrate your book launch. Thank you for inviting me to sit at your table.

Jaime King, every song I think of you, every prayer starts with you. How we found each other in this huge world will always be a sacred gift I love forever. My beautiful blond sister.

Jana Kogen Breitbarth for finding me and loving me. Bonnie Liedtke, Julie Taylor, and Andrea Pett-Joseph for taking me on.

Dr. Burt. You saved my system. Thank you.

Thank you, John Danhakl.

Jennifer Grey, there isn't enough love.

Matthew Perry, for looking the part of Cary Grant the night we met, and for being my real true friend ever since. Thank you for getting me home safely as you recovered yourself.

Jamie Lynn Sigler, the total knockout. Thank you for being an example and my beautiful friend.

Christina Applegate, one of my messy sisters and (looks like) forever friend. *Gah,* I'm probably on my way over to get in bed actually. Nah, too tired, love you. Night.

Ann Eagleton and Winch and Pretzel and Jim, I don't think I could have made it without you coming here to Cali every summer for our walks in the sand. You will always be in our memories and now my favorite texting mom.

JLCurtis, your hand could not have come sooner.

Azura Skye, you know you are my favorite and your talent is so ethereal and stunning and raw and dignified. As are you. God I love you. And thank you for being at every stage of my life here.

Jason Schwartzman, you are beloved.

Gia and Jacquie, as are you.

The Strickers. Boundless love and thanks, you held me at my worst. You hold us still. We can't wait for our next trip with you.

Kelly Jennings and HRH Nibbles. You both know how I feel, but it doesn't cover it.

Britney, you did it. So much love to you, the Queen, the Lion. How does a girl get in touch with Britney Spears?! Xo, Saintly.

To David Weber, the tall and handsome man I loved dearly.

Bill Nighy, my most elegant friend, I hope we dance one day very soon. Thank you for your beacons of hope through the years, love and oceans.

The Cranbrook Kingswood mix tape of everything I love. For the Fab Four, Fran, Sue, and Kelly. And Chip, Chris Keogh, Art Tavee.

Todd "Meathead" Kessler, you will always amaze me with your writing. Your mind. I am so proud of you. Love, Archie.

Acknowledgments

Art and Caroline, my personal photographers, please carry on. With massive love.

James Toner, where are you?

Christine Goodale. Thank you for changing my life. In the best way. Photography saved me. You seeing me saved me. I loved your art rooms. And you.

Gina Ferrari. "Watercolored Iris" is due for an update. My idol as a wee Blair, I love you still.

Skunks. From *Rushmore* to now . . . I feel we've been through it all together. Thank you. I love you and cannot wait for the best in your life.

Quinn Olmsted Spilsbury. You saved me from the possum, from the Monster, from the bitch monster, and another monster. You are forever my Pugsley and I your Wednesday. Those early years of Arthur, we saved each other until you found your love, your own family. And a beautiful family you have. Always and always BFF, Squish.

Lori Petty. I mean, I can't sometimes. And I know you always know what I mean. Thank you for having me in your movie. And meeting my first children, Chloe and Jennifer. It's been a whole thing, and I hope to find you again, my friend.

Ellen Pompeo, from our NYC days to now, you have always been top shelf.

Constance Zimmer, I am overjoyed to be your friend, thank you.

Karen "Spring Break" McCullah, the biggest jolt of sunshine.

Janey Lopaty. I love Janey From Juicy. I love Janey.

Amanda Anka, and Tanda . . . all blessings already are . . . but you make them bigger.

Sharon Stone, your brain, your being, your strength . . . thank you for being there when I most need it. Coming over to float and hang, I'll tell you in person.

Thaiba, my yellow heart, thank you.

Hoora Smart and Julia Chastain, my beautiful girls of Instagram, I love you.

Courtney Ferguson. Rest in Peace, angel girl.

Jim LeBrecht. I love our friendship so much. My admiration is boundless.

Andraéa LaVant. Formidable and stunning and patient with me. I will never greet your service dog in the same manner. Now that I have my own, I do not know how you did not drive over my feet in frustration. More to come! Love you.

Keah Brown. To see you smiling across the room was the best surprise on a fall night in the Hamptons, you anchored me and I love you. Thank you for your talent and friendship.

To the disability community. I'm humbled and honored to be one part of a representation. I am an ally. Thank you.

Selma Blair is an actress best known for her roles in *Legally Blonde*, *Cruel Intentions*, *The Sweetest Thing*, and *Hellboy*. Blair was named a *Time* Person of the Year in 2017 as one of their Silence Breakers, and she was nominated for a Grammy Award for Best Spoken Word Album for her narration of *Anne Frank: The Diary of a Young Girl*. She is the subject of the documentary *Introducing, Selma Blair*, which reveals Blair's intimate and raw journey with multiple sclerosis. Blair lives with her son in Los Angeles.

A NOTE ON THE TYPE

This book was set in Adobe Garamond. Designed for the Adobe Corporation by Robert Slimbach, the fonts are based on types first cut by Claude Garamond (ca. 1480–1561). Garamond was a pupil of Geoffroy Tory and is believed to have followed the Venetian models, although he introduced a number of important differences, and it is to him that we owe the letter we now know as "old style." He gave to his letters a certain elegance and feeling of movement that won their creator an immediate reputation and the patronage of Francis I of France.

Composed by North Market Street Graphics
Lancaster, Pennsylvania

Printed and bound by Bang Printing, a CJK Group Company
Brainerd, Minnesota

Designed by Anna B. Knighton

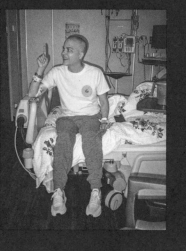

Anything

When I was very much littler,
I asked my mom what I would get
when she died.

There was a filmy, frothy thing she wore.
I couldn't wait to have it.
I also wanted her pear shaped diamond,
what she promised to my sister Katie,
whom I already didn't like.

The two sapphire rings dad bought her
that would look so good on my fingers,
were going to my sister Lizzie.
I didn't know why.

I remember her saying my half sister, Mimi,
could have all her clothes which meant I
wouldn't have her filmy, frothy dress.

I asked her: "When you die,
                        what will I get?"

And because I was her favorite,
she said: "Anything you want.
                        Anything your little heart desires.
                        Anything that is left
                                        when I'm gone."

I fell asleep at night
dreaming of Aything.